THE PONDS OF KALAMBAYI

The Ponds of Kalambayi

A Peace Corps Memoir

Mike Tidwell

AUTHOR OF *BAYOU FAREWELL*

LYONS PRESS
Guilford, Connecticut
An imprint of Globe Pequot Press

Lyons Press is an imprint of Globe Pequot Press.

Lyrics from "Mr. Tambourine Man" by Bob Dylan are reprinted by permission of Warner/Chappell Music, Inc. © 1964 by Warner Bros. Inc. All Rights Reserved.

Project editor: Julie Marsh
Page layout: Justin Marciano

Library of Congress Cataloging-in-Publication Data

Tidwell, Mike.
The Ponds of Kalambayi: an African sojourn / Mike Tidwell.
p. cm.
ISBN 1-55821-078-4 (cloth)
ISBN 1-55821-447-X (paperback)
1. Kalambayi (Zaire)—Social life and customs. 2. Peace Corps (U.S.)—Zaire—Kalambayi. 3. Kalambayi (Zaire)—Description and travel. 4. Luba (African people)—Social life and customs. 5. Tidwell, Mike—Journeys—Zaire—Kalambayi. 6. Fish-culture—Zaire—Kalambayi. I. Title.
D7665 K24T53 1990
967.51'23—dc20   90-40035
                                                                       CIP

ISBN 978-0-7627-7366-4
Printed in the United States of America
10 9 8 7 6 5 4 3 2 1

For Mbaya Bukasa. And for Karen.

This country where people were dying in chains—why did God not take a hand? Why did he not open a way to men? This world was blocked, stopped-up, done for. It needed someone a lot cleverer than men to get it out of this one. This hole. The huge hole of madness that was forming here; the plagues, the downpour.

—SONY LABOU TANSI, IN *THE ANTIPEOPLE*

ACKNOWLEDGMENTS

Many thanks to Karen Sundberg, without whose patient love this book never would have been written, and to the people of Kalambayi, to whom I've accumulated considerable debts of hospitality. Thanks also to Shabtai Klein, Chris Dege, Ann Rittenberg, Andy Thorpe, Jon Lane, Karyn Robinson, my agent Jean Rosenthal, and Peggy and Ted Krautter for special assistance; Chuck Reineke, Wayne Tidwell, Sandy Remancus, Brandt Witte, Bob Keys, and Melissa Jordan for manuscript suggestions. Finally, special thanks to Frank Reiss and Alex Johnson, who believed in the project as much as anyone and gave time and support beyond the reach of just expression.

Two characters in this book have been given fictitious names. The first is the director of the fish training program in chapter 1. The second, a Zairian, appears in a later chapter and has been disguised because the information he gives could provoke reaction from Zaire's watchful police apparatus.

Introduction, 2011

As I pen these words, reflecting on a book I wrote as a young man, I'm reminded of L. P. Hartley's famous lines: "The past is a foreign country. They do things differently there." The metaphor is eternal, of course, reconfirmed each time we stumble upon that long-lost box of photos or forgotten journals in the attic.

But imagine the feeling when those old photos and journals were themselves recorded overseas, when a meaningful part of your past actually *took place* in a foreign country. Such is the doubly exotic feeling I get as I write this new introduction to *The Ponds of Kalambayi*, my Peace Corps memoir first published more than twenty years ago.

Yes, much has changed in the nation where most of this book took place. Even the country's name has changed. After the fall of the dictator Mobutu Sese Seko in 1997, and during a prolonged and brutal civil war, the country was renamed the Democratic Republic of the Congo (DRC). I have, however, kept the old country name—Zaire—throughout this edition for practical and historical purposes.

More than three million people died during the Congo civil war of 1996–2003, mostly in the eastern part of the country, several hundred miles from the setting of this book. The war disrupted the economy nationwide, resulting in a per-capita income today of just $174 and a life expectancy of only forty-eight years. Yet the country's population has managed to skyrocket despite the ravages of war. Reflecting trends across much of sub-Saharan Africa, the population of the DRC has nearly doubled from thirty-eight million in 1990 to seventy million today.

Much has changed in my own life, too. I was a twenty-eight-year-old unpublished author in 1990 when I walked five blocks to a post office—no Internet then—and mailed this manuscript to my New York publisher for actual *typesetting*. I've since gone on to write five more books, raise a son to young adult, devote myself to the cause of environmental protection, and finally, in 2005, quit drinking alcohol for good (I mention this as an update on my struggles, described in chapter 17, to fight off a village-brewed moonshine called *tshitshampa*).

But in all this time, I never went back to Kalambayi, never returned to the dusty and destitute region of central Congo where the Peace Corps sent me to teach fish culture from 1985 to 1987. I've wanted to go back. Very badly. But Africa is a faraway place and the civil war and ensuing economic chaos have made the Congo a particularly dangerous place to visit. I've exchanged sporadic letters with a handful of Kalambayan villagers over the years, knowing that someday—perhaps when my son is safely grown and a more predictable order settles over the country—I will return.

Meanwhile, in the blink of an eye, the Peace Corps itself has grown old. Hard to believe it's celebrating its fiftieth anniversary in 2011. Many Americans will be surprised to learn this, thinking of the agency as an idealistic wave that came and went with the 1960s. But the Peace Corps today serves seventy-seven different nations with more than eight thousand active volunteers. Sadly, the DRC is not one of those nations. The agency pulled out of the Congo in 1991 as the country's political strife deepened in the run-up to civil war.

The idea for the Peace Corps was first popularized by President John F. Kennedy. Here was Kennedy's vision: The Peace Corps would take volunteers from the "solution" nation—America—and ask them to work hard to transfer knowledge and technology to the "problem" nations in the developing world. This arguably paternalistic view, forgivable for the era, has nonetheless led more than two hundred thousand Americans to serve as volunteers abroad. This in turn has produced tens of millions of people worldwide who today are slightly better fed, clothed, sheltered, and educated than they would otherwise be. I'm genuinely proud to have been part of that effort.

But revisiting my own Peace Corps story twenty years later, I realize Kennedy's original vision has been sadly turned on its head. We in the United States have become the world's leading "problem" nation. We are now a direct and daily burden on all of the world's poor, threatening to unravel whatever help we've managed to provide in the past. How are we doing this? Simple: We are destroying the world's atmosphere with greenhouse gas pollution. We are changing the climate.

Re-reading *The Ponds of Kalambayi* now I'm struck by how many pages I devote to describing the coming and going of the central African seasons. In the chapters that follow you'll see that pretty much everything in this centuries-old, village-based culture is dependent on the annual wet season and dry season arriving and departing on time. Without reliable rains, there is no planting of subsistence crops in September and January. Without a long dry spell beginning in June, there is no hunting for wild pigs and antelope in August. Even a slight deviation from these ancient patterns leads straight to hunger. Period.

And that's precisely what's happening worldwide. Our weather systems are deviating from ancient patterns. The planet is rapidly warming. Satellite cameras show Arctic ice in full-on retreat while sea levels rise and precipitation patterns alternately veer toward biblical flooding and unrecognizable droughts across Africa and the rest of the world in recent years. One measurement of change in Africa is Mount Kilimanjaro. Eighty-five percent of its glacial ice has vanished since 1912, including nearly one third just since I left the Peace Corps in 1987. The mountain will very soon be completely ice free for the first time in eleven thousand years.

We know what's driving the climate crisis: our daily consumption worldwide of oil, coal, and natural gas. But we Americans consume far more than our share while we do very little as a nation to solve the problem.

Meanwhile, the villagers I write about in this book are almost entirely innocent in this climate equation. Coal-fired electricity versus wind power? They don't *have* electricity in Kalambayi. SUVs versus hybrid cars? They don't *have* cars—none at all, or functioning roads for that matter. Africa as a continent, with roughly one billion people, contributes less than 4 percent of the world's greenhouse gases.

But America, with less than 5 percent of the world's population (311 million), generates *a staggering 25 percent* of the world's total greenhouse gases. In a perfectly fair world, we'd get 25 percent of all the planet's atmospheric heating beamed right down upon our nation's borders. If that were the case, if the world were fair, then America would already be completely wrecked. Florida would already be a series of islands. Kansas would already be a scrub desert.

But since we can *share* the warming with Africa, share it with Bangladesh and Pacific Island nations that will literally disappear, we in America don't seem to care so much. We aren't moved to full action. Year after year, our government refuses to cap carbon pollution at home while essentially blocking international treaty efforts abroad. We thus knowingly let climate destabilization unfold on all the world's continents, promising agricultural, ecological, and social chaos to billions of poor and innocent people like those in this book.

So on the fiftieth anniversary of the Peace Corps, as I reflect on my own service years ago, I realize it's time to resurrect JFK's original vision by becoming a solution nation again. As a young man, I thought I had to go overseas to help the world's poorest people. That strategy produced a few fish ponds in Africa and the book you now hold in your hands. But today, as my hair grays and the years pile on, I know I can best serve the people of Kalambayi by working hard right here where I was born. Simultaneously, I believe this book has never been more important, describing as it does the universal struggles and vulnerabilities and indomitable spirit of much of the still-poor world. But today, these same stories move me to fight for electric cars and solar panels all across America, and for wind farms along our U.S. coastlines.

We're in a race against time, to be sure, to cut carbon pollution fast enough and so save our planet. But we're picking up speed, and I'm optimistic because here's what I know: If the past is a foreign country, so is the future. People will do things differently there.

—MIKE TIDWELL, AUGUST 2011, TAKOMA PARK,
MARYLAND

INTRODUCTION, 1990

HOW DO YOU PACK FOR A TWO-YEAR TRIP TO AFRICA? I KNEW what I needed to take but not how to carry it all. I considered a suitcase for a while, but eventually decided against it. Its unwieldy bulk would surely prove out of place against Africa's dusty landscape. Next, I considered a backpack. But again there was a problem. I couldn't find one large enough for my swelling list of supplies.

It was while rummaging through a closet at my father's house that I happened upon a solution. I was looking for a pair of misplaced boots when, wedged between a vacuum cleaner and a pile of yellowed newspapers, an old duffel bag caught my attention. I pulled the bag out and took it to the back porch. There pummeled by a broomstick, it shed its layer of dust and presented a durable blue canvas. Across one side of the canvas I found my family name stenciled in black, disciplined letters. T-I-D-W-E-L-L. It was my father's old Air Force duffel bag, orphaned in storage for more than twenty years.

When I asked my father if I could take the bag to Africa, he readily agreed. He had forgotten about the bag and seeing it now brought back memories of his service. Among these was the most terrifying day of his life: October 22, 1962. On that day, he told me, he jumped out of bed, put on his uniform, ran onto the tarmac of a Strategic Air Command base in Arkansas, and started loading nuclear bombs onto B-47s. It was day nine of the Cuban missile crisis and President John F. Kennedy had ordered an unprecedented full alert, commanding all the planes loaded and into the air. To the sound of sergeants shouting "this is not a drill, this is not a drill," my father and several dozen other young airmen breathlessly watched the last plane take off, certain that their trembling hands had just delivered nuclear Armageddon to a tense and waiting world.

Twenty-two years later, standing next to the closet from which I had just retrieved the old duffel bag, my father and I contemplated the tangled web of irony. The president who had guided the planet to the brink of nuclear destruction—John F. Kennedy—had, in the same administration, founded the Peace Corps to help save the planet from poverty and war. Now that organization was sending me to Africa as a volunteer. For J.F.K., my father loaded nuclear bombs onto B-47s. For J.F.K., I would teach destitute village farmers how to build fish ponds for food.

And now I was ready to go. I had my duffel bag. There remained only the task of filling it with the things I would need in Zaire, my country of service. Formerly the Belgian Congo, Zaire stretches high and wide across the remote center of the continent, embracing an area where living conditions are appallingly difficult. Just how difficult was brought home to me in a letter I received from Washington as I was preparing to leave: "Pack as if you were going camping for two years," it said.

The letter boiled the waters of my imagination. I began to pack. Into the duffel bag I stuffed a mosquito net for the clouds of insects waiting to assault me, a Swiss army knife for the wild pigs I would hunt, a flashlight for the sultry nights without electricity, a pair of boots for the roadless valleys I would work in.

I hadn't gotten very far in my packing, however, when I suddenly stopped. Something was wrong. I stepped back from the Air Force bag and give it a long look. Taking it might be a mistake, I thought. Having just read a yard of books on Zairian history, it now occurred to me that the bag's blue military color might cause uneasiness among Zairians who remember 1960. In that year the U.S. Central Intelligence Agency helped orchestrate the assassination of Patrice Lumumba, Zaire's first and only democratically-elected prime minister. Lumumba was the shining Kennedyesque figure of Zairian history. He was young, intelligent, bursting with vision. Then the C.I.A.

brought about his death. An authoritarian government, fervently backed by the United States, eventually gained control after the assassination and has ruled in Zaire ever since, oppressing its people and destroying the economy.

These thoughts and apprehensions went through my mind as I held my father's duffel bag. I emptied it and was about to put it back in the closet when a second examination made me reconsider the rejection. The bag had faded over the years to a blue-white tone that seemed sufficiently anonymous for my purposes. As a further test, I took it back outside where the mid-day sun rendered the anemic blue even less conspicuous. In the end, I decided to go ahead and use it. I took the old duffel bag, this veteran of the Cuban missile crisis, with me on my two-year trip to Africa as a development worker sent to alleviate poverty my country had helped create.

Bending and arching, looking curiously confused, the Congo River makes its way through central Africa, crossing the equator twice. It's an enormous river, dominating both geography and human life in Zaire. In his famous novella *Heart of Darkness*, Joseph Conrad wrote of the Congo: "There was in (the world) one river especially, a mighty big river. That you could see on a map, resembling an immense snake uncoiled, with its head in the sea, its body at rest curing afar over a vast country, and its tail lost in the depths of the land."

Actually, the Congo has several tails. A dozen major tributaries spill into its serpentine body. These tributaries are themselves fed by other rivers, each farther and farther lost in the depths of the land. One such branch, running through the grasslands of south-central Zaire roughly 1,000 miles east of the Congo's main body, is the Lubilashi River. On a map the Lubilashi appears as an unremarkable ribbon meandering among others. But on the ground it is wide and powerful; an impressive river. At one point along its banks live 20,000 people banded together in a chiefdom called Kalambayi. Like the river along which they live, the people of Kalambayi are lost, their lives barely touched by the probing hands of the twentieth century. To this place I journeyed with my newly acquired duffel bag.

One way to understand what it means to be lost in sub-Saharan Africa is to visualize the continent in terms of concentric circles. The outermost circles, near the coasts, generally have the highest levels of economic development. They pass through Lagos, Libreville, Johannesburg, Nairobi. But as one moves inward geographically in Africa, one moves downward in income. On the way to the center of the continent, one passes through ever-tightening circles of poverty until, inside the final, smallest ring, one finds Kalambayi: a 400-square-mile patch of simple mud huts and barefoot people. From this place, the Indian Ocean is roughly the same distance to the east as the Atlantic Ocean is to the west. To the north and south, respectively, the Sahara Desert and Port Elizabeth, South Africa, both lie about 1,500 miles away.

So sits Kalambayi, Africa's bull's eye. Far removed from the continent's periphery, clinging to the banks of a lost river. It endures in stubborn obscurity. There are few places in the world where the people are as poor and the life as traditional.

For two years, I lived among the Kalambayan people. I spoke their language and taught many of them how to raise fish. My goal was to increase family protein consumption. But what I gave these people in the form of development advice, they returned tenfold in lessons on what it means to be human. There, at the center of the continent, they shared with me the ancient spirit of Africa's heart. They shared its hopes, its generosity. Above all they shared its unbending will to survive in the face of adversities so severe I nearly lost my life more than once just passing through.

I'M STILL NOT SURE I'M GLAD I EVER MET RAYLEEN MCGARITY. I do know one thing, however. I'll never be as impressed again when my father or an uncle tells of tests of manhood performed for soldier-eating boot-camp sergeants. I won't be as impressed because I butted heads with Rayleen McGarity for ten weeks and I was tough enough. I made it. Many of the problems I faced in Africa were admittedly more formidable. But Rayleen came first. She was my baptism. She was proof of what terrible, dark forces the world could create. After her I was ready to go to the Third World.

Rayleen was fond of a certain saying. "If you give a man a fish, he eats today," she told us fledgling trainees. "But if you teach a man how to raise fish, he eats forever." It grew a little stale from overuse, but we her students agreed enthusiastically each time she repeated the saying. Then again, we had no choice.

Rayleen McGarity's job was to train young Americans to be Third World fish culture extension agents for the Peace Corps. She taught people how to teach other people how to eat fish forever. In the process, for ten weeks at the University of Oklahoma campus at Norman, she presided over one of the most devastating, mind-taxing, ego-crunching, fear-inspiring boot camps ever administered by a civilian.

"I want to make something clear from the beginning," she announced to us thirty-one unsuspecting volunteers our first night in Oklahoma. "You people weren't sent here to have fun. You were sent here to teach yourselves how to raise fish, and no one," she continued, pacing, "is going to leave this program, except to go home, until I know he or she is tough enough to get the job done overseas."

So began a period of my life that, despite my best efforts to forget, comes back in dark memories of lack of sleep, of psychological games, of superhuman training tasks, and of clinging, in the end, to a lowest-common-denominator desire to survive, nothing more. This was the angst thirty-seven-year-old Rayleen McGarity wrought in the deepest parts of her trainees. But if they could still walk and talk and spell their names after ten weeks, Rayleen sent her underlings overseas to get the job done. She sent people from Michigan to Guatemala, people from Vermont to Nepal, people from Texas to the Philippines, and she sent me—a moderately naïve, twenty-two-year-old from Georgia—to Zaire.

We didn't call her "sergeant" or "captain" or anything like that. To us, privately at least, she was known simply as Mama Thunder. She didn't look all that tough. She was about five feet tall, wore horn-rim glasses, and had a short, shapeless haircut that looked like she had done it herself. Compounding this odd appearance was a habit of dress that featured, most days, a black leather flight jacket worn incongruously above plaid double-knit pants.

But when she spoke, when Mama Thunder spoke, one heard the resonance of power and knew the truth. She didn't use many words to get her points across. Someone with so much authority doesn't have to. A simple question usually would do.

"What are you doing, Peter?"

It was Rayleen. It was her voice. Someone had taken a false step and was caught in her crosshairs.

"I mean, just what in the heck are you doing?"

Peter Kittany, trainee, Blytheville, Arkansas, was, it was plain to see, using a hand scale to weigh thousands of tiny live fish taken from his assigned training pond.

"I'm weighing my fish, Rayleen," he said.

"What were your instructions, Peter?"

"My instructions were to count my fish."

"So why are you weighing them?"

"Because there are thousands and thousands of fish in this pond," he said. "If I just count the number of fish in one pound and then multiply that figure by the total number of pounds, I'll know approximately the total number of fish. It's a lot easier that way."

"What were your instructions, Peter?"

"But I can't possibly count them all, Rayleen. There are too many."

"Count them, Peter," she said. "Count every one of them, and do it today."

Thus ordered, Kittany drained his pond to ankle's depth and with a dip net began capturing and counting his fish and placing them one by one in basins of holding water. Tilapia, the bluegill-like fish native to Africa used in the training program, are formidable procreators capable of producing thousands of offspring in a matter of months. Peter's pond was thus chock-full of babies no bigger than matchsticks, all of them squirming and slinging mud with deft accuracy into the face of anyone unfortunate enough to wander near.

"One, two three ...," Peter began counting. He counted and counted. When it got dark and all the other trainees went home, he put a flashlight in his mouth and kept going with both hands free. Later, it began to rain and an absurdly violent Oklahoma thunderstorm crackled overhead. But flashlight between his teeth, Peter didn't stop counting. Three thousand, five thousand, seven thousand ... on and on it went.

Sometime in the middle of the night, one of Rayleen's assistants appeared on the pond bank.

"What are you doing Peter?"

"I'm counting my fish," he said.

"Good," the assistant said. "Good. Count them all."

That was how Rayleen operated, cold and fastidious, demanding feats that had no apparent utility and then waiting for compliance, rebellion, or stark mental collapse. There was no need to know the exact number of ten thousand–odd fish in Peter Kittany's pond. It had no experimental value or purpose in the strict sense of training. But that wasn't the point. When Rayleen cornered a trainee and handed him a ludicrous job, she was more or less saying: "Do it or go crazy. And if you're going to go crazy, at least do it here before we waste money sending you overseas."

If there was one thing she really loved for this purpose, something guaranteed to push a trainee to the fragile edge of sanity, it was a good riddle. That was how the training program began, with a riddle. Those who could solve it stayed. Those who couldn't took the next plane home.

The morning after her sobering first-night speech, when we trainees first began to sense that something weird and calamitous was imminent, Rayleen led us to an off-campus classroom and told us to sit down and shut up.

"The training has now begun," she said. "There will be no talking."

With no further instructions, she sat on a stool in the front of the room, folded her arms, and began staring at us. We in turn began staring at each other, wondering what in the world we were supposed to do and thinking increasingly paranoid thoughts. Nothing was happening. Rayleen was just staring at us. It was some sort of test, we believed, and we had to figure it out before dementia froze our minds. Were we supposed to draw pictures? Do jumping jacks? No one knew. Minutes passed, then hours. Still we sat, stupidly, nervously, all thirty-one of us in a room. We broke for lunch and came back and did the same thing all afternoon. No talking, no nothing.

Toward the end of the second day, something happened. Rayleen stood up, walked over to a trainee and unceremoniously led her out of the room. Without explanation, the two returned after a few minutes and sat down again. No one said a word. After a while, the same thing happened with another trainee. The pair left the room and came back. This went on five or six times, and then I was tapped. Rayleen led me down a hall and through a door where we stood outside by some bushes next to the building.

"What's your name?" Rayleen asked abruptly, pressing her face a bit too close to mine.

Huh? My name?

I told her.

"Where are you going?"

"Zaire," I said.

"Where are you now?"

"Norman, Oklahoma."

"What are you doing here?"

"Training to be a fish culture extension agent," I said.

"I'm sorry," she broke off. "Your last answer is unsatisfactory. Go sit back down and think about it."

Unsatisfactory? What did that mean? I had told her the truth. I was a trainee. What could be wrong with that response?

Not knowing the answer, I went back to the room and silently thought about Rayleen's questions for a long time. The next day, I was again summoned outside and presented with the same questions.

"What is your name?"

"Where are you going?"

"Where are you now?"

Then the last one: "What are you doing here?"

Confused, I changed yesterday's answer a bit.

"I'm trying to learn how to raise fish," I said.

She paused. Something about the answer was right, but something was still missing. But what? What did she want me to say? The chance passed.

"Unsatisfactory," she said. "Go sit down."

Meanwhile, some trainees had left the classroom with Rayleen and had not come back. The rest of us, still sitting silently in the room, saw them only during meals at the campus cafeteria. Their shoes and pants, we noticed, were mysteriously covered with mud and thorns and things of the forests. But we weren't permitted to question them or to discuss the training with each other under any circumstances.

The next morning at the bushes again:

"What are you doing here?" Rayleen asked me.

She was growing impatient. I had been doing a lot of thinking in class and had remembered something she had said during her first-night speech about trainees being expected "to teach themselves how to raise fish."

Rayleen, her hands stuffed into her flight jacket, her face horribly close to mine, was waiting.

"I'm here to, well, uh, teach myself how to raise fish," I said. It worked. I said something right.

"Okay," she said. "Go on. What do you need to raise fish?"

What? There was more?

"Well, I guess, first of all, I need fish."

"No. I can't accept that," she said. "Go back and sit . . ."

I was blowing it. What was wrong? What did I need to raise fish? What did she want me to say?

A better answer came.

"Water," I said quickly. "I need water to raise fish."

Water. The password. That was what she wanted to hear.

"Very good," she said, looking pleased behind her horn-rim glasses. "Now get going and find it."

"Find what?"

"Water," she said. "Go find a place with water where you're sure you can teach yourself how to raise fish, and when you find it, sit down and wait and I'll be by to pick you up for lunch."

"But where? What water? Which direction?"

"Just find it," she said.

With no further instructions, she turned and went inside, leaving me alone in a state of total bewilderment.

I dithered by the bushes for a few minutes, trying to digest what Rayleen had just said. "Find a place with water where you're sure you can teach yourself how to raise fish." Hmmmm. I took a deep breath and, with the state of Oklahoma suddenly looking like a damn big hiding place, began looking for a place, any place, to raise fish.

My first strategy was to find a creek and to follow it. After a ten-minute walk I found one that ran through some woods by a golf course. Not really sure what I was doing, I began looking for a good place to build a rock dam on the creek and stock fish behind it: a place that, perhaps, Rayleen also knew and later would come by to pick me up for lunch. But after three hours of fruitless searching, I gave up and went to the cafeteria. My shoes and pants were covered with mud and thorns and things of the forest like the other trainees.

For three days I covered, on foot, large sections of Cleveland County, Oklahoma. I'd leave campus every morning and head in a different direction, following creeks and rivers I hoped would lead to a lake or some other suitable place to raise fish. I was certain that somewhere out there a place was waiting for me and I had to find it quickly or admit defeat to Mama Thunder and go back home. Late in the morning of the third day, along a two-lane county road about seven miles outside of Norman, I happened upon a responsible-looking five-acre lake with two children fishing along the far bank. This is it, I thought. A place where I'm sure I can teach myself how to raise fish. Rayleen must know this great place, too. Buoyed by my luck, I sat down next to the road and waited for her to come pick me up for lunch. But I waited and waited. Twelve o'clock rolled around— lunch time—and still no Rayleen. She never came. It wasn't an acceptable place.

Dejected and hungry and feeling awfully stupid, I began hitchhiking back to campus. A man in a sky-blue Volkswagen Beetle saw me along the road and pulled over. I told him where I was headed and he waved me in.

"Whatcha doin' way out here on foot?" he asked as we drove off. He was in his mid twenties.

I figured it was pointless to tell him the truth, that I had been sitting alongside this rural road waiting for a woman named Mama Thunder to come pick me up for sandwiches. But the more I thought about it, the more I realized his question really didn't have an answer. What *was* I doing way out here on foot? What *was* all this wandering leading to? I didn't have a clue. I was Rayleen McGarity's senseless, meandering subject, wound up and let loose in the wilds of Oklahoma.

To make conversation, I told the driver in the most general terms that I was training to do work in Africa for the Peace Corps. As I spoke, I noticed a heart-shaped card hanging from his rearview mirror that read: "God is love." Oh no, I thought, here it comes.

"What a selfless dedication of your life to others," the driver said, proceeding to tell me more about his Christian faith than I thought possible during a fifteen-minute car ride. "I can tell that the Lord is at work in your life. He's called you to Africa."

Well, no, I thought. Not really. I wasn't the kind of person he thought I was, and I discreetly tried to tell him so. I wasn't a Christian out to save souls or a career social worker out to transform the world. To be sure, I was keenly concerned about the suffering that plagued Africa and I wanted to contribute part of my life to reducing it. I was also motivated by a concern for our species. If we don't respond to help a desperate neighbor, are we in the end capable of saving ourselves? During those same autumn weeks we trainees were trying to leapfrog Rayleen McGarity on our way to Africa, the first footage of the 1984–1985 Ethiopian famine reached the West. We read about the tragedy in copies of the *Dallas Morning News* and our commitment to service in Africa grew.

Still, I was uncomfortable with the do-gooder image. I wasn't a crusader. My goal was to help a few villagers on that continent live slightly better lives. There was nothing more spectacular about it than that.

The motivation was also partly selfish. Four years of college had just produced a diploma with my name on it, but no clear instructions on how to proceed. According to widely accepted social timetables, it was time to start paying taxes and voting and putting a little something into a 401(k) retirement plan each month. It was time, in short, to be a real person. But each time I looked inside myself, no real person seemed to be lacing up his boots, ready to step out. Where was he? Who was he? What kind of work would he do? I wasn't sure. Living in Africa, stripped nearly naked of my own culture, I hoped to give my deepest feelings a chance to produce some answers. I hoped to travel my inner continent, in other words, and come back with a better-focused picture.

"Good luck to you, friend," the driver said a few minutes later, dropping me off on a campus sidewalk after telling me repeatedly what a great person he thought I was. "God bless your work in Africa."

"Thanks," I said sincerely.

But as he drove away, I wondered if I would ever have work in Africa for God to bless. After the morning experience at the lake I was growing more confident that my Peace Corps service would end right where it had begun—in Oklahoma. I walked to the campus cafeteria and ate lunch with the other trainees, all of us sullen and dirty.

To be honest, I wasn't sure about the five-acre lake to begin with. Something was wrong with my thinking and I knew it. We trainees couldn't be expected to raise fish at thirty-three different Cleveland County lakes and creeks. That, it was now clear, was absurd. I had to rethink Rayleen's instructions and approach them for what they were: a puzzle to be solved. "Find a place with water where you're sure you can teach yourself how to raise fish and, when you find it, sit down and wait and I'll be by to pick you up for lunch." After a lot of careful thought I came to the following conclusion: There must be one place with thirty or so small ponds strung together like a fishery station. A place with water, a place where we could learn how to raise fish and a place where Rayleen could tell each trainee with confidence that she would pick him up for lunch when he found it. And, I theorized, if such a place existed, someone at the university's biology department probably knew where it was.

"Excuse me," I said to the department secretary behind her disk. "I'm a fisheries trainee, and I'm looking for the Peace Corps fish station."

She looked up at me and then past me, apparently to make sure we were alone.

"Do you have identification?" she asked.

I showed her.

"Come with me." She got up and led me down a hall and into a small, empty conference room. She shut the door.

"Look," I said, suddenly feeling nervous and guilty about what I was doing, "am I allowed to be here and asking you this? Because if not, I'll just turn around and walk away."

The secretary looked at me with all the earnestness of a parent. "No, no relax," she said. "It's okay. You're all supposed to come here sooner or later and ask for directions."

It was that simple.

A large map of the university hung on the conference-room wall. The secretary pointed to a spot at the far end of campus.

"Take the north-line bus," she said. "It's faster."

Twenty minutes later I was sitting on the bank of a fifty-by-twenty-five-foot fish pond, chewing on a blade of grass and happily contemplating a school of tilapia. There were thirty-two ponds altogether, a station just as I had suspected. About ten other trainees had already found the place. Promptly at noon, Rayleen pulled up in a black subcompact car and offered me a ride to lunch.

"Mike," she said as I got in.

"Yes, Rayleen?"

"Are you sure you can teach yourself how to raise fish here?"

"Yes, I'm sure."

"Good," she said.

⁓

There were four or five trainees who didn't solve the riddle that first week. They just kept stomping through the Oklahoma woods until Rayleen finally sent them home. Most protested, some even cried and begged. But they weren't tough enough for Rayleen, so they couldn't stay. In the end, ten of the thirty-one original trainees didn't finish the ten-week program. The stress got some, fatigue others. Some just couldn't stomach Rayleen anymore and asked to leave.

My roommate, Bob Weid, from Albany, New York, lasted six weeks. Like the rest of us, he was assigned a pond to feed and manage, and he was required each week to determine the growth rate of his fish. This was done by draining the water to a low level and then netting and weighing the fish. One week, to save time, Bob adjusted his pond's drain pipe in the evening so it would slowly drain half the pond water overnight. But he miscalculated. The next morning his pond was completely drained and all his fish were dead.

Making her ritual inspection of the ponds at 6:00 a.m., Rayleen quickly spotted the disaster and approached Bob. She walked in short deliberate steps, her hands tucked inside her flight jacket, affecting the air of a baseball manager on his way to remove a failed pitcher from the mound.

"Bob," she said, staring dumbfounded into the empty pond. "What are you going to do now? Your fish are all dead. They're all dead, Bob."

"It was an accident, Rayleen," Bob said, looking terrified as he picked up stiff, milky-eyed fish corpses from the pond-bottom mud. "Believe me. It won't happen again."

It didn't happen again. After a few days we never saw Bob again.

For the rest of us, the rigorous training went on. The hardest part of the program was that nothing, no new information or skill, was taught outright. Instead, problems were presented—"How can you get water from this stream over to that pond site?"—and with Rayleen's riddles and Socratic method, we taught ourselves how to raise fish. We learned how to survey land, stake water canals, and design ponds. We learned how to stock ponds and how to feed fish properly. Eventually we learned a great deal. But one thing we never figured out was Rayleen McGarity. She was too complex.

Rayleen the fun lover: "Today, guys, we're going swimming," she informed us one morning. Great, we thought. Then we discovered what she meant. We were required to spend an entire, miserable hour staring at the bottom of a swimming pool and treading water using a floating survival technique called drown-proofing.

Rayleen the unpredictable: "I've decided that today there will be no talking at lunch. No one is allowed to say anything to anyone. Is that understood?"

"But why?"

"Beginning now."

Rayleen the cold one: "Rayleen, today is Thanksgiving, and we thought that maybe we could have the day off to cook and have a big dinner together."

Request denied. Dinner as usual at the campus cafeteria.

Rayleen the slightly psychotic: "Pretend you're a rock," she told a trainee one day, making the point that a development worker must be able to adapt to odd situations. "Get down on the ground and be a rock, with a rock's personality and mannerisms, and make it convincing."

Although her training style was unorthodox, at times even mean, there was no doubting the fact that Rayleen did what she did out of a deep, abiding love for the Peace Corps idea. She had spent twelve years as a volunteer in the African state of Togo, doing everything from raising fish to building roads to digging wells. So much time in the Third World had left inside of her a hard-earned knowledge of poverty's sadness and an understanding of how hard it is to change. But change was always possible, she told us. By making us tough and competent, she wanted us to continue the work she had begun. These good intentions stayed with me after I left the training program, but they didn't dilute memories of the fierce martinet who dominated and made my life miserable for ten never-ending weeks. To my horror, Rayleen continued to haunt me after Oklahoma. She figured in some of my worst dreams long after I had reached the distant remove of rural Africa.

The training finally ended on December 5th. There was snow on the ground, the first of the season, when we woke up and Rayleen drove us to the airport. Through her we had taught ourselves how to raise fish, and now she was letting us leave.

"Now for goodness sake don't just give away the fish over there," she reminded us that last day. "Teach those people how to eat fish forever."

As we boarded the flight that would take us to New York and eventually Africa, Rayleen stood in her flight jacket and double-knit pants and, to our immeasurable surprise, hugged each trainee goodbye. She hugged me in my turn, wrapping her arms tight around my shoulders. And when she let go and pulled away, I noticed something. Mama Thunder was crying.

2

HAVING ENDURED THE OKLAHOMA TRAINING PROGRAM AND
the subsequent eighteen-hour flight to Zaire, I eventually
settled down to live in Lulenga, a village on a hill next to the
Lubilashi River. Tucked inside the folds and ridges of central
Africa's sprawling grasslands, Lulenga was one of thirty-three
villages comprising the chiefdom of Kalambayi. This was where
Rayleen sent me to build fish ponds for two years.

To see the Lubilashi flowing just below my village, you had
to walk one hundred yards from my front door, past a jumble of
mud-box houses and stout palm trees, to the edge of the village.
There, if the grass wasn't too high, you could watch the slow-
moving water as it cleaved through green hills, making its way
to the Congo River one thousand miles away.

There were almost always a few dugout canoes being man-
euvered across the river by men with long bamboo poles. The canoes
carried people and goats and sacks of corn. Along the riverbanks,
children fished with nets for clarias, a hard-to-catch catfish with
outlandishly long whiskers and a body that can grow as large as a
man. On both sides of the two-mile-wide valley, villages tilled small
farm plots. They used short-handled hoes and fought occasional
battles with hippopotamuses that lifted themselves from the brown
river at night to eat corn and manioc meant for humans.

This riverine world was particularly beautiful in the late
afternoon when the sun began to fall and the sky and clouds
played host to streaking colors of jade green and burnt orange. So
sublime was this period between about 5:00 and 6:00 p.m. that
in Tshiluba, the melodious and complex language spoken by the
Kalambayans, it was known as "the time of day when even ugly
people look beautiful." Watching the sun cast its last rays over a

distant ridge, watching those rays pass above green-gold grass to the upturned faces of children along the banks and the gleaming black skin of bathers in the current, I knew the expression was true. Nothing unattractive was possible at that hour.

I was the only one of the five hundred or so inhabitants of my village not to live in a thatch-roofed mud hut. I lived instead in a sagging cinder-block structure built by Belgian colonists thirty years earlier. One end of the fifteen- by forty-five-foot building was divided into the three small rooms of my living quarters. I shared the other two-thirds of the building with fourteen tons of locally grown, handpicked cotton. The cotton was piled to the ceiling—a million, dirty-white bolls—waiting to be trucked to the regional capital. This was my home. I lived in a cotton warehouse. It was the best the people of Kalambayi could provide.

A rusting, corrugated tin roof covered the warehouse, and when it rained it sounded like fistfuls of pocket change being dropped from the African sky. Heavy storms made conversation inside the house almost impossible. But in the morning, when the storms ended, the metallic roar gave way to a rhapsody of women's voices hanging in the air outside my windows. Mine was the only tin roof for miles around, and village women came after storms to scoop rainwater from clay pots stationed under the roof's edges. Dressed in *pagnes*, the colorful wrap-around skirts of African style, the women gossiped and joked and sang as they transferred the water to enamel basins. When the basins were full, the women lifted them onto their heads and walked away, exhibiting a strength and balance that mystified me.

Lukusa Mandako, my supervisor in the Zairian Department of Agriculture and Rural Development, first brought me to this place in a yellow, four-wheel-drive Land Rover with a spare tire fastened to the hood. He was waiting for me at the airport when my plane landed in Mbuji Mayi, the capital of Kasai Oriental province. This was Zaire's central-most province and home of the Baluba tribe to which the Kalambayans belonged. After leaving Oklahoma I had spent ten weeks studying French and Tshiluba at a state university in eastern Zaire. From there I had flown to Kinshasa, the Zairian capital, before boarding a plane for the interior.

Approaching Mbuji Mayi from the air was like looking down and preparing to enter a dream. The tall savanna grass covered the land like an interminable textured carpet, spreading out over lumpy hills to the horizon. Here and there, clusters of palm trees rose up from the grass, drawing the eye to the pointed roofs of village houses. A network of footpaths and narrow dirt roads connected the villages one to another. As the plane descended farther, I could make out people walking along paths, transporting goods on their heads to unknown destinations. I could see men farming with hoes in rectangular fields. Along rivers, women washed clothes.

Lukusa was standing on the Mbuji Mayi landing strip ready to greet me when I emerged from the plane with the other passengers. He led me through the airport terminal—a pale, one-story building with the decrepit look of an old train depot—and we exited onto a dirt parking lot on the other side. After loading my duffel bag, shortwave radio, camera, and two handbags into the government Land Rover, we set off through the urban sprawl of Mbuji Mayi, a grubby diamond-mining town with dirt roads. A sensory overload of tin-roofed hovels, streetside merchants, and wheezing, overworked Mercedes Benz trucks passed before us until, twenty minutes later, we entered the bush and I began seeing on the ground what I had seen earlier from the air.

A thick-set man with a soft, round face, Lukusa presented an air of ease and self-confidence behind the wheel. After ten years with the department, he was accustomed to the infrastructural ambushes of the rural interior. He managed the seventy-mile, dirt-road drive to Kalambayi well, plunging into the bush several times to get around bad sections of road and twice freeing the vehicle from mud with the help of a shovel and wood planks placed under the tires for traction.

But Lukusa's most impressive feat came at the Lubilashi River. We arrived and found two narrow, twelve-foot-long planks leading from the riverbank to the deck of a pre–World War II pontoon ferry. I got out of the cab, certain that anything sort of complete accuracy would send the vehicle sliding off the planks and into the river. After two false starts, Lukusa lined up the tires and gunned the engine. The rear tires spun violently. The planks bowed slightly under the weight. I swallowed hard. At last the Land Rover made it onto the ferry.

Lacking a motor, the small, raft-like ferry floated slowly across the river along a shore-to-shore steel cable that took us to the southern shore of Kalambayi. I sat on the hood of the Land Rover during the crossing and was overcome by the feeling that I was living a magazine ad for some machismo-brand cigarettes. Water murmured beneath the pontoons. Grass houses, hacked from the rioting savanna, dotted the riverbanks. The sky fixed the land with an unblinking blue stare. I was in Africa.

We left the ferry and began the two-hour drive to Lulenga. The farther we traveled the more barbarous the roads became. Soon they really weren't roads at all, but simply loose federations of holes and gullies stretched over hilltops and down into valleys. The level of poverty seemed to follow the state of the roads, getting worse with every mile. We passed lean, hard-eyed men carrying spears and women carrying underweight babies strapped papoose style on their backs. Older children, dressed in clothes so threadbare they looked moth-eaten, rushed out to greet us yelling "*Machini! Machini!*" It was the Tshiluba word for truck, something people saw infrequently in this bush-choked region.

As the Land Rover lurched and heaved past a succession of villages, I asked Lukusa about the house I would be living in. He assured me it was a permanent structure with a cement floor: a comfortable place, he said. I was glad to hear this as I watched the monotonous string of mud-and-stick huts pass by my passenger window. Comfortable, he said. I imagined a house with white walls, a veranda, perhaps a hammock inside and papaya trees visible through arch-shaped windows. These visions were still developing in my mind as we rounded the last turn and entered Lulenga. Then they evaporated.

"Jeeesus," I said.

Lukusa drove the Land Rover to the front of my house-to-be and turned off the engine. Silently, we stared through the windshield at a nightmare. The living quarters of the old cotton warehouse had been unoccupied for years except for the periodic intrusions of village delinquents who carved their names on the flaking plaster walls and slung mud balls at the building's exterior. The house had no door or windows or finished floor, nor did it resemble in any way a place inhabitable. Inside, on the floor, were piles of sand and cement where local masons had begun, but only partly finished, repairing the interior.

"Hmmm. *Ça c'est bizarre*," Lukusa said, getting out of the Land Rover. "I was told by the village chief that his house would be done by now."

Somehow, *bizarre* wasn't quite the adjective I was thinking of. The data my brain was registering screamed out for something with more descriptive kick.

"*Incroyable*," I said. That was a better word. It meant unbelievable. I repeated it over and over again. "I'm finally here, ready to move in with all my stuff, and I don't even have a place to live, Lukusa. What am I going to do?"

He turned to me and, judging by the look on his face, recognized the signs of a man approaching hysteria. "*Restez tranquille. Restez tranquille*," he said. "I'll take care of it. It's all right."

It took Lukusa about two hours to call together the village men and hammer out an agreement to have the house finished.

"Three days," the villagers said. "Give us three days and we'll get it done." I was skeptical. We unloaded my belongings from the truck and put them inside the house of the village chief. Lukusa informed me that a motorcycle and two hundred liter barrel of gasoline would be delivered for my use within a few days.

Then, clearly not appreciating half as much as I did the fact that he was leaving me in the middle of nowhere without even a decent house to live in, Lukusa shook my hand, wished me good luck, and drove away. I watched the Land Rover taillights bounce into the distance. When, on my tiptoes and stretching my neck and straining my eyes, I could no longer make out the vehicle, I turned around and realized for the first time I was opposite a large crowd of villagers staring with five hundred pairs of eyes at the first white person ever to live in their village. I waved and mumbled an awkward greeting and began taking slow, backward steps toward the warehouse. Then I turned and entered hurriedly through the doorless doorway.

It took longer than three days to repair my house: several weeks longer, in fact. But eventually it received a door and windows, and the floor was cemented. And although the plaster on the walls continued to crack and crumble, and there was no electricity or running water, the warehouse grew to be home. Resigned to my fate, I settled into mute companionship with fourteen tons of cotton.

———

Mbaya Bukasa almost died when he was fourteen years old. There's no way to know the exact day or place, but sometime during his fourteenth year Mbaya took a few swallows of water from a stream or a river or a calabash cup and he got sick. He got diarrhea. He lay on a reed mat outside his family's two-room hut and frequently got up to run to a mud outhouse around back. He lost weight. He lost energy. For weeks it continued.

With the family's meager savings, Mbaya's father bought various black-market medicines that filter into the bush. When these failed, he paid a village healer to cure his son. The cure never came. Months went by. Finally, after more than a year of poor health, when Mbaya's body had shrunk and he began, near death, to vomit and defecate blood, his father sold the family's only goat and borrowed a wobbly bicycle. Slowly, he pushed Mbaya twenty miles over hills and through rivers to a Belgian Catholic mission in the town of Ngandajika to the south. There, a European doctor found a tropical parasite ravaging the boy's intestines. Mbaya never remembered the name of the disease; there are so many that attack villagers. He received the proper medication and spent a month recovering at the mission.

During his year-long illness, Mbaya fell far behind in his schoolwork and, embarrassed by his age, he did what most children do when they become severely sick in Kalambayi: He never went back to the village schoolhouse. He was eighteen years old and had a fifth-grade education when he came to my house looking for a job. His illness had left him with a slight build and an excessively boyish look for his age. "Please give me work," he said.

My government living allowance was an extravagant $70 per month. In local currency that translated into 7,000 zaires, a zaire being the country's basic unit of currency. I told Mbaya I would give him 10 percent of my allowance, $7 a month, if he would draw my drinking water from the village source, wash my clothes, and help me buy and cook food from the village markets. These were things I couldn't possibly do myself and work full-time as an extension agent.

Mbaya agreed to the arrangement, I think, both because $7 was a lot of money in Kalambayi and because on that first day he came inquiring about a job the interior of my house was thick with the soothing, moody sounds of American folk-rock music. The music was spilling out of a small cassette player I had brought from home. He didn't tell me at the time, but Mbaya on that day fell in love with a legend.

A few months later, when I was lying in bed exhausted from a day's work and Mbaya was in my house's small kitchen building a cooking fire, I listened as he began clumsily whistling a tune that sounded dimly familiar. My mind began casting about, trying to place the music. Was it a Western song or a local village tune? I wasn't sure. Mbaya kept whistling and I began whistling softly along with him. Finally, I seized upon lyrics, English lyrics. First I placed ". . . I'm not sleepy. . . ." Then came ". . . play a song for me. . . ." Then, at last, I had it. ". . . in the jingle jangle morning I'll come fooollowing you."

Dylan. He was whistling Bob Dylan.

"Mbaya," I yelled from my bedroom, seeking confirmation, "what song are you whistling?"

From the kitchen there came only silence as, I suspected, he tried to make sense of my still poor pronunciation of Tshiluba.

"*Wambi tshini*?" he asked. "What did you say?"

"The song," I repeated. "What song are you whistling?"

"I don't know," he said. "It's something your *tshisanji* sings a lot."

Tshisanji was the Tshiluba word for cassette player. I picked up the *tshisanji* lying next to my bed and put in a tape.

"This song?" I asked, fast-forwarding to the right spot.

The music played. Bob Dylan sang:

"Hey Mr. Tambourine man, play a song for me . . ."

"Yes, yes. That's it," Mbaya yelled from the kitchen. He came into my room and we sat on my bed with our backs against the cinder-block wall, opening ourselves wide to the music. As it turned out, none of my other tapes impressed Mbaya very much: only Dylan. He loved Bob Dylan.

"*Musambu muimpa wa dikema*," he said as the tape rolled on. "This is such great music."

We both grinned, feeling suddenly closer after having discovered about each other a common taste, a common sensitivity. For two years the process continued. We tended to laugh at the same things, we thought alike in many ways, and we grew to prize the friendship that developed between us. There was separating us a cultural cleavage of almost interplanetary distance. But uniting us, stripped of language barriers and man-invented biases, was a tie tantamount to brotherhood. We were both Bob Dylan freaks.

So it was that for $7 a month Mbaya Bukasa came to work for me. He practically lived in my house, and paying his salary proved to be one of the best investments I ever made. He was honest and he worked hard. But there was more to it than that. I spent a lot of time ill in Kalambayi and it was Mbaya who pulled me through the worst episodes.

In a Western industrialized country like the United States, good health is more or less a birthright for a large majority of the population. Clean living conditions, nutritious food, and access to basic medical care mean that most people stay healthy most of the time. But in Kalambayi, as in much of Africa, good health is not a birthright. It falls instead somewhere between a wish and a struggle. At any given time you are almost as likely to be ill as well.

Unlike the villagers among whom I lived, I had money to buy enough meat, fruit, and good vegetables to ensure a nutritious diet. I also took vitamins and had a first-aid kit full of basic medicines. Even with these advantages, though, I got sick. Sanitation conditions in the villages were generally poor. It was often hard to avoid contact with people carrying contagious diseases. Eventually, I just got used to being at least mildly ill much of the time. But the various illnesses that attacked me found a body strong and well fed and ready to fight back with paid-for antibodies. Almost no one else in Kalambayi was as lucky. To note my own illnesses serves only to illustrate the gravity of theirs.

I had been in Africa for less than a month when I got my first case of malaria. There is no single word for malaria in Tshiluba. When smitten, a villager simply says, "My whole body is sick." That's the best way to describe it. Along with the fever come headaches and awful body aches. It took me one or two days of sweating in bed to get over each of the five cases I eventually got.

It took much longer, however, to recover from a case of hepatitis I picked up from one of my neighbor's children a year after arriving in Kalambayi. This virus causes inflammation of the liver and turns one's urine black and one's skin a disturbing yellow. The sickness left me with the energy level of a ninety-year-old invalid. I couldn't work for a month.

But like everyone else in Kalambayi, I suffered most from the water. Over a two-year period, unclean drinking water in the villages deposited inside of me a host of intestinal diseases including giardia, dysenteric amoebas, round worm, hook worm, and shigella. Carrying bottles of boiled water everywhere I went was of little use. In every village men drank gourds of palm wine and manioc beer laced with the local water. Refusing to drink with the men would have been interpreted by many as a rebuff, thus complicating my efforts to gain their confidence. So I drank. I drank the wine and the beer and the local water. And I paid the price.

Usually, at the start of an attack of diarrhea and stomach cramps, I was able to get to the Catholic health clinic in Ngandajika—three hours away by motorcycle—in time to avoid debilitating symptoms.

But it was different when I got bilharzia. The water-borne parasites of this disease had most likely entered my body a few weeks earlier while I was helping a farmer net some fish in a pond. For several weeks I didn't know I was seriously ill. I didn't know the parasites had already begun attacking my bladder and intestines. I began to have short bouts of abdominal pains and diarrhea, but the symptoms lasted only a few hours and then went away. I didn't grow concerned until one morning I woke with fever. I broke out my thermometer and took my temperature. It was 100 degrees. At almost the same moment my stomach sent unambiguous instructions to my feet to run to the outhouse around back. I remained there for a good five minutes. I wasn't well.

I was supposed to work that morning with a village farmer who lived a short distance from my house on the other side of a stretch of bush. I decided to walk over and tell him I was ill. Along the way, I suddenly felt like someone had punched me in the stomach. I entered the tall grass along the footpath to relieve myself. After I had done so, I was startled. There was blood in my stool. I turned around and went home and took my temperature again. It had risen to 101. I knew I had to get to the Catholic mission that day, but I decided to rest a while until the fever went down some. Wearing a pair of shorts and a t-shirt, I got in bed.

You are never as far away from home as when you get sick in a foreign country. I hid myself under the sheets and, with my body hot and my stomach hurting, grew lonely and intensely aware of the geography of my situation. I was six thousand miles from where I was born and grew up. It had been a month since I received my last letter from home and it would probably be another month before I got the next one. Now, worse, I was sick and there was no one around to talk to—at least no one who spoke English, the language I spoke without lapsing into fits of frustration and self-anger over not being understood.

I was a foreigner. In the more isolated villages all the children under six years of age ran away horror-stricken at the sight of me, having never seen a white person before and convinced I was a ghost or some macabre creature that had slithered out of the river. It was disturbing to inspire so much fear just by walking through a village. But now I was the one a bit afraid. My fever didn't seem to want to break.

A village rooster crowed loudly outside my open front door, waking me from a short sleep. I got up and got punched in the stomach again. I ran to the outhouse and came back and took my temperature. 102 degrees. It was around noon. I went back to bed.

I was feeling really hot all over now. My head was hurting. I thought about a thousand things, all of them related to being home and being healthy. I dozed off and after a brief sleep woke up again. I looked around. At first I thought I was at the Peace Corps office seventy miles away in Mbuji Mayi. Then I thought I was at a volunteer's house thirty miles to the south. Then, for a brief moment, I wasn't sure where I was or what I was doing. I was totally confused. It was a feeling, I realized later, that wasn't altogether new. I had had it before. In Oklahoma. In the woods. Rayleen McGarity. The same fear of being lost. The same feeling that something was terribly wrong.

After a moment, I gathered my thoughts. I remembered I was in bed, ill with fever. My anxiety subsided some. But staring at the rusting tin roof above me I grew sad and depressed, not just over my own condition, but over that of everyone in Kalambayi. "Find a place where you're sure you can teach yourself how to raise fish," Rayleen had instructed me. Finding the ponds had been a frustrating and disorienting experience. But I had found them. It had been a neat little victory, a happy crescendo.

But I was no longer in Cleveland County, Oklahoma. I was in Kalambayi and my job was to bring development. But where do you begin here? There was so much poverty and sickness. Even I was sick. The riddle was too complicated.

I had been sleeping for a couple of hours when I woke up. It was late afternoon and I was on fire. I put the thermometer in my mouth and waited. In a strange way, the bed sheets felt tremendously heavy on my skin. They were pushing down, trying to crush my body. I couldn't understand it. I took out the thermometer and looked at it. A white rush of fear filled my brain. The thermometer read 104 degrees.

"When the body temperature runs above 103 degrees there is a real risk of cerebral damage to the patient." I immediately remembered reading those words some months earlier in a Peace Corps health manual. The words now seemed written across the gray bar of mercury I was staring at. 104 degrees. How profoundly, unbelievably serious, I thought. I can't be this ill, not 104-degree-temperature ill. Could it go to 105? Do people really get temperatures that high? And God, 106. What happens to the body at that temperature?

My thinking suddenly grew scattered and illogical—a chaos of panicked constructions. My body was too hot. My head was a fog. My only cogent thoughts were: I am in a grave condition and I must get to the mission, I must get help. I took my temperature again. Again it was 104 degrees.

I stood up and felt very dizzy. I sat back down on the edge of the bed and rubbed my face with my hands. My fingertips were like red-hot coals. My face was even hotter. I stood up again. I had a three-hour motorcycle ride ahead of me. Where were my clothes? My shoes? My glasses? I walked unsteadily out of the room.

I heard a voice.

"Michel."

It was Mbaya. Mbaya was there. He had called my name. He was standing in front of me.

"I'm very sick," I said.

He put his hand to my cheek. "My God," he said.

"I've got to leave," I mumbled, unsure really of what I was doing. I was shivering spasmodically.

"No, Michel. You can't."

Forcing me, he led me to a chair in the sitting room and made me sit down. Then he disappeared. When he came back he helped me to my feet and led me into the kitchen. He had placed a single wooden chair in the middle of the room and had removed everything else from the dirt floor. He began speaking.

"Go over to the chair," he said.

"Take off your shirt," he said.

"Sit down," he said.

When the first bucket of cold water crashed over my head and spilled down my chest to the floor I screamed. Mbaya was killing me. Unfathomable extremes of hot and cold were savaging my skin for control, creating a pain like nothing I had felt before. I understood what was happening, but it was too much. It was beyond human tolerance. I stood up.

"Sit down," Mbaya said, pushing me back onto the chair. "We've got to do this."

I began waking from my torpor, which made the pain even worse. The second wave of water was colder and the shock even greater than the first. Again I voiced my agony. There was a third wave and a fourth wave and then Mbaya took a towel, folded it in half and began fanning me with it. The air was outrageously cold and I shivered and writhed. After about five minutes, Mbaya got the thermometer and I took my temperature. 104 degrees. More water, more fanning.

After fifteen minutes, my temperature budged down to 103.5. Mbaya kept going, pouring water on me and then mopping my head and arms and chest with a soaked towel before fanning me for long periods of time. Slowly, stubbornly, the fever dropped. Near nightfall it was down to 100.

Mbaya and I were both exhausted. I dried myself off and went into my room and lay in bed. He squatted on the damp kitchen floor and cooked his dinner over a charcoal fire. The next morning I found him on top of a sleeping bag next to my bed. Sluggishly, I got dressed. My face was puffy and red. The stomach cramps and diarrhea were still with me, but I was now only slightly feverish. I was able to travel.

I woke Mbaya and, with my head more lucid than it had been the day before, thanked him sincerely. I was leaving for the Catholic mission, I told him, and would return when I was well. As I pulled away on my motorcycle, I looked back and saw him standing in the doorway of my house. He was staying behind. I had gotten sick and now I was leaving to get help. I would cross the Lubilashi and continue on until I reached a Belgian doctor at a distant Catholic mission. And, if I wanted to, I could keep going. I could go all the way home and leave Kalambayi forever. Eventually, that's what I would do. I had a two-year contract to work in Africa. I was a visitor. But Mbaya had to stay. Kalambayi was his home. He would get sick again.

3

BEFORE PULLING AWAY IN HIS LAND ROVER AND LEAVING ME and all my gear at the crumbling cotton warehouse, Lukusa had called me over to the cab. "You might need this," he said, handing me a rolled up piece of paper. It was a creased and yellowed map of Kalambayi made by Belgian cartographers a decade earlier.

That night by kerosene lamp, I unrolled the map and took a close look. The paper crackled under my hands. I moved my finger from left to right, reading the names of villages and trying to memorize their locations. Next, I traced the rivers. There were three main ones, and following them with my finger I suddenly realized something. By a fluke of geography, Kalambayi was an island. Except for a short, uninhabited stretch to the north between Lake Kasasa and Mount Kasenga, every inch of the chiefdom was surrounded by rivers. To the south, wide and brooding was the Lubilashi. To the east and west, respectively, were the Lualu and Luvula Rivers. After almost touching fifteen miles to the north, these two rivers entered the Lubilashi forty miles apart, completing the land's vaguely bell-shaped boundary. In the center, surrounded by water on a rambling parcel of dense grass, lived the Kalambayans—islanders.

A few days after examining the map, I took it with me to the top of a large, black rock that sat outside Lulenga on the ridge. From this high point I compared the bending shape of the Lubilashi below me with the bending shape of the Lubilashi on the map. The two corresponded, and I took this as an indication that the Belgians had done an accurate job. My map was reliable.

It felt strange standing on the rock and having both the map and the land it represented before my eyes. With the aid of the paper, I suddenly could sense the rivers of Kalambayi all around me; I could sense the isolation, sense the island. Just knowing that there was virtually no way to enter or leave the chiefdom without crossing a river somehow made the Lubilashi's opposite shore seem farther away. The canoes moving through the water seemed different too: smaller now, like sticks floating in a narrow sea.

It wasn't long after I arrived in Kalambayi that I learned the effect these rivers had on life in the chiefdom. The drownings began. There were more than two dozen during the two years I lived there. In most cases the victims were tossed from canoes while trying to cross the rivers. This usually happened after storms when the water surged and turned dirty orange, making crossings even more hazardous than they were under normal conditions.

Two weeks after I unpacked my bags, there was a multiple drowning outside Lulenga. The Lubilashi had become swollen with rain and storm winds were still blowing hard when Ngoyi Lusangu lost control of his canoe and it tipped over in the middle of the river. He and three of his passengers drowned, their bodies recovered miles downriver. A dark, fearful mood settled over the village after the deaths. There was a gathering of men in the chief's compound to determine how the accident happened.

Lengos Mpombola came by my house after the meeting had ended. He was a young, handsome-faced man who lived five huts down from me.

"What was decided?" I asked him.

"It was Mambamuntu," he said. "The chief decided Mambamuntu tipped over the canoe and held the men under water until they died."

Mambamuntu, he explained, was a mermaid, a voluptuous, black-skinned mermaid with usual mermaid features: shirtless, buxom, half woman, half fish. Local superstition held that the creature inhabited the rivers around Kalambayi, quietly stroking through the water and taking people's lives from time to time as a show of power. The myth inspired fear and reverence among all

Kalambayans. Villagers knew that when crossing the rivers they might look down and see more than their own faces looking back.

A few nights after the Lulenga drownings, a group of village men went down to the Lubilashi with drums. Within an hour, a faint, rhythmic beat began traveling back to the huts. Before going to bed I walked to the big rock outside the village and peered down through the darkness at the gathering. I could see a bonfire along the riverbank, its thin, orange glow looking mysterious and forbidding in the black air. I could hear the continuing beat of drums, eerie and thumping, filling the valley with a sense of loss. The men had gone down to the river to dance and sing and sacrifice a chicken to Mambamuntu, the mermaid. They had gone to plead that their island be left alone, that their people be allowed to cross the rivers without accidents, without death.

The history of Kalambayi was for many years one of independence and seclusion. Inside their ring of rivers, with land stretching away endless and unknown in every direction, the people lived aware of little beyond their own affairs. It was only toward the end of the nineteenth century that things began to change. The Kalambayans were discovered. First came a brief period of Arab slave raiding, then came the Europeans.

Belgian colonists under the hire of King Leopold II arrived in Kalambayi in dugout canoes along the Lubilashi in the late 1880s. After a nasty struggle with the paramount chief, they declared administrative control over all the villages. The white foreigners had come with orders to end African savagery and replace it with a European version. King Leopold had claimed the Congo River basin as his personal colony and from it he intended to squeeze enough wealth to satisfy his royal tastes back home.

But change came slowly on the island. There were no immediately exploitable resources such as rubber or ivory, so the people were spared many of the early outrages committed in other parts of the colony. They were spared the death-inducing slave labor and the cutting off of villagers' hands as punishment for failing to meet rubber quotas. Instead, things in Kalambayi continued pretty much as before. People farmed and hunted in their centuries-old fashion with only periodic interference from their European overlords.

Years later, however, the Belgians discovered something about the island that made them grow suddenly excited: This place in the middle of the continent was one of the best spots in the world to grow cotton. The rainfall pattern was perfect. The abrupt change each May from dependable rains to an equally dependable three-month dry season was a cotton farmer's dream. If seeds were planted five months before this change, the rains would coax the plants out of the earth and give healthy beginning to the formulating buds. Then, just as the tender cotton bolls began to emerge, the rains would stop, allowing the bolls to mature into dry, fluffy fibers of a quality even better than cotton grown in Mississippi, where year-round rains soak the bolls and prevent such excellence.

The trick, of course, was timing. If the cotton was planted too early, the bolls would emerge during the rainy season and become damaged. If it was planted too late, the rains would end before the buds had matured enough to give optimal bloom.

"Christmas Day is best," a Belgian cotton agronomist in charge of Kalambayi's production later told me. "If you plant cotton here on Christmas Day, you'll have a superb harvest in July. It's all been worked out scientifically. That's what we've always tried to get these people to understand."

Thus, on or around Christmas Day 1925, cotton seeds were dropped into the Kalambayan soil for the first time. A colonial decree required every capable man to tend a fifty-by-fifty-meter plot (later raised to fifty-by-one-hundred). The harvests were sold at a fixed price to a Belgian company that exported to Europe. If a villager resisted cultivation, he was forced to lie on the ground and expose his buttocks to twenty lashes from an elephant-hide whip. No one resisted for long.

The initial cotton production in Kalambayi was so profitable—for the Europeans, anyway—that the operation expanded rapidly. After a few years, villagers were beating back the grass and planting cotton each Christmas as if they had been doing it all their lives.

Things began to change at an accelerated pace on the island in the early 1930s. To support the growing cotton production, the Belgians needed more roads, and building roads to and through Kalambayi meant conquering rivers. To the south near Kabala, a pontoon ferry—the same one I would use fifty years later to enter the chiefdom—was attached to a steel cable pulled high and tight above the Lubilashi. The ferry allowed trucks to cross in thirty minutes what before, depending on the rains, had been impossible even in a canoe. Bridges were built across the island's other rivers, and trucks came more frequently. They carried seeds, tools, insecticides, and fertilizer for the cotton. They carried dynamite to break up brick-size rocks and cement to hold the rocks together in the walls of cotton warehouses, administrative buildings, and a Catholic mission.

It wasn't long before no one really thought of Kalambayi as an island anymore. To the south was a ferry. To the west a steel-beam bridge stretched 150 feet across the Luvula River. To the east a series of rock-archway bridges crossed the Mujimbayi and Mvunai Rivers and finally the steep-banked Lualu. Between the bridges and connecting most of the villages were dirt roads built with hand tools by the villagers themselves under orders from the cotton company.

By the mid 1950s the process was complete. The island had been transformed. Its once-formidable waters, now passing obediently under bridges and giving silent buoyancy to the ferry, were virtually forgotten.

There was, mostly after the Second World War, a feeling on the part of the Belgian colonists that perhaps their relationship with the Kalambayan people ought to include more than just requiring them to plant cotton each Christmas Day. It might also be good to try to raise the people above their Iron Age standard of living. The best way to begin this, the Belgians decided, was to take advantage of the area's many streams and creeks. If dammed up, the water could be used to fill fish ponds. Protein deficiency was a serious problem in the area, and a diet of fresh fish would certainly improve health conditions. Besides, it might help the Kalambayans farm more cotton.

Consequently, Belgian fish culture extension agents began visiting Kalambayi twice a week in the mid 1950s. In their Land Rovers they brought shovels and wheelbarrows, and under their supervision villagers built several hundred small five-by-five-meter ponds throughout the area. The agents stocked the ponds with tilapia and the villagers became fish farmers.

At first, the people were excited about their new ponds. They gathered along the banks and looked down at the fish, hopeful of the improvement the tilapia might bring to their lives. But the concept of fish culture was profoundly foreign to them, and, in the end, the necessary instruction on how to manage the ponds and feed the fish was limited or nonexistent. The Belgians more or less stocked the ponds and left. Eventually time and rainwater wore down the earthen dikes. Most of the ponds broke open, expelling their water. Those that didn't only served as prisons for slow-growing, unattended fish.

By the time I came to live in Kalambayi thirty years later, there was only one pond with fish still in it from the old Belgian project. It sat at the bottom of a steep valley near the village of Kalula and had long since melted into the surrounding bush.

"It's my pond," said seventy-year-old Makoyi Mufedi after his two sons carried his arthritis-racked body three miles to my doorstep. "The fish are old, but they're still there, and you're welcome to come look at them."

I took him up on his offer and was dismayed by what I saw. Fish culture in Kalambayi had been reduced to a level of absurdity. On important occasions such as funerals or a call from a special visitor, Makoyi's sons would carry their father down to the pond where the old man, and no one else, would perform the ritual. He would stand next to the water, drop in a handful of live termites, and wait. As soon as the fish arrived, positively agog over the food, he would launch sharp arrows into their blue-gray bodies with a large bow. When he had a half dozen fish or so, his sons would carry him back to the village.

The only man in Kalambayi who still had a Belgian pond wasn't a fish farmer. He was a harpoonist.

The problem was that the Belgians, in their time, had done exactly what Rayleen McGarity had warned us trainees not to do. They had given away the fish. They had failed to spend the necessary time teaching villagers how to farm fish on their own forever.

Now it was my turn.

━━━ ⌒ ━━━

Equipped with a motorcycle from the United States Agency for International Development and administrative support from the Zairian Department of Agriculture and Rural Development, I set out to really show the people of Kalambayi something about fish culture. I was an extension agent for the government's *Projet Pisciculture Familiale*, or Family Fish Project.

Six days a week, I left my house around 7:30 a.m. and rode as much as forty miles over unspeakably eroded dirt roads and down narrow paths. I visited villages and expounded the virtues of fish culture to anyone who would listen. At first, most of the men I approached gave me a chair, pulled out a bottle of palm wine, nodded politely as I spoke, pulled out another bottle of palm wine, and then said: "No thanks. We've got enough work to do already." Around six o'clock, exhausted from equal parts of sun, foreign language, and palm wine, I'd return home.

It was after a few weeks of this, not long after watching Makoyi Mufedi shoot arrows at his geriatric fish, that I met Ilunga Mbumba, chief of the village of Ntita Kalambayi. I was riding my Yamaha 125 Enduro through an uninhabited stretch of bush when he appeared from out of the ten-foot-tall grass along the trail, signaling for me to stop. Had he not waved, I'm pretty sure I would have stopped anyway. Ilunga had been out hunting antelope and he presented a sight worth inspecting. In one hand he carried a spear, in the other a crude machete. On his head was a kind of coonskin cap with a bushy tail hanging down in back. Around his neck was a string supporting a leather charm to ward off bad bush spirits. Two underfed mongrel dogs circled his bare feet, panting.

When I stopped and saw Ilunga that first time, I saw a man living, it seemed to me, in another century. Inside the tall grass from which he had just stepped, the clock ran a thousand years slow if it registered any time at all. Unable to help myself, I stared at him openly, taking him in from head to toe. He, meanwhile, stared back at me with the same wide-eyed incredulity. And no wonder. With my ghost-white skin and rumbling motorcycle, with my bulging safety goggles and orange riding gloves, with my bushy brown beard flowing out from under a banana-yellow crash helmet—with all this, I suppose I had a lot of nerve thinking of *him* as a museum piece.

For a moment we just kept gawking, Ilunga and I, mentally circling each other, both of us trying to decide whether to burst out laughing or to run for safety. In the end, we did neither. We became friends.

"My name is Ilunga," he said, extending his hand.

"My name is Michel," I said, shaking it.

We smiled at each other another moment before Ilunga got around to telling me he had heard my job was to teach people how to raise fish. It sounded like something worth trying, he said, and he wondered if I would come by his village to help him look for a pond site. I said I would and took down directions to his house.

When I found Ilunga at his village home the next morning, he was forty feet in the air in the crown of a palm tree, squatting on branches and chopping nuts from the tree's trunk with a large hatchet. His muscular upper body was shirtless and wet with sweat.

"Hello," he yelled down as I approached the tree.

"Hello," I answered, careful to give the torrent of falling palm nuts a wide margin.

"I'll be down as soon as I finish this small bit of work," he said. "Have a seat."

Fair enough, I thought. I sat down on a log bench under an orange tree and looked around. Ilunga's house was dirty and extremely small, with only two rooms. The walls consisted of palm branches lashed together in a lattice frame and plastered with mud. The grass around the house had been cleared, leaving a dirt surface on which roamed a few scrawny chickens and goats. Scattered about the compound were the limited possessions typical of Kalambayan families: calabash bowls, woven reed mats, knives, assorted woven baskets, a few spears leaning against a tree, an enamel basin used for carrying water. I surveyed this scene and waited for Ilunga to finish his work. An hour later, he was still chopping and I was still waiting.

"Excuse me, chief," I yelled up.

The chopping stopped.

"Yes?"

"I thought you wanted to look for a place to build a fish pond this morning."

"Oh, yeah," he said, "I do."

He began chopping again. I was beginning to think my ability to speak Tshiluba was even worse than I had feared. We weren't communicating.

"Chief," I yelled up. "If you want a pond, why don't you climb down, and we can start looking?"

"Okay," he said.

Chop, chop, chop.

I sat down again. The morning was getting off to a bad start and I was getting impatient. Twenty minutes later—just as I was contemplating cutting down the palm tree myself and asking Ilunga man to man, eye to eye, if he wanted a fish pond or not—he quit working and, like a telephone lineman, descended barefoot, one peg at a time, on a heavily knotted bamboo pole.

"Welcome," he said when he reached the ground. "Welcome to my village."

"Thank you," I answered. I stood, ready to go. "Shall we start looking for a pond site?"

"No, not yet. We must eat first."

I sighed and sat back down. Like most of the villagers I met on the road, Ilunga wanted to feed me and take care of me. I was his guest. His wife, the cook, was off fetching water at the village source and it was forty-five minutes before she returned, accompanied by their three young sons. It took another hour and a half for her to gather firewood, start a fire, and prepare a meal of sweet potato leaves and dried antelope meat. With this she served a large bowl of *fufu*, a dough-like food made from corn and manioc flour. We ate with our hands from communal bowls placed on the ground.

After the meal I was on the verge of suggesting we leave right away when Ilunga pulled out a bottle of clear liquid corked with a corncob plug. The sight didn't stagger me with joy. It was *tshitshampa*, a popular, corn-based liquor brewed in crude stills throughout Kalambayi. The drink was taken straight, in small glasses, and had a face-numbing, body-blasting strength like nothing I had ever drunk before. Ilunga thought it best we have a few shots before work. I was still in the process of getting used to the stuff, and told him to pour me a modest dose.

Downing it, I decided to ask Ilunga a few questions, taking advantage of the prolonged relaxation. I was curious to know how he had become a village chief at such a young age. He was only thirty.

"This," he said, pointing to the bottle of *tshitshampa.*

"What do you mean?"

"This killed my father. *Tshitshampa.*"

He proceeded to tell a horrifying story. It had happened on a night three years earlier when his father got extremely drunk with some men on the other side of the village.

"By the time he came home, the rest of us were already asleep inside the house," Ilunga said. "We're not really sure how it happened, but somehow he was so drunk he stumbled and fell on top of a cooking fire outside the house that still had burning coals. He fell on the fire and couldn't pull himself off. The next morning I found him chest-down on top of ashes. He was dead. His neck and chest were covered with burns so bad I can't describe them."

I shuddered trying to imagine such a thing.

"How could anyone be that drunk?" I asked.

"I don't know," he said, "but he was."

Ilunga seemed curiously unfazed by the story. Indeed, within minutes he reached for the *tshitshampa* again and offered me another shot. I looked at the bottle and then at him and then shook my head no.

I also asked Ilunga why he wanted to build a pond. He was my first serious customer, and understanding his motives might help me persuade other men to join the fish project. He told me he had tried a number of different ways to make money for his wife and three sons. Like most village men, he had spent time prospecting for diamonds in Mbuji Mayi. But the work was dangerous and low-paying, and he gave it up. He also farmed cotton, which was obligatory, still forced on the villages by the Belgian cotton company. But there was little profit in cotton; prices were depressed. As for hunting wild game, the results were limited and unpredictable. Animals were getting more scarce as villages grew.

"So I thought a fish pond might help," Ilunga said, rising to put away the bottle of *tshitshampa*.

He looked at me.

"Are you ready to look for a place?"

I laughed. It was past noon.

"I'm ready," I said.

⌒

Into the bush we went, hunting for a pond site.

"The first thing we need," I told Ilunga, feeling the ghost of Rayleen McGarity hovering over me, "is water. Do you know a good spot where there's a small stream or a spring?"

"Follow me," he said.

Machetes in hand, we stomped and stumbled and hacked our way through the savanna grass for two hours before finding an acceptable site along a stream about a twenty-minute walk from Ilunga's village. Together, we paced off a pond and staked a water canal running between it and a point farther up the stream. Then, with a shovel I sold him on credit against his next corn harvest, Ilunga began a two-month journey through dark caverns of physical pain and over-exertion. He began digging. No bulldozers here. The task of carving out a pond from the valley-bottom floor was left to the farmer himself.

There is no easy way to dig a fish pond with a shovel. You just have to do it. You have to place the tip to the ground, push the shovel in with your foot, pull up a load of dirt, and then throw the load twenty or thirty feet to the pond's edge. Then you have to do it again—tip to the ground, push it in, pull it up, throw the dirt. After you do this about fifty thousand times, you have an average-size ten-by-fifteen-meter pond.

In many ways, the work is like a marathon. If you go too fast, you invite physical ruin. If you go too slow, you may never finish. You have to pace yourself. You have to dig a few hours each day, carefully spreading out the pain over time. But no matter what, you can't take a break. You can't stop. Not even for a week. To do so is to risk losing the rhythm of the fight and so become suddenly overwhelmed by the task at hand. Once the shovel enters the soil the first time, the work must continue every day—tip to the ground, push it in, pull it up, throw the dirt—again and again, meter by meter, fifty thousand times, until the marathon is over.

But Ilunga, being a chief and all, wasn't content with an average-size pond. He wanted one almost twice that size. He wanted a pond fifteen-by-twenty meters large. I told him he was crazy as we measured it out. I repeated the point with added conviction after watching him use his bare foot to drive the thin shovel blade into the ground.

"A pond this big is too much work for one person," I said. "It'll kill you."

"See you next week," he said.

"It's too much Ilunga."

He started digging.

"Okay," I said. "*Bon chance.*"

I left him at the pond site and began heading toward the village, hearing every ten seconds as I walked away the sound of a shovel-load of dirt hitting the ground after traveling twenty feet through the air.

For me, it was painful visiting Ilunga each week. This was the part of the fish culture process I had been dreading ever since arriving. I'd come to check on the pond's progress and find Ilunga grunting and shoveling and pitching dirt the same way I had left him the week before. I groaned inwardly at the sight of his clothes, ragged, full of yawning holes that revealed a glistening, overworked body. I calculated that to finish the pond he would have to move a total of four thousand cubic feet of dirt. Guilt gnawed at me. This was no joke. He really was going to kill himself.

One week I couldn't stand it any longer. I found Ilunga at the pond site with his body covered with the usual mixture of dirt and sweat.

"Give me the shovel," I told him.

"Oh no, Michel," he said. "This work is too much for you."

"Give it to me," I repeated, a bit indignantly. "Take a rest."

He shrugged and handed me the shovel. I began digging. Okay, I thought, tip to the ground, push it in, pull it up, throw the dirt. I did it again. It wasn't nearly as hard as I thought. Stroke after stroke, I kept going. About twenty minutes later, though, it got hot. I began wondering how, at 8:30 in the morning, the sun had suddenly reached noontime intensity. I paused to take off my shirt. Ilunga, thinking I was quitting, jumped up and reached for the shovel.

"No, no," I said. "I'm still digging. Sit down."

He shrugged again and said that since I was apparently serious about digging he was going to go check on one of his fields. "Good idea," I said.

Shirtless, alone, I carried on. Tip to the ground, push it in, pull it up, throw the dirt. An hour passed. Tip to the ground, push it in, pull it up . . . throw . . . throw the . . . dammit, throw the dirt. My arms were signaling that they didn't like tossing dirt over such a great distance. It hurts, they said. Stop making us do it. But I couldn't stop. I had been digging a paltry hour and a half. I was determined to go on, to help Ilunga. How could I expect villagers to do work I was incapable of doing myself?

Sweat gathered on my forehead and streamed down my face as I continued, shoveling and shoveling. About thirty minutes passed and things started to get really ugly. My body buckled with fatigue. My back and shoulders joined my arms in screaming for an end to hostilities. I was no longer able to throw the dirt. Instead, I carried each load twenty feet and ignobly spooned it onto the dike. I was glad Ilunga wasn't around to see this. It was embarrassing. And God was it hot. The hottest day I could ever remember. Even occasional breezes rustling through the surrounding savanna grass didn't help. And then I looked at my hands. Both palms had become blistered. One was bleeding.

I took a short break and began digging again. The pain resumed, cracking out all over my body. Fifteen minutes later, my hand finally refused to grip the shovel. It fell to the ground. My back then refused to bend down to allow my arms the chance to refuse to pick it up. I was whipped. After just two hours of digging, I was incapable of doing any more. With a stiff, unnatural walk, I went over to the dike. Ilunga had just returned, and I collapsed next to him.

"I think I'll stop now," I managed, unable to hide my piteous state. "Take over if you want."

He did. He stood up, grabbed the shovel and began working—smoothly, confidently, a man inured to hard work. Tip to the ground, push it in, pull it up, throw the dirt. Lying on my side, exhausted, I watched Ilunga. Then I looked hard at the spot where I had been digging. I had done nothing. The pond was essentially unchanged. I had moved perhaps thirty cubic feet of dirt. That meant 3,970 cubic feet for Ilunga.

After the brief digging experience, my weekly visits to the pond became even more painful and my awe of Ilunga grew. Day after day, four or five hours each day, he kept going. He kept digging his pond. He worked like a bull and never complained. Not once. Not when he hit a patch of gravel-size rocks that required a pickaxe and extra sweat. Not when, at the enormous pond's center, he had to throw each shovel-load twice to reach the dikes. And not when he became ill.

His hand was on fire one morning when I arrived and shook it.

"You're sick," I said.

"I know," he said and resumed digging.

"Then quit working and get some rest."

"I can't," came the reply. "I've got to finish this pond."

Several weeks later, Ilunga drove his shovel into the earth and threw its load one last time. I never thought it would happen, but there it was. Ilunga's pond, huge, fifteen-by-twenty meters and completely finished. We hollowed out a bamboo inlet pipe and positioned it in the upper dike so canal water could enter the pond. Three days later, the pond was gloriously full of water. Using my motorcycle and two ten-liter carrying *bidons*, I transported stocking fish from another project post twenty miles to the south. When the last of the three hundred tilapia fingerlings had entered the new pond, I turned to Ilunga and shook his hand over and over again. We ran around the banks hooting and hollering, laughing like children, watching the fish and marveling at what a wonderful thing a pond was. Where before there had been nothing, just grass and scrub trees, had come watery life.

To celebrate, I had brought a bottle of *tshitshampa*, and Ilunga and I began pouring each other shots and slapping each other on the back and talking entirely too loud for two men sitting alone on a pond bank in the middle of the African bush. A warm glow spread from our stomachs to our limbs and, soon, strongly, our heads. Ilunga expressed his dream of digging three, no six, no twelve more fish ponds, and I concluded that there was no biological reason why, if fed properly, tilapia couldn't grow to be the size of Land Rovers. At one point, we decided to assign names to all of Ilunga's fish. Straight-faced, signaling each other to be quiet, we crouched next to the water and began naming the first few fish that swam by. After four fish, though, we lost track of which fish had which names. This struck us as absolutely hilarious for some reason, and we fell on our backs and stamped our feet and laughed so loud we couldn't stand it.

Oh, sweet joy, the pond was finished. Ilunga had done it. He had taken my instructions and accomplished a considerable thing. And on that day when we finally stocked the pond, I knew that no man would ever command more respect from me than one who, to better feed his children, moves four thousand cubic feet of dirt with a shovel.

I had a hero.

———•———

Not long after Ilunga started building his pond, two other men—Kalambayi Katanda and Ngeleka Muzangu—decided to dig at the same site. Soon all three ponds stood connected side to side, full of water and tilapia. It was done. We had created, in our estimation at least, a full-fledged fish farm.

And now that the construction phase was over, it was time for the most important part of my job: teaching the men how to eat fish forever. I continued visiting the site every week, and the farmers and I would walk endless circles around the banks. We would note the fishes' growth and discuss proper feeding and management techniques. All the while, I used the same Socratic method on them that Rayleen McGarity used on me. I tried never to divulge information outright, but made the men work for it by thinking through a long series of questions.

When, after long sessions like these, we ran out of things to talk about, the farmers and I would plop down on the grassy dikes and grow silent and just watch the water, placid before us, its surface broken only now and again by a diving insect or a surfacing fish, then growing smooth again. As we watched, the sun beamed down and the water sparkled with a wondrous poetry of reflected light.

Of all my time in Africa, I loved these quiet moments by the ponds the best. There's something about bodies of water, something about rivers and lakes and oceans and ponds, that seems to hold and heal the human soul. Near them one stops and stares in a way similar to sitting by a log fire at night. Maybe it's the liberating effect of the water's open surface that does this or the intrigue one feels at being at the edge of something unknown below. Or maybe it's the tug of a strange, subconscious desire to return to a watery womb. Whatever the attraction, it's clear that water has the power to make one grow contemplative and content. It casts a spell of serenity. That's the way it affected the village farmers and me. For long stretches of time, with all of Africa suddenly quiet around us in the late morning sun, we would lose ourselves to the ponds.

During my first few months, men from other villages grew interested in fish culture. They stopped me along footpaths or visited me at my house, and together we stocked a growing number of ponds. I was encouraged by the quick interest. But the work wasn't easy. Fish culture was no less foreign to the villagers now than it had been thirty years earlier with the Belgians. Getting the farmers to understand it and do it right was difficult, especially with the older men.

Consider, for example, the case of pond-stocking method versus Monsieur Bukasa Dikumbi. Government researchers for our project had established that the best way to stock tilapia was to add one two-month-old fingerling for every square meter of pond surface. A one-hundred-square-meter pond, in other words, required one hundred stocking fish. Easy enough. But Bukasa, a salty, sad-eyed, sixty-five-year-old father of twenty, worked on the principle of, hell, just throw the fish in helter-skelter, the more the better. The notion of precision lay outside his understanding.

"Let me put it this way," I told Bukasa one day, trying to explain. "If we want to stock one fish for every square meter, and our pond has, let's suppose, just one square meter of surface area, how many fish should we stock?"

"One," he said.

"Yes," I said. "That's right. Very good. Now, if we have a pond with two square meters, how many fish?"

"Two."

"Ten square meters?"

"Ten."

"One hundred square meters?"

"One hundred."

"And if our pond has 150 square meters like your pond, Bukasa, how many fish?"

"My pond?"

"Yes, your pond."

"At least three hundred or four hundred," he said.

So it went. Bukasa smiled and I winced and we started over again.

Still, the farmers and I made progress and fish culture continued to expand. To the west, in the village of Bena Mbaya, a group of men built a 150-foot-long dike that dammed a stream in a flat, narrow valley and created a half-acre reservoir that fed ponds. Villagers there eventually dug twenty ponds set end to end in an awe-inspiring, uninterrupted necklace of water. Elsewhere, ponds were built to the north in Tshipanzula, to the east in Kanda, to the south in Kalula. The simplicity of the project had great appeal. To get started all you needed was a shovel, which you could borrow; water, which was free; and $1 to $3 to buy the stocking fish. After that you were set up in perpetuity. It was working. Fish culture was starting to take off in Kalambayi.

Then the crisis came.

"Birds are eating my fish," Chief Ilunga told me one day when I went to visit him. "They're eating all my fish and there's nothing I can do about it."

It was true. A trio of kingfishers—beady-eyed birds with long, sinister beaks—was living in trees near Ilunga's pond and growing fat off the tilapia below. Worse, Ilunga wasn't alone. More than half the fish farmers in Kalambayi were suddenly telling tales of kingfishers swooping down and plucking fish from the water with terrifying effectiveness. The birds, it seemed, had abandoned their usual haunts along Kalambayi's rivers and had migrated en masse to the cornucopia of good eating offered by fish ponds. Some farmers estimated they were losing half their fish.

Since beginning my extension work, I had done my best to prepare the men for this attack and others like it. Stocking a pond and feeding the fish are not the whole of fish culture, I warned them. There's much more to it than that. As soon as the fish enter the pond, a stealthy army of rogues begins plotting attack. Birds, turtles, frogs, toads, giant lizards, snakes, and even certain kinds of insects arrive at water's edge and—first looking left and then right—enter to reap what they haven't sown. From the day he stocks his pond to the day he harvests, a fish farmer must be vigilant. He must be a warrior.

The project farmers had already adopted several techniques for killing attackers. Spears took care of frogs and toads, who were the easiest opponents and made for the best sport. I spent many a lively hour gigging these would-be fish-eaters along pond banks with farmers. As for turtles and lizards and most other predators, a well-placed stone from a slingshot usually did the job.

But in this ancient contest of thinking man versus natural calamity, birds are the real sons of bitches.

"Every time I try to sneak up to the pond, no matter how slowly or quietly, the birds see me coming and fly away with fish dangling from their beaks," Ilunga told me. "I can't get close enough to do anything about it."

For an entire month, Ilunga tried everything he could think of to kill the birds. He spread a handmade net across the top of the pond banks to tangle up the birds' feet. But all he caught was a large owl whose stomach, when he cut it open, was full of frogs. A friend. Next, he placed several homemade, spring-released mousetraps around the pond. He used fish as bait, but got no takers. One morning, he hid himself in the tall grass next to the pond and waited with an ancient, muzzle-loading rifle he had bought for two goats from his brother-in-law.

"The birds knew I was there and didn't come to the pond," he told me later. "Then, in the afternoon, one came out onto the bank and I pulled back the hammer. But just when I was about to shoot, I heard my brother Tshibamba come running down the path screaming, 'Hey, bird, get away from there.' He had come to draw water from the stream. The bird took off. I stood up and fired after it and missed. I should have shot my brother instead."

The birds never fell for that trick again.

Meanwhile, the carnage continued and Ilunga grew increasingly despondent. I did too. Rayleen had covered a lot of topics in Oklahoma but killing kingfishers wasn't one of them. Flat out of ideas, I started feeling like I was letting Ilunga and the other farmers down. How in the world were they supposed to make any money if these stupid birds kept eating all the fish?

Eventually, though, Ilunga got an idea so simple I berated myself for not having thought of it sooner. He built a scarecrow. He made it out of straw, dressed it in old clothes, and put it next to the pond. It worked. For the next several days the birds stayed away. But then a funny thing began to happen. One morning while feeding his fish, Ilunga noticed flecks of white bird droppings on the scarecrow's forehead and right cheek. After a few days, the droppings grew to cover the scarecrow's straw hair and much of its face. The kingfishers were back. Too shrewd to stay scared for long, they now were using the scarecrow's head as a launching pad from which to spot and kill fish. In the process, they were disdainfully releasing their bowels. The metaphorical implications weren't lost on Ilunga.

"They're mocking me," he said. "The chief of this village is being mocked by a bunch of birds. I can't stand it any longer."

At this point the solution was right under our noses, but it was another week before we realized it.

"You know," I said to Ilunga as we sat, feeling beaten, at the ponds, "if the birds keep landing on the scarecrow's head, why don't you try hiding a trap in its hair?"

He gave me a sidelong look.

"It won't work," he said darkly.

"How do you know it won't work?"

"Because I know. I've done everything. These birds are immortal."

"Try it," I said.

He finally agreed. He parted the scarecrow's polluted hair and placed a mousetrap on its head, lightly covering the trap with straw. When he had finished we headed back to the village.

After a month of failing in every imaginable way, Ilunga with this technique killed all three kingfishers in two days. The birds landed with typical irreverence on the scarecrow's head only to die in a flurry of feathers and straw as the spring-released trap did its job. After the third kill, a messenger arrived at my house in Lulenga bringing word that dinner was being prepared at Ilunga's home and the chief requested my presence. An hour later, Ilunga and I were picking the last of the kingfishers' bones and finishing a large bowl of *fufu*.

The crisis was over. Word of Ilunga's technique spread quickly, and it wasn't long before little straw men—their faces covered with bird droppings—kept silent and effective guard over fish ponds throughout Kalambayi.

After four months, the project farmers had pushed fish culture far beyond Makoyi Mufedi, the old man with the Belgian-era pond and the arrow-dodging fish. There were now close to two dozen ponds strung along the streams and springs of twelve different villages. Families were eating more protein and the upcoming harvests promised money for new clothes, school fees, and medicine. It was just a start, of course, but the progress was exciting. People in Kalambayi now were producing something beyond the subsistence level and doing it on their own, exclusively for their own benefit. There were no high-priced fertilizers to buy, no cotton company setting prices, no one taking a cut but the farmers themselves.

Still, not all was well. The project's success was sketched in pencil across a canvas of greater failure. Crippling the land and complicating everything was a problem: Kalambayi was becoming an island again. The entire infrastructure of bridges and roads developed by the Belgian cotton company years before was falling apart, a victim of post-independence neglect. It had been happening slowly and for a long time and now the process was nearly complete. Rivers which for years had passed without incident under bridges and around the land's perimeter were reasserting their former authority. Roads which had traversed the territory, connecting every village, were dying a slow death by erosion. For me, an extension agent whose job it was to visit every quarter of the chiefdom, this caused blinding headaches.

A case in point was the Mvunai River. It flowed seven miles from my house near Kalambayi's eastern border. It wasn't a huge river; just big enough and volatile enough to make folly of the work of Belgian engineers. In the late 1950s, the Belgians designed and built an important 150-foot-long bridge that crossed the Mvunai and made possible commercial contact between Kalambayi and several tribes to the east. For many years, transport trucks passed this way almost daily, loaded with manioc and cotton and people.

But ten years before I arrived a heavy rainstorm made the Mvunai go crazy. The river turned muddy and angry and eventually jumped its banks, contemptuously chopping and slicing earth as it went. The high left bank to which the bridge was connected collapsed and disappeared in the torrent, removing itself like a cape pulled from a charging bull. When the spasm had ended, the river followed a whole new path, passing neatly around the bridge in a self-fashioned curve to the left. The bridge itself was left standing, foolishly, on a newly formed sand bank. High and dry, it jutted out toward the river, going nowhere and crossing nothing.

Meanwhile, farmers in three villages on the other side of the Mvunai wanted to raise fish, so every Friday I went. This despite the fact that putting a Yamaha 125 in a narrow, fifteen-foot-long canoe can only be described as something just shy of madness. With the help of other men at the river, I would lift the motorcycle into the canoe and lean it severely on its side with the tires on the floor and the handlebars actually hanging over the water past one gunwale. I then would sit on the opposite gunwale, providing a delicate counterweight that kept the canoe from tipping over.

Every week the local canoe operator, a skinny eighteen-year-old kid named Mbumba, would take me across the river this way, with the old stone bridge still standing not one hundred yards away, its sides covered with dirt and vines except here and there where exposed stones, like eyes, watched us struggle. The canoe would rock slightly from side to side as it crawled across the river. "Slow down!" I would yell to Mbumba who stood behind me, poling us across. "You're rocking again." I was sure that sooner or later I would ride my motorcycle to this river, put it in the canoe, start across, and wind up walking home with a terrible letter to write my boss. "Dear Lukusa . . ."

The Mvunai bridge was just one exhibit. There were others. For lack of spare parts, the pontoon ferry near Kabala spent more than half its time out of service, preventing vehicles from entering Kalambayi from the south. To the east, the wood-plank surface of the Luvula River bridge had aged so much that the bridge's continued use was uncertain. Many truck drivers refused to cross it. The drivers who did had no guarantee they would get very far on the other side; things were no better in the interior.

Indeed, across the island, the cases of infrastructure decay seemed to multiply every day. They piled up higher and higher like some crude monument to the second law of thermodynamics. The chiefdom was proof, in other words, that all things left to themselves proceed in such a direction that disorder and randomness increase. And accelerating this process of deterioration in Kalambayi was water. A substance both heavy and fluid, it could behave, as in the case of the Mvunai Bridge, like an enormous moving mallet. It moved across the land and through rivers, destroying things seemingly at will. I came to appreciate this fact with undiluted certainty one morning as I plunged, on my motorcycle, four feet under water to the bottom of Tshiyumbu Creek.

Flowing just shy of Kalambayi's northern border, Tshiyumbu Creek ran through a stretch of land where villages ended and an interminable landscape of bush and hills began. The road through this area had long since surrendered to converging phalanxes of grass and scrub trees. Only a footpath remained. The path was passable on motorcycle as long as you sped up a little when approaching the creek and plowed through its one-foot-deep, fifteen-foot-wide waters. I passed this way every week on my way to work in the village of Bena Ngoyi until the fateful day when, speeding up a bit as usual, I entered the creek and dropped, like a stone, four feet to the bottom. Splash. I was under water, lying on my side, my leg pinned under the motorcycle, and my ears listening to the single-cylinder engine gurgle, make bubbles, and die.

Rushing water from a severe storm two days earlier had deepened the creek and increased its disorder and randomness. By the time I came along it was nothing but a watery booby trap waiting patiently in ambush. I quickly freed my leg and stood up in the chest-high water, gulping air. Swearing passionately, I pulled the motorcycle onto the shore. I tried kick-starting it and watched as water shot out the exhaust pipe as if coming from a giant squirt gun. For several hours I removed and dried motor parts. By the time I had the motorcycle running again it was too late in the day to do anything but turn around and go back home. I learned my lesson, though. It never happened again. With a caution bordering on paranoia, I began wading through every creek I came to, no matter how familiar, before driving across.

Kalambayi, the island. Just add water. That's all you had to do. Add water and the rivers and dirt roads and paths came alive. That's alive as in thinking, moving, scheming, changing. In just one hour a good rainstorm could create fascinating new examples of erosion—exposing new rocks, crafting new bumps, forging new gullies. Then, the next day, another storm would worsen and rearrange the obstacles with the ease of a magician moving shells about on his table. Riding a motorcycle on such roads was like piloting a paint shaker. Stay left here. Keep right there. Damn! Where did that hole come from? The motorcycle gets stuck in mud, bogged down in disorder, mired in randomness.

It wasn't long before I began waking up each morning in terribly depressed moods, dreading the ride before me that day. With the grim routine of a gladiator preparing for a fight, I would lace up my leather riding boots, pull on my protective gloves, put on my helmet, and fasten the chin strap tight. Then, driving slowly, as carefully as I could, I would set off to work, bouncing and slipping and sliding along the way. I fell at least once a week, tumbling from my motorcycle and hitting the ground after encountering an unexpected rock or surprise puddle. I must have presented quite a sorrowful sight many mornings, pulling up to villages covered with mud, my face pale, perhaps a new scrape or bruise on my arm from a fall along the way. Out of necessity, I began carrying a shovel with me to dig my way out of bad spots. One fish farmer, Katombe Jean, offered additional assistance. He tied a leather charm to my handlebars to protect me against the evil roads spirits that were obviously attacking me.

None of this did much good, though. The roads continued to grow worse, hideously worse, after each storm. Transport trucks from the regional capital began coming less frequently to pick up produce in the villages. The island's surface was too damaged for the tires to negotiate. Surplus corn and manioc rotted in storage.

Something had to be done, I decided. The chiefdom was literally returning to bush. Wondering if I might, in my position, be able to pull some strings, I went to the village of Kabala where stood the local administrative office of the national government and the national political party, which were the same thing. The office was inside a one-story, cinder-block building and, like everything else in the area, was in an advanced stage of decline. Various types of vines slithered up the cracking exterior walls, with some vines actually entering the building's side windows. When I arrived, two workers were nailing tin patches onto the rusting roof and a woman was building a crude cooking fire right outside the office door.

"Yes, I can file an emergency request for road repair," Bashiya Mulumba said when I put the question to him inside. He was the government functionary who managed state affairs in Kalambayi.

"You can?" I said, a little surprised by his quick and confident response.

"Yes, sure. It's no problem. But I'll need five hundred American dollars to do it."

"Five hundred dollars? For what?"

"For the paper and ink and stamps and typewriter ribbon it will take to fill out the forms."

"You need five hundred dollars worth of supplies just to make one request?"

"Of course," he said, "things are expensive in this country."

He must have taken my look of shock and disgust for bargaining theatrics because he promptly lowered his price.

"Okay, I can probably do it for two hundred and fifty."

I shook my head and told him that, as much as I wanted to help keep the government office properly equipped, I didn't have that kind of money. Then, with the most insincere tone I could muster, I thanked him for his time and turned to leave.

"Well, how much money *do* you have?" he asked as I was heading for the door.

I slapped my pockets. "Nothing," I said. "I don't have any money at all."

I hadn't expected my visit to Bashiya to be quite the exercise in futility and attempted bribery it turned out to be. With time, though, I learned well that Bashiya's job had nothing to do with serving Kalambayi and everything to do with generating pocket money for his party bosses in Mbuji Mayi by taxing villagers to the height of their ability to pay.

Two weeks later, I decided to bypass Bashiya and go straight to the cotton company officials in Ngandajika thirty miles away. They were the ones who really called the shots in Kalambayi anyway. Since independence, the Belgians had maintained a controlling interest in the cotton company and, with government approval, had continued the policy of forced cultivation in and around Kalambayi. I wanted to see if the company could dispatch a bulldozer to at least repair some of the worst stretches of roads in the chiefdom. Road repair had been one of the company's responsibilities since it conquered the island more than half a century before. It had provided the work trucks, shovels, and cement needed to keep things working.

But this was no longer possible, I was informed when I inquired at the company office. Jean Luc, a tall, twenty-six-year-old Belgian supervisor dressed in matching khaki shorts and shirt, told me the company was more or less broke; it was all but washing its hands of Kalambayi. To cut operation costs, the company had stopped spending money on infrastructure repair several years earlier, he said. With an air of defeat and exasperation, he went on to explain that, in addition to the cost of operating in a country aswarm with corruption, cotton prices had dropped 100 percent in the past twenty-five years. In a final, nightmarish blow, the Chinese government had recently liberalized its country's internal markets and entered world competition with massive new production, making a bad price even worse. "Think of it," Jean Luc implored me in a tone full of smug ridicule. "One billion people using ten billion fingers to pick cotton. We're doomed."

There just wasn't much money in cotton anymore. I saw with my own eyes the blueprints of a plan to repair the Mvunai bridge. "But no funds," Jean Luc said. "Not now. Maybe never." The company would continue investing as little money as possible in Kalambayi, getting its cotton out as best as it could on what roads and bridges still functioned.

With all my hopes for road repair thus thoroughly crushed, I left the cotton company office and headed home, sensing that I was in for a long, long two years in Kalambayi. I reached the Lubilashi and crossed in a canoe where the ferry lay broken for lack of cable. Riding down gnarled roads on the other side, I passed Kalambayan villagers toting goods on their heads and pulling goats on hemp-rope leashes. The people had virtually no understanding of why things were falling apart, I realized. They didn't know why cotton prices were depressed, didn't understand the vagaries of world commodity markets. Nor did they know the first thing about China and the millions of new Chinese farmers growing cotton. All they knew was that the price they were getting for their cotton was low and that company officials, if they came at all, came late to pick up harvests.

And, like me, they knew that long sections of roads throughout their chiefdom were fast regressing to mud sloughs. Except for motorcycles (mine and the Catholic mission's), motorized traffic now had decreased to a trickle. Villagers were growing increasingly discouraged. Many were ready to turn to fish culture, and I was ready to teach them, ready to battle the roads to reach them. But even by motorcycle, it grew harder and harder to get to many villages. Sometimes it was impossible.

Only at the last moment, for example, did I see the palm tree that left me banged-up one morning and my motorcycle in need of multiple repairs. The tree had fallen during a storm the night before and lay across the road, three feet off the ground. When I rounded the curve early the next day, I gasped. Frantically, I applied the brakes. But I didn't stop. I started sliding through mud. I watched the tree grow closer and closer, and in those terrifying few seconds when I knew I was going to hit and there was nothing I could do about it, all the frustration and anxiety of working in this rotting backwater, of trying to push forward a system clearly moving in the opposite direction, shot through me in searing climax.

There was a sickening, cracking sound when the motorcycle hit. I went flying forward. My wrist hit the tree trunk. My thigh slammed into the speedometer. Then the next split second was a blank. I don't recall actually going over the handlebars and over the tree. The next thing I knew I was on my back, lying in a cold puddle of muddy water with the gray sky above me and pain rifling through my bruised limbs.

It took several days to recover from the accident physically and even longer to recover mentally. With distressing vividness, the image of the approaching palm tree played itself over and over again in my head until I found myself beating back thoughts of breaking my work contract and leaving Kalambayi for home. How was I supposed to get anything done if I kept plummeting into creeks and slamming into trees? How, in this place of traps and obstacles and stagnant villages buried under a stagnant economy, was I supposed to keep from killing myself, much less teach men how to raise fish?

I wasn't sure. In fact, my job was beginning to seem close to impossible. But I decided I had gone through too much in Oklahoma and too much in Kalambayi these first few months to leave now. Besides, every time I pulled into villages and saw those skinny four-year-old children with the orangish hair and puffy cheeks of protein starvation, I knew I couldn't leave without taking their faces with me. I didn't want that baggage. I didn't want those faces forever asking me if I had really done everything I could to stay. So I resolved to stick things out. I resolved to live with it, all of it—the roads, the erosion, the accidents. And I did. With time I learned to better handle the roads, and the falls became fewer. But no amount of determination could diminish the daily strain. It was always there on the way to work, at every creek and at every curve in the road.

And there were the stormy nights. There were the nights when I worried myself sick as the pocket-change rain fell from the sky. It bounced off my tin roof, filling my rooms with a nervous white sound. On such nights, I worried about fish ponds flooding and breaking open. I worried about how I was going to get to work the next morning. I wondered what jig the roads were dancing that night and what new clothes they would wear the next day. Were the raindrops I was hearing on my roof going to roll to the bridgeless Mvunai River, or would they do more damage to Tshiyumbu Creek? Maybe they would just rush down to the nearby Lubilashi and join the torrent that pulls on the ferry ten miles away until, at least twice a year, the shore-to-shore cable snaps like a rubber band.

And when the beating rain would grow louder on my roof and I could no longer think, I would fall asleep and often dream worse things. The bad things that worried me so by day would come true.

Shadowy and thick came one dream, in haunting black and white. Outside my village, on a hill in the pouring rain, the fish farmers of Kalambayi were huddled together and looking down in paralyzed seriousness at the Lubilashi several hundred yards away. All the farmers were there, two dozen of them: Chief Ilunga, old man Bukasa, even the men from Bajila Membila on the far side of Kalambayi near Katanda. They stood in the angry, slanting wetness and watched a truly terrifying thing: Every pond from every village in Kalambayi somehow had been connected end to end in a quarter-mile-long chain that ran parallel to the Lubilashi's near bank and perilously close to the river's now rain-swollen waters. Two dozen ponds, each full of fish and each worth fifty thousand shovel-loads of dirt, were no more than a few feet from a giant moving mallet.

At first, I didn't know the farmers were there. A few villagers spotted them standing in the rain, and, thinking it odd, came to my house to tell me. I ran to the edge of the village and saw the men on a knoll about one hundred yards down the slightly sloping valley. I yelled out for them to come take shelter at my house. But with the rain smashing down everywhere on the shoulder-high grass, the farmers didn't hear me. Then I noticed their heads intently turned toward the river. I followed their gaze and shuddered. The water was now almost touching the dikes.

There was no path leading to the small clearing where the farmers stood, so I began working my way slowly through the thick grass. At first I parted the tall blades with my arms, slipping and stumbling through. Soon the grass became more dense, and I had to tuck my head under my arms and move like a plow. When I finally reached the farmers, no one turned to speak to me. They just kept looking down with baleful stares at the river and the delicate string of ponds below. I joined them. The rain continued crashing down. The river raged on.

Then it happened. With impossible quickness, as if yanked up by a string, the river rose and covered the ponds. The chain disappeared from beginning to end. Our horror was so great when this happened that the farmers and I flinched back as if feeling a sudden burst of heat against our faces. We watched, helpless, our heads recoiled, as water raced above where the ponds had been. Then, after no more than ten or fifteen seconds, the water retreated in the same strange and sudden way it had risen. The ponds were visible again. But the chain had been damaged, dikes were broken, and not one pond still held water. The fish were gone. The rain still poured.

She was there too, somewhere, standing among us. I knew she was there and she had seen what had happened. I tried to find her in the crowd, but in the heavy rain, with my mind shaken by what had happened, my eyes wouldn't focus; no face was distinguishable. I bumped against vague bodies for a while until finally I just yelled out for her to hear. "I didn't just give away the fish," I cried. "But there's been a flood, Rayleen. There's been a flood."

4

As I pressed on, determined to make fish culture work on this sinking island, I had more to worry about than just roads taking my life. People in villages across Kalambayi were trying to kill me too. They were feeding me too much. With little in the way of possessions, but driven by a congenital desire to share what they could, villagers gave me *fufu*—teeming, steaming metric tons of it.

Fufu, again, was the doughy white substance served at every meal. Women made it by pouring corn and manioc flour into boiling water, stirring the mixture with wooden spoons, then lumping the gummy results into calabash bowls where it assumed a size, shape, and weight not unlike small bowling balls. It had little taste, but filled you up and that was its purpose: to compensate for the dishearteningly small servings of manioc leaves or dried fish that came with it. Kayemba Lenga told me a funny fable about how Kalambayan ancestors stole the recipe for *fufu* from mosquitoes long ago. Now, in protest, the bothersome insects buzz one's ears every night. Not being overly fond of *fufu*, nor the recurring malaria protesting mosquitoes had already given me, I asked Kayemba half-jokingly if it wasn't possible to give the recipe back.

But it wasn't possible. *Fufu* was as much a part of the landscape as the grass and rivers. In every village, around every corner, it was there, waiting for me, widening my waistline. Without exception, the villagers I visited each day insisted I have some before moving on. As in most traditional societies, the giving was ungrudging and automatic—born of kindness— and saying no simply was out of the question.

A fairly typical day:

I arrive at Bukasa's house at 8:00 a.m. and a bowl of *fufu* awaits me, releasing hot wisps into the morning air. "Come," he says. "Sit down. You need to eat before we go to the ponds." We eat and leave for work. At the ponds I meet Kayemba and Mulundu Ilunga who cheerfully drag me back to their houses for large, back-to-back servings. I thank them afterwards and leave for the next village, Bena Ngoyi. By the time I pull up to the huts it's 1:00 p.m.—lunchtime. Two more bowls of *fufu*. Sluggishly, my shirt buttons threatening to launch, I move on to Milamba for a quick look at a pond and a torturous sixth bowl. At the end of the day I'm transporting my bulk home under depressed tires when a man in Kalula flags me down. He wants to discuss digging a pond. We sit and talk, and when I rise to leave he tells me to wait. I panic. "No seriously," I protest. "I'm not hungry. Really, no please. Please don't." But he knows I'm just being polite. He has two wives and they *both* bring out *fufu*. I wash my hands. *Bon appetite*, he says.

This was something I hadn't counted on. I had expected a lot of challenges living in rural Africa, but being incapacitated by too much generosity, too much *fufu*, just wasn't one of them. And *fufu* wasn't the only thing weighing me down. Relentlessly, Kalambayans shared all their food, unloading on me whatever happened to be around when I rolled into view. They put oranges in my hands, peanuts in my pockets, stuffed sugarcane in my knapsack.

"It won't fit," I told Kayemba one day as he tried to tie an entire regime of bananas across my motorcycle handlebars. "I'll crash. Just give me five. That's enough."

"No, it's all right," he said. "I've got another regime in the house."

"I'll crash, Kayemba. Don't do it." I wasn't just being polite this time. He yielded and sulked for a moment until the absurdity of his attempt caught up with him and we both laughed so hard tears welled in our eyes.

It was truly overwhelming, all this giving. The Kalambayans were some of the poorest people anywhere in the world, and yet they were by far the most generous I had ever met. Indeed, each time I thought I had been offered everything they had to share, something new was laid at my feet.

Barely three months after I moved into the Lulenga cotton warehouse, the village chief, Mbaya Tshiongo, appeared at my door dressed in his threadbare trench coat and ripped tennis shoes. He was a meek, doddering septuagenarian with whom my previous contact had been limited to conversations in the market where I told him repeatedly that, yes, everything was fine and, no, I didn't need anything. Now he had come to my house with something more dramatic on his mind. Standing at his side were his four eligible daughters, shy and fresh as daisies.

"Michel," he began, leathery half-moons sagging under his eyes, "you live in my village and I am responsible for you. Take one of my daughters. You're alone. A wife will make your life better. Choose one and she will stay with you."

Half the people in the village were standing behind the chief waiting to see who I would choose. Flattered and panicked in equal measure, my chest thumping, I fumbled for a way out of this with minimal loss of face. I walked up to the chief, put my arm around his shoulders and quietly guided him inside, where I explained things: "I can't accept, chief. Really. They're beautiful women. But I'm fine by myself. I don't need a wife right now."

A cloud of perplexity crossed his face. He tried to reason with me. "But you *do* need a wife, Michel. Every man does. Look, I'll waive the dowry. You won't even have to pay me anything. Just take one." But I wouldn't budge. Standing to leave, the chief asked me to at least promise to let him know if I ever changed my mind. I said I would.

After the crowd dispersed and Chief Mbaya led his daughters, now wilted by rejection, back home, I was left alone in my house convinced there really were no limits to what these people would have me have. The intense desire to give moved me to admiration, especially because I knew villagers shared with each other with almost the same zeal they did with me, the visitor. It was a social habit lacking in my own culture and I was curious to know what it was, exactly, that produced it in Kalambayi.

Kazadi Manda, a lean, square-jawed fish farmer in Ntita Konyukua who had a mile-wide smile, provided part of the answer early one morning about a week later. We were sitting at his pond, tossing stones at toads and watching his tilapia eat a batch of papaya leaves spread across the liquid light of the pond's surface. His fish, like those of Chief Ilunga and the other new farmers, were coming along nicely, getting fat for the upcoming first harvests. After talking shop for a while, Kazadi and I turned our attention to other matters. I told him about Chief Mbaya coming to my house with his daughters.

"You're joking," he said. "He just walked up and said pick one and you refused?"

"Yes."

"But why? Why didn't you take one? It *is* a little strange that you live alone in that warehouse the way you do, don't you think? Nobody can understand it. Don't you want a wife?"

"Of course," I said. "Someday. If I can find the right person. But I barely knew these women."

"So?"

"I can't marry a woman just like that. I have to be in love first and she has to be in love with me. It takes time."

Kazadi didn't get it. The look of blank incomprehension on his face told me the relationship I was talking about didn't exist in his universe. He had no conception of the self, of the individual. Nor, by extension, did he fully understand the Western notion of romantic love between an individual man and woman.

"You don't get married for love," he told me. "You get married because you need a woman to cook your food and bear your children. Love is what you feel for your whole family. The happiness of your children and brothers and parents and grandparents—of all of them together—is what brings your own happiness. You can't get that by yourself or from a woman."

"So until I have a lot of children and a big group of relatives all around me I can never hope to be happy?" I said.

"That's right."

"Never?"

"Never."

Sitting at the pond, listening to Kazadi pass on this truth with the conviction of an inspired cleric, I began to better understand the fabric of life in Kalambayi. The family was indeed paramount. Kazadi was wed to his relatives. And because each village was nothing but a collection of several extended families, and because it was often difficult, due to their size, to tell where one family began and another left off, this concern for the group was extended in large measure to include all members of the village and, ultimately, all people. Everyone treated everyone else more or less like a relative, whether he was or not. Everyone was taken care of, even Kalambayi's strange, white, American visitor—me.

Kazadi and I talked a while longer before spreading a final bundle of papaya leaves across the pond. When we finished he told me he wanted to harvest some peanuts from his field a short distance away. I didn't have to be in the next village for another hour, so I offered to help. He led the way up the valley.

It was a brilliant morning, warm and cloudless, with the sun poised low and the tawny hills around the valley almost cloth-like in their softness. A group of brown weaverbirds bobbed about a nearby tree. In the distance two women washed clothes in the drowsy sunlight, singing as they worked. Mornings like this served to remind me that it didn't rain every day in Kalambayi. It just seemed that way to me during my first few months because of all the destruction storms wrought. In truth, the sky was much more often blue than gray, and once I reached the villages and got off the roads, I usually enjoyed the fine weather and my new life working outdoors.

Kazadi and I moved through a stand of banana trees, then a cotton field, then a stretch of grass that left our pants wet with dew by the time we reached his small plot of peanuts. We walked to the distant-most corner of the field and went to work, pulling the plants from the ground with our hands. The soil was poor here, sandy as in most of Kalambayi, and the stems lifted easily. Working fifteen feet apart, we placed the plants in separate piles, first shaking dirt from the dangling shells. When each pile had roughly twenty plants, I figured we had about as many as Kazadi could carry comfortably back to his family. But he kept going. I did the same.

A moment later he finally stopped and tied the piles together in a large bundle. I went down to the spring to wash my hands. When I walked back up the hill to my motorcycle, the entire bundle of peanuts was tied, to my surprise, above the rear fender. Kazadi was hoeing in a field a little farther up. He stopped to wave goodbye. "They're raw," he said, pointing to the peanuts, "so boil them first and add a little salt before you eat them."

⌒⌒

Curiously, this habit of giving in Kalambayi didn't rub off on me. Even as I watched, and was moved by, the sacrifices villagers like Kazadi made to keep me stocked with produce and filled with *fufu*, I didn't do the same. I didn't reciprocate. I accepted the food and other gifts when I could, but the idea of spreading around my own wealth in the same free and automatic manner didn't take hold. I hadn't been sent to Kalambayi to become like the people exactly. I taught fish culture. I shared an expertise. That was enough.

So on the off chance that I was hungry at the end of the day, I didn't eat in my yard like most people, inviting passers-by to join me. I took my tin of sardines and plate of fried rice and stayed inside behind a curtain pulled across the front door. I was glad to be alone and eating something other than *fufu*, glad to be listening to the BBC's "Globe Theatre" blessedly broadcast in English over my shortwave radio. If someone came while I was eating, a friend or fish farmer, I stood at the door and told him that, well, I was having dinner and could he please come back later. Lifelong experience at suburban dinner tables had taught me that mealtime visitors meant embarrassment. You made apologies and they went away or waited until you finished.

I didn't really care or really wasn't conscious of the fact that the villagers around me thought this habit was a little strange, a bit obscene, even for a visitor. Mbaya, my worker, didn't tell me. Nor did any of my neighbors. And no one said anything about the fact that I smoked whole cigarettes by myself, not passing a portion of each one to other men in my company as was the local habit. I just did these things. Just like I socked away money, saving as much of my living allowance as I could for the beer and *pommes frites* it would buy on my next trip to Mbuji Mayi.

To be sure, I had made a lot of changes since arriving—adapting to strange foods, learning to bathe in cold rivers, surrendering my native tongue for two years. But my attachment to the word "mine" was strong and stubborn. Whatever the villagers did, I had my things, I needed my things, and I didn't give them away. So much was this attitude a measure of who I was and the Western culture that produced me that during my early months it simply never occurred to me to try to change.

I suppose it's no wonder then that I treated Mutoba Muenyi the way I did. She was a beggar—a haggard, unkempt, insane beggar who roamed pretty much aimlessly through the villages of Kalambayi, sleeping in other people's huts or in cotton storage houses. Mbaya told me she was the daughter of a nearby village chief and had been made crazy years ago by the curse of a disgruntled husband.

I did my utmost to avoid Mutoba on those occasions she came to Lulenga and stood under the cluster of palm trees in the center of the village, babbling nonsense in her high-pitched voice while gesturing for food and money. I avoided her because I've never handled beggars well. They intimidate me. I had moved through the streets of enough American cities to know that the usual response when confronted by a bedraggled panhandler is to hang on to your money and keep walking.

So when I turned to answer a tap on my shoulder one afternoon in the Lulenga market and saw Mutoba—clothes unwashed, teeth rotten, arms motioning toward the avocados I was buying—I ignored her. When she followed me through the market, creating a scene, I told her to stop and quickly made my way home, embarrassed by her presence. A few weeks later she appeared again, this time planting herself at my door, asking for money. Again I shooed her away. It wasn't until our third encounter that things began to change. Mutoba involved me in a small nightmare. She made me pay, in a sense, for all my previous behavior.

❧

It happened in Lulenga, early one morning in June. The village was silent and still in the predawn darkness, everyone asleep, when Mutoba crept to my house, pressed her face inches from my door and started singing loudly. Her harsh voice woke me like cymbals crashed above my bed. The song she sang was improvised, with lyrics telling how she was hungry and how I should give her something to eat.

Sleepy and annoyed, I lay in bed listening, cringing at the thought that half the village was doing the same thing. My clock said 5:45. "Ssssshhhhh," I hissed from my room, "be quiet. Go away. I don't have any food."

But the singing didn't stop. Not after five minutes. Not after ten. It went on and on, bludgeoning the morning quiet. Then something terrible happened. With mounting urgency, pushed on by the impurity of the local water, my body began signaling that it had something to contribute to the backyard outhouse—now. Cursing, I got up, grabbed my flashlight and began looking for the padlock to my door. Because the outhouse was around back, I would have to lock the front door on my way out, preventing Mutoba from entering while I was away. But suddenly there was a problem. I couldn't find my padlock. With my bowels approaching critical mass and Mutoba's hideous singing continuing outside, I searched everywhere, finding nothing. I had misplaced the lock.

There was nothing left to do but go outside. I opened the door. There she was. My flashlight revealed Mutoba's bare feet, her startled eyes. She didn't move. She just kept singing as I shut the door behind me. I dared not go to the outhouse now, leaving this crazy woman unwatched by an unlocked door. I sprinted past her one hundred feet to the far end of the cotton warehouse. There, off to the side in a patch of knee-high grass next to a palm tree, I turned facing her and lowered myself to my haunches. All the while I kept my flashlight fixed warily on her at the doorstep. I squatted and Mutoba sang, each of us staring with equal shock at the spectacle before us.

And that's how most of the village found us. To my yard they came—mamas and papas and children rubbing sleep from their eyes. They filed out of their houses to see what all the commotion was about. A minute or so after the performance started, just as the rising sun was providing rosy light by which to see, there were several dozen thunderstruck people gathered along the edges of my yard, watching the mad showdown between crapping foreigner and crowing bag lady.

I was beside myself with humiliation and anger by the time I finished and stood. I walked straight to Mutoba. With the crowd looking on, I yelled at her to leave immediately. She, in turn, yelled back, called me a *muena tshitua* over and over again. It was a name I had never heard before. After a moment, she finally left. The crowd, guffawing and embarrassed by all the ugliness, walked away.

About thirty minutes later, while I was sitting inside my house still trying to figure out what had just happened, Mbaya came by. He already had heard about the affair with Mutoba, but insisted I recount the story in full.

"You look a little ill," he said when I had finished.

"I feel ill."

Then I asked him a question: "What's a *muena tshitua*?" The words had stuck in my mind since Mutoba spoke them. "She called me a *muena tshitua*. What's that?"

Mbaya grew noticeably uncomfortable at this and heaved a forced laugh. "Oh, it's nothing," he said. "You didn't know."

"Know what? What does it mean? What did she call me?"

Reluctantly, he told me. Mutoba had delivered one of the most serious charges one can make in Kalambayi. "A *muena tshitua*," he said, "is someone who doesn't share. She said you were stingy."

There was a brief pause after this, a few seconds when Mbaya avoided my eyes and I folded my arms. Hanging in the silence and permeating Mbaya's awkward manner seemed to be the suggestion that the *muena tshitua* label wasn't such a bad fit, that perhaps Mutoba was right.

"But how could I give her anything?" I asked him, breaking the silence. She had come at an outrageous hour, singing like a wild soul and wresting me from sleep, I said. Running her off was the only thing I could have done.

But even to myself my argument sounded a bit feeble. There were no mitigating circumstances to explain my other encounters with her, nor my conspicuously selfish behavior in general.

When I finished, Mbaya responded cautiously. Like most Kalambayans, he was often hesitant to openly criticize or correct. He softened what he was about to tell me by stressing that he thought I was basically a great guy and I shouldn't worry too much about what a deranged old woman told me. Then, delicately, he explained that I hadn't done the right thing that morning. It was all right to shoo Mutoba away, but the proper response was to give her a little food or whatever she needed first. That's what most people did.

He was right, of course. The same villagers who vigorously plied me with *fufu* and peanuts everywhere I went also took care of Mutoba. It wouldn't occur to them to do otherwise. She couldn't farm or provide for herself, so when her clothes became too torn, someone, somewhere, gave her new ones. When her filth became excessive, someone placed a piece of soap in her hand. And almost always, when mealtime came, someone gave her food. The sense of familial generosity flowing through every village protected her.

But wrapped up in my own notions of privacy and propriety, trying to live in this culture without really being a part of it, I gave nothing to Mutoba. My problem, in a big sense, was greed. Not just greed toward the things I wanted to keep for myself, but toward this whole two-year trip abroad. I wanted to take as much from this African world as I could, to learn and experience, without surrendering any large part of myself, without making significant changes like replacing the faulty moral compass I had come with with one that made more sense in this poor setting. Clearly, this resistance was bound to fail me. I had no desire to "go native," to become like a typical villager in every way. But to have any meaningful experience here, to leave with true friends and true insights, I had to let go of some strong habits. I had to rip something out in order to add something new.

This wasn't the message Mbaya had in mind, really, when he tried to educate me on that strange morning Mutoba Muenyi came to my house, but it's the one that started to sink in. His message, though not in as many words, was more simple: "You've been here long enough, Michel. It's time you stopped being such an appalling tightwad."

─── ❧ ───

So, like learning to navigate bad roads and speak the local language, I had to learn to share in Kalambayi. I had to learn to put aside my excessive concern for my own interests and to open up my house and cupboards to people who did the same for me. Needled with shame after my talk with Mbaya, I began with Mutoba. The next time she came to my house—this time knocking on a moon-lit evening—I shuffled into the kitchen and brought back a papaya and some dried fish. On following visits, I gave whatever else I had on hand. Weeks went by and there were other changes. I stopped the awkward practice of blocking my door when friends and neighbors came at dinnertime. When they arrived, they entered and ate with me. There was always more rice or *fufu* in the kitchen I could eat later. Similarly, I stopped smoking whole cigarettes. I started passing half of each one I lit up to whatever men happened to be around me at the time.

And, eventually, I took the big step. A good part of my $70 monthly salary started sneaking away from me. It found its way to my closest friends, people who began to represent something of my own extended family: $5 to Kazadi Manda to buy malaria medicine for his daughter; $3 to Mbaya's brother to pay school fees; fifty-cent gifts of dried fish to poorer farmers whose children I knew had eaten nothing but manioc leaves for weeks. Saving money for a row of cold beers in Mbuji Mayi gradually lost its importance.

As time passed, it grew easier and easier to let go of what I had. The reason was simple: I had a lot. Like most people who go overseas to do development work, I did so expecting to find out what it's like to be poor. But awakening to my surroundings after a few months, I discovered that that's not what happens. Instead you learn what it's like to be rich, to be fabulously, incomprehensibly, bloated with wealth. No one in Kalambayi could afford to share more than I.

Into this jumble of backwater villages, where every man had a mud house, a hoe, and ten kids, I came stomping and rattling with a motorcycle and cassette tapes and books to read and boots to wear and a bed to sleep on. I had two kerosene lamps and kerosene to put inside them. I had tools to fix my motorcycle and a two-hundred-liter barrel of gasoline to make it run. I had a tin roof over my head. I even had a white, dish-like object which, if launched properly, would spin furiously and float parallel to the ground for long distances.

"What's it called?" Mbaya asked the first day I pulled it out from under my bed.

"Frisbee," I said.

"Freeze-beee," he repeated.

I was stuffed with treasure.

More impressive than all of this, however, was the fact that I had so many clothes. Never mind the motorcycle, clothes were something the Kalambayans could really relate to because they, too, wore them and spent money on them. That I could go an entire week and not wear the same shirt twice was, in this African setting, the gleaming pinnacle of affluence. Not counting the rags he farmed in, a typical village man owned only one shirt and one pair of pants. These he bought secondhand in village markets after the clothes had traveled to Africa from the West in fifty-kilo bales. The village man wore the clothes every day and washed them every day until they became so faded and torn he strained to maintain dignity in the village. At fifty cents a shirt and seventy-five cents a pair of pants, there was little else he could do. He couldn't afford more.

In a strange way, this consequence of poverty proved useful to me when I arrived in Kalambayi. It helped me remember people. If I forgot faces, I could often place names simply by using clothes as memory cues. For example: white jersey with Washington Redskins helmet always meant Mukadi; red polyester shirt with large tear above breast pocket meant Kayemba; pale t-shirt emblazoned with HILTON HEAD IS WHERE IT'S AT meant Kabamba. It was a sad but useful phenomenon.

Later, the fact that Kalambayans have so few clothes was of even greater utility. It helped me catch the thief who broke into my house. Despite the common habit of sharing, the chiefdom was no Shangri-la of social harmony. There was plenty of bickering and feuding between villages and between villagers. And, as in all societies, there were thieves.

I had gone to Mbuji Mayi one weekend, and Mbaya was spending the night in my house, sleeping in my bed, when the break-in happened.

"I heard something in the kitchen, and I woke up," he told me when I returned. "Then I heard a louder noise and I knew someone was in the house and stealing things. I jumped up and ran out of the bedroom. The thief heard me, and he ran out of the kitchen at the same time. It was so dark we collided in the sitting room and fell to the floor. I grabbed him around the waist and started screaming, 'thief, thief, help.' He started making his way to the door, dragging me, but I held on and kept screaming. Then we both fell out the door and onto the ground outside. It was really dark out. No moon. I couldn't see anything. I just hung on. He was wearing a trench coat, so I held on to that. Then the coat came off in my hands. He had shaken it off, and when I looked up, he was gone. People nearby heard the noise and came out of their houses. I had the coat in my hands, and I told them what had happened. 'Go get Michel's lantern,' someone said. I ran in the house and came back. Now there was a whole crowd of people standing around the coat. I lit the lantern and held it up to the coat. 'It's Kaja,' everyone said together. 'It's Kaja.'"

Kaja Tshitemba. He was the son of the river ferryman, and we had his coat. Thus, we had him. He might as well have left behind an autographed picture. Nowhere more than among the very poor is there meaning to the saying "the clothes make the man." I showed the coat to Chief Mbaya, who recognized it immediately. He ordered Kaja to produce a goat and a chicken as restitution. These I gave to Mbaya.

Not all the acts of thievery committed against me in Kalambayi were as easily solved, though. It took me several weeks, for example, to figure out who was stealing my garbage. The pit I dug behind my house when I arrived was not filling up with the rubbish I regularly put in it. In fact, it was virtually empty.

One day, having just disposed of a fresh bucket of garbage, I decided to do some maintenance work on my motorcycle near the side of my house and in view of the pit. There, secretly watching through a space between the carburetor and the cylinder, I saw what was happening to my garbage. Less than ten minutes after it entered the pit, it was being divided up by a group of four children from the family next door. Nine-year-old Ditu, carrying his infant brother on his back, took all the used batteries. These, I later learned, would be used to jerry-build charges for muzzle-loading rifles. Masengu and Mbelu seized tin cans that would serve as drinking cups. They also took crumpled cigarette packs whose paper would be used to roll local tobacco. Finally, Miteo, the oldest of the group, picked up a copy of *Newsweek* magazine, and the next day George Shultz's face was providing protective cover on his exercise book as he walked to school.

When the children had finished their plunder, there was a second wave of attackers. A chicken, two goats, and a mongrel dog came and devoured the remaining pile of coffee grounds, fish bones, and assorted fruit rinds. By the time I had finished removing and cleaning the carburetor on my motorcycle, it was over. The garbage was gone. The pit was empty again.

I suppose it was never garbage to begin with, though. The notion of throwing things away made little sense in a society that possessed so little, a society where people wore the same tattered clothes and farmed the same sandy soil every day. From that soil came the only thing of real value that anyone owned: food. The life of planting, cultivating, and harvesting crops filled stomachs, but it did so little else that my garbage pit assumed the status of a trove. Still, remarkably, people shared what little they had. It was an admirable social trait, one I was trying hard to adopt myself. But, I was about to discover, it meant big, big trouble for fish ponds.

5

"My wife has left me, and I've got to harvest my pond," Chief Ilunga said. It was two o'clock on a Sunday afternoon and he was breathing hard. He had just walked the five miles from his village of Ntita Kalambayi to my house in Lulenga. He had walked quickly, stopping only once to drink *tshitshampa* with friends along the way. Now his speech was excited, full of the fast cadence of personal crisis. "My wife has left me, and I've got to harvest my pond. I've got to harvest it tomorrow and use the money to get her back."

It was a dowry dispute. Ilunga's father-in-law claimed Ilunga still owed $30 in bridewealth from the marriage to his daughter five years earlier. To emphasize the point, he had ordered his daughter home to their village thirty miles away. She had obeyed, taking with her all the children. Now Ilunga was humiliated and alone, with no one to cook his food or wash his clothes. He needed money fast.

The development was something of a blow to me, too. Never had I expected the first fruits of my extension work to go toward something as inglorious as roping in a runaway wife. But that's what the Fates had snipped off. I told Ilunga I would be at his pond the next morning to help with the harvest.

Ilunga's wife had picked a bad time to leave him. His pond was in its fifth month of production, one month short of the gestation period considered best for harvesting. Still, after only five months, things looked good. Ilunga had fed his fish like a man possessed, and as far as we could tell a considerable bounty waited below.

Part of the pond's success was due to a strategy I had developed not long after arriving in Kalambayi. The plan was simple: get Ilunga and the other farmers to feed their fish with the same intensity they fed me *fufu*, and they would surely raise some of the biggest tilapia ever recorded.

"Imagine a fish is like an important visitor who has traveled over mountains and through rivers to see you," I had told Ilunga after he finished his pond. "If, when you set a meal down in front of that visitor, he finishes all the food in two or three minutes and then stares back at you from across the table, how do you feel?"

He grimaced. "Terrible," he said. "The visitor is still hungry. He should always be given more food than he can eat. He shouldn't be able to finish it. That's how you know he's full."

"Exactly," I said.

Exactly. Every day for five months, Ilunga dumped more food into his pond than his fish could possibly eat. He covered the surface with sweet potato leaves and manioc leaves and papaya leaves and the fish poked and chewed and started to grow.

Helping things out was an unexpected gift. Two months after we stocked the pond, an official of the United Nations Children's Fund in Mbuji Mayi donated two sturdy wheelbarrows to the Kalambayi fish project. The wheelbarrows were blue with UNICEF painted neatly on the sides in white. When I called all the farmers together to present the tools, the shiny steel basins and rubber trees inspired a great amount of whistling and head-shaking. I felt as if I had just delivered two mint-condition Mack trucks. The men ran their hands along the rims and grew dizzy contemplating the wealth the tools might bring. Using the village of Kabala as a dividing point, the farmers split up into two committees representing the upper and lower stretches of the Lubilashi. After establishing rules for their use, the men took possession of the wheelbarrows.

Ilunga, as much as anyone, parlayed the UNICEF largess into bigger fish. He used the upper Kalambayi wheelbarrow to gather leaves and termites for fish food. To fill his pond's stick compost bins he went most Thursdays to the weekly outdoor market in Ntita Konyukua. There, he used the wheelbarrow to collect manioc peels and fruit rinds and the other rubbish village markets leave scattered about the ground. These materials rot quickly in pond water, stimulating a plankton growth essential for intensive tilapia culture. But to get the goods, Ilunga had to swallow his pride. He had to hunt through the crowd of marketers and bend over and compete with hungry dogs and goats and chickens along the ground. It was something of a spectacle. Ilunga was thirty years old and the chief of a village—and he was shooing away goats to get at banana peels in the marketplace dirt. People started to talk. After a while, one of Ilunga's brothers tried to dissuade him of the practice. "You're embarrassing yourself," he said. "The pond isn't worth this."

But Ilunga didn't listen, just as he hadn't listened back in the beginning when I told him he was digging a pond so large it might kill him. He kept going to the market. Stares and whispers didn't stop him.

Most amazing was the fact that Ilunga was doing all this work in addition to tending his fields every day like everyone else. He was squeezing two jobs from the daily fuel of protein-deficient *fufu*. Eventually it started to show. I walked to his house one afternoon and found him outside, fast asleep in the coddling embrace of the UNICEF wheelbarrow. He had lined the basin with a burlap sack and reposed himself, his arms and legs drooping over the edges. From the trail fifty feet away, I watched. The imagery was potent, almost unbearable with its themes of hope and struggle and want all bound up in that exhausted face, those closed eyes, those dirty black limbs hanging down to the ground. God, how I had set Ilunga's soul ablaze with my talk of rising out of poverty, of beating back the worst aspects of village life with a few fish ponds. He had listened to me and followed every line of advice and now he lay knocked out in the hold of a donated wheelbarrow. Deciding it would be criminal to wake him, I walked away, praying like hell that all the promises I had made were true.

And now we would find out. It was time for the denouement: the harvest. Five months had passed, Ilunga's wife had left him, and we would discover what had been happening all this time under the pond's surface. I was anxious because, in a way, owning a fish pond is like owning a lottery ticket. Unlike corn, which you can watch as it grows, or, say, chickens, which you can weigh as they get big, there is no way to positively assess the progress of a pond until you harvest it. The fish are under water, so you can't count them or get a good look at them. You just have to work and work and wait. You hang on to your lottery ticket and wait for the drawing, never sure what number will come up until you drain the pond.

Ilunga and I had a pretty good idea his fish were big, of course. God knows they had been given enough to eat. We also had seen lots of offspring along the pond's edges. But the water was now so well fertilized and pea-green with plankton that neither of us had seen a fish in nearly two months. (Ilunga had refused to eat any fish in order to maximize the harvest.) We knew the tilapia were there, but how many exactly? How big? And what about the birds? How many fish had the thieving kingfishers taken? We would soon know all the answers. An unacknowledged, icy fear ran through both of us as we agreed that Sunday afternoon at my house to harvest his pond the next day.

It was just past 6:00 a.m. when I arrived for the harvest. Ilunga and his brother Tshibamba were calling and waving their arms as I moved down the valley slope toward the pond. "Michel, Michel. Come quickly. Hurry, Michel." I had driven my motorcycle to Ilunga's house in the predawn dark, using my headlight along the way. Now, as I finished the last of the twenty-minute walk to the valley floor, the sky was breaking blue and a crazy montage of pink and silver clouds lay woven on the horizon. The morning beauty was shattered, however, by the cries of the men waiting for me at the pond. They were yelling something I didn't want to hear. It was something my mind refused to accept.

"There are no fish, Michel," they said. "Hurry. The fish aren't here."

I reached the pond and cast an incredulous stare into the water. They were right. There were no fish. The men had spent most of the night digging out a vertical section of the lower dike and slowly draining the water until there now remained only a muddy, five-by-five-foot pool in the lower-most corner of the pond. The pool was about six inches deep. And it was empty.

Tshibamba was screaming, running along the dikes and pointing an accusing finger at the pond bottom. "Where are they?" he demanded of the pond. "Where are the fish?"

Ilunga was past the yelling stage. He gazed at the shallow pool, his face sleepy and creased, and said nothing. He was a wreck, as forlorn and defeated as the pond scarecrow ten feet to his left with its straw limbs akimbo and head splotched with bird excrement.

"Wait a minute," I said to the men, suddenly spotting something at one end of the pool. "Look!"

I pointed to a fan-shaped object sticking out of the water and looking a lot like a dorsal fin. We all looked. It moved. A fish. Before we could celebrate, other fins appeared throughout the pool, dozens of them, then hundreds. The pond water, which had continued all the while to flow out through a net placed over the cut dike, had suddenly reached a depth lower than the vertical height of the bottom-hugging fish. The fish had been hiding under the muddy water and were revealed only at the last moment and all at the same time, a phenomenon of harvesting we eventually became nervously accustomed to in Kalambayi. Ilunga's fish—big, medium, and small—had been corralled by the dropping water into the small pool where they waited like scaly cattle. They looked stupid and restless. "Yeah, now what?" they seemed to ask.

Ilunga showed them. He threw off his shirt and made a quick banzai charge into the congested fray, his arms set to scoop up hard-won booty. There ensued an explosion of jumping fish and flying mud, and Ilunga absorbed the rat-tat-tat of a thousand mud dots from his feet to his face. By the time his hands reached the pool, the fish had scattered everywhere into the surrounding mud like thinking atoms suddenly released from some central, binding force. Ilunga raised his empty hands. He looked up at us—his face covered with mud dots, his feet sinking into the pond-bottom gook—and flashed a wide smile. The harvest had begun.

"The small ones," I yelled, hurriedly discarding my shirt and shoes. "Get the small fish first to restock with."

I jumped into the pond and, like Ilunga, was immediately pelted with mud. Two more of Ilunga's brothers had arrived by then, and together, five strong, we gave battle with the tenacity of warriors waging *jihad*. We chased the flapping, flopping, fleeing fish through the pond-bottom sludge. When we caught them, we stepped on them and throttled them and herded them into tin buckets. Ilunga took charge of capturing and counting three hundred thumb-sized stocking fish and putting them in a small holding pond. The rest of us collected the other fish, segregating the original stockers, which were now hand-sized, from the multitudinous offspring. The work was dirty and sloppy and hypnotically fun.

So engrossed was I in the harvest, in fact, that I barely noticed the tops of the pond dikes were growing crowded with onlookers. By the time we finished capturing all the fish, people had surrounded the square pond bottom like spectators around a boxing ring. A quarter of the men, women, and children in the village had come to see the harvest. I was impressed by their show of support for Ilunga's work.

Ilunga ordered the crowd to clear back from a spot on the upper dike. Filthy like pigs, we carried the fish out of the pond in four large buckets and set them down at the clearing. We rinsed them off with canal water and began weighing them with a small handheld scale I had brought. The total came to forty-four kilos. It was an excellent harvest. After only five months, Ilunga had coaxed three hundred tilapia fingerlings into forty-four kilos of valuable protein. It was enough to bring home his wife and then some.

Whistling and laughing, I grabbed Ilunga by the shoulders and shook him and told him what a great harvest it was. I had expected a lot of fish, but not this many. It was marvelous, I told him, simply marvelous. He smiled and agreed. But he wasn't nearly as happy as he should have been. Something was wrong. His eyes telegraphed fear.

Tshibamba made the first move.

"Go get some leaves from that banana tree over there," he told a child standing on the pond bank.

When the child returned, Tshibamba scooped about a dozen fish onto one of the leaves and wrapped them up.

"I'm going to take these up to the house," he said to Ilunga. "It's been a while since the children have had fresh fish."

"Yes, yes," Ilunga said. "Take some."

"I'll have a little, too," said Kazadi, Ilunga's youngest brother, reaching into a bucket.

"Go ahead. Take what you need."

Then a third brother stepped forward. Then a fourth. Then other villagers. My stomach sank.

It was suddenly all clear—the crowd, the well-wishers, the brothers of Ilunga who had never even seen the pond until that morning. They had come to divide up the harvest. A cultural imperative was playing itself out. It was time for Ilunga to share his wealth. He stood by the buckets and started placing fish in the hands of every relative and friend who stepped forth. It would have driven Rayleen McGarity stark raving mad. He was just giving the harvest away.

There was no trace of anger on his face as he did it, either. Nor was there a suggestion of duty or obligation. It was less precise than that. This was Ilunga's village and he had a sudden surplus and so he shared it. It just happened. It was automatic.

But the disappointment was there, weighing down on the corners of his eyes. He needed the fish. Getting his wife back had depended on them.

Caked in mud, I sat on the grassy bank and watched an entire bucket of tilapia disappear. Fury and frustration crashed through me with the force of a booming waterfall. All that work. All my visits. All the digging and battling kingfishers. All for what? For this? For a twenty-minute free-for-all giveaway? Didn't these people realize the ponds were different? Ilunga had worked hard to produce this harvest. He had tried to get ahead. Where were they when he dug his pond? Where were they when he heaved and hoed and dislodged from the earth four thousand cubic feet of dirt?

I knew the answer. They had been laughing. They had been whispering among themselves that Ilunga was wasting his time, that moving so much dirt with a shovel was pure lunacy. And they laughed even harder when they saw him bending over to pick up fruit rinds in the marketplace in competition with goats and dogs. But they weren't laughing now. Ilunga had proved them wrong. He had raised more fish than any of them had seen in their lives, and now they were taking the spoils.

The fish continued to disappear and I began bursting with a desire to intervene. I wanted to ask Ilunga what the hell he was doing and to tell him to stop it. I wanted to turn over the bucket already emptied of fish and stand on it and shoo everyone away like I had shooed Mutoba Muenyi those first few times she came to my door. "Giving is virtuous and all that," I wanted to tell the crowd. "But this is different. These are Ilunga's fish. They're *his*. Leave them alone. He needs them."

But I said nothing. I summoned every ounce of self-restraint in my body and remained silent. This was something between Ilunga and his village. My job was to teach him how to raise fish. I had done my job. What he did with the fish afterward really was none of my business. Even so, I didn't have to watch. I went over to the canal and washed up. Ilunga was well into the second bucket when I told him I was leaving.

"Wait," he said. "Here."

He thrust into my hands a large bundle of fish.

Oh, no, I thought. Not me. I'm not going to be party to this gouging. I tried to hand the bundle back.

"But these fish are for you," he said. "You've taught me how to raise fish, and this is to say thank you."

"No, Ilunga. This is your harvest. You earned it. You keep it."

He gave me a wounded look, as if I had just spit in his face, and suddenly I wanted to scream and kick and smash things. I couldn't refuse his offer without devastating him. I took the fish and headed up the hill, feeling like a real parasite.

"Wait for me at the house," he said as I walked away.

It was 8:30 when I reached the village and stretched out, dizzy with disappointment, on a reed mat next to Ilunga's house. He arrived about thirty minutes later with his sister Ngala, who had helped at the harvest. Both of their faces looked drained from the great hemorrhaging they had just gone through. Without even the benefit of loaves of bread, they had fed a mass of about fifty villagers, and now Ngala carried all that was left in one big tin basin. I estimated there were about twenty-five kilos. To my dismay, though, Ilunga wasn't finished. He scooped out another couple of kilos to give to older relatives who hadn't made it to the pond. Then he sent Ngala off to the market in Lulenga with roughly twenty-three kilos of fish, barely half the harvest total.

At the going market price of 100 zaires a kilo, Ilunga stood to make 2300 zaires ($23). It was far short of what he needed to get his wife back. Far short, in fact, of anything I could expect village men to accept as fair return for months of punishing shovel work and more months of maniacal feeding. The problem wasn't the technology. Ilunga had produced forty-four kilos of fish in one pond in five months. That was outstanding. The problem, rather, was generosity. It was a habit of sharing so entrenched in the culture that it made me look to the project's future with foreboding. What incentive did men like Ilunga have to improve their lives—through fish culture or any other means—if so much of the gain immediately melted into a hundred empty hands? Why work harder? Why develop? Better just to farm enough to eat. Better to stay poor like all the rest.

After Ilunga's sister left for the market, I couldn't hold my tongue any longer. We were alone at his house.

"I can't believe you gave away all those fish, Ilunga. Why did you even bother digging a pond if all you were going to do with the harvest was give it away?"

He knew I was upset, and he didn't want to talk about it.

"Why did you dig a pond?" I repeated.

"You know why," he said. "To get more money. To help my family."

"So how can you help your family if you give away half the fish?"

"But there's still a lot left," he said. "You act like I gave them all away."

I suddenly realized he was about ten times less upset by what had happened than I was. My frustration doubled.

"What do you mean there's still a lot left? There's not enough to get your wife back, is there? You gave away too much for that. Your pond hasn't done you much good, and I guess I've wasted my time working with you."

The last sentence really annoyed him.

"Look," he said, "what could I have done? After I drained my pond I had hundreds and hundreds of fish. There were four buckets full. You saw them. If my brother comes and asks for ten fish, can I say no? For ten fish? That's crazy. I can't refuse."

"No, it's not crazy, Ilunga. You have six brothers and ten uncles and fifty cousins. And then there are all the other villagers.

You're right. Ten fish aren't very many. But when you give ten to everyone you have little left for yourself."

"So what would you have done?" he asked me. "Would you have refused fish to all those people?"

"Yes," I said, and I meant it.

"You mean you would have taken all the fish and walked past all those people and children and gone up to the house and locked the door."

"Don't say it like that," I said. "You could have explained to them that the pond was your way of making money, that the harvest was for your wife."

"They already know I need my wife," he said. "And they know I'll get her back somehow."

"Yeah, how? You were counting on the harvest to do that, and now it's over. You gave away too much, Ilunga. You can't keep doing this. You can't feed the whole village by yourself. It's impossible. You have to feed your own children and take care of your own immediate family. Let your brothers worry about their families. Let them dig ponds if they want to. You've got to stop giving away your harvests."

Thus spoke Michel, the agent of change, the man whose job it was to try to rewrite the society's molecular code. Sharing *fufu* and produce and other possessions was one thing. With time, I had come around to the habit myself, seen its virtuosity. But the ponds were different, and I had assumed the farmers realized that. Raising fish was meant to create surplus wealth, to carry the farmers and their immediate families to a level where they had more for themselves—better clothes, extra income. That was the incentive upon which the project was built. It was the whole reason I was there.

So when Ilunga harvested his pond that early morning and started giving away the fish, I wanted to retreat. I wanted to renounce my conversion to the local system and move back to the old impulse I had arrived with, the one that had me eating secret, solitary meals and guarding my things in the self-interested way prized by my own society.

"Stop the giving"—that was the real, the final, message I wanted to bring to Ilunga and the other fish farmers. Stop the giving and the community-oriented attitude and you can escape the worst ravages of poverty. Build a pond and make it yours. And when you harvest it, don't give away the fish. Forget, for now, the bigger society. Forget the extended family. Step back and start thinking like self-enriching entrepreneurs, like good little capitalists.

But Ilunga didn't fit the plan. Nor did any of the other farmers who harvested after him. "If my brother comes and asks for ten fish, can I say no?" he had asked. His logic was stronger than it seemed. Like everyone else in Kalambayi, Ilunga needed badly the help fish culture could provide. What he didn't need, however, were lessons on how to stay alive. And that, I eventually grew to understand, was what all the sharing was really about. It was a survival strategy, an unwritten agreement by the group that no one would be allowed to fall off the societal boat no matter how low provisions ran on board. No matter how bad the roads became or how much the national economy constricted, sharing and mutual aid meant everyone in each village stayed afloat. If a beggar like Mutoba Muenyi came to your house in the predawn darkness, you gave her food. If you harvested a pond and fifty malnourished relatives showed up, you shared what you had. Then you made the most of what was left. If it was $23, that was okay. It was still a lot of money in a country where the average annual income is $170 and falling. It might not pay off a marriage debt, but $23 satisfied other basic needs.

In the end, despite my fears, sharing didn't destroy the fish project. Farmers went on building and harvesting ponds, giving away 20 to 50 percent of their fish, and selling the rest to earn money for their wives and their children. It was a process I simply couldn't change and eventually I stopped trying.

And perhaps it was just as well Ilunga and the others weren't in a hurry to become the kind of producers I wanted them to be. They might develop along Western lines with time, but why push them? The local system worked. Everyone was taken care of. Everyone *did* stay afloat. Besides, there were already plenty of myopic, self-enriching producers in the world—entrepreneurs and businesses guided by the sole principle of increasing their own wealth above all else. So many were there in fact that the planetary boat, battered by breakneck production and consumption, was in ever-increasing danger of sinking, taking with it the ultimate extended family: the species. There seemed to be no survival strategy at work for the planet as a whole as there was for this small patch of Africa, no thread of broader community interest that ensured against total collapse. Indeed, sitting in my lamplit cotton warehouse at night, listening to growing reports of global environmental degradation over my shortwave radio, the thought occurred to me more than once that, in several important respects, Kalambayi needed far less instruction from the West than the other way around.

At the moment, however, no one needed anything as much as Ilunga needed his wife. He had given away nearly half his fish and now the opportunity had all but vanished. I stopped back by his house after the market closed in Lulenga and watched him count the money from the harvest: 2,000 zaires. Even less than I had thought. I reached into my pocket and pulled out all I had, 200 zaires. I handed it to him. He was still short.

"What are you going to do?"

"I don't know," he said. "I've got to think about it."

Three days later, on my way to Tshipanzula, I pulled up to Ilunga's house to see what solution he had come up with. I was surprised when he wasn't there and his neighbors said he had gone to Baluba Shankadi, his wife's tribe.

Another week went by before I saw Ilunga again. It was in the market in Ntita Konyukua and he was standing under a mimosa tree, gesturing and talking with two other fish farmers. As I made my way through the crowd of marketers, getting closer, I saw Ilunga's wife standing behind him, carrying their youngest child.

"How?" I asked when I reached him, shaking his hand, delighted by the sight of mother and child. "How did you do it?"

At first he didn't answer. He talked instead about his pond, telling me he had returned the day before and now was trying to track down the UNICEF wheelbarrow to start feeding his fish again.

"But your wife," I said. "How did you get her back?"

"Oh, yes, she's back," he said. "Well, I really don't know how I did it. After you left my house that day I still needed 800 zaires. One of my brothers gave me a hundred, but it still wasn't enough. I tried, but I couldn't come up with the rest of the money so I decided to leave with what I had. I walked for two days and reached my wife's village and handed the money to my father-in-law. He counted it and told me I was short. I told him I knew I was but that I didn't have any more. Then I knew there was going to be a big argument."

"Was there?"

"No. That's the really strange part. He told me to sit down, and his wife brought out some *fufu* and we ate. Then it got dark and we went inside to sleep. I still hadn't seen my wife. The next morning my father-in-law called me outside. Then he called my wife and sons out from another house. We were all standing in the middle of the compound, wondering what to do. Then he just told us to leave. 'That's it?' I said. 'It's over?' He told me yes, that I could go home. I didn't think I understood him correctly, so I asked him if he was sure he didn't want any more money. 'No, you've done enough,' he said. 'Go back to your village.' I was afraid to say anything else. I put my wife and sons in front of me and we started walking away before he could change his mind."

6

THE HOUSES IN KALAMBAYI WERE SMALL. TWO MEN WORKING every day for two weeks could build one. They were square structures, typically fifteen by fifteen feet at their base, with six-inch-thick mud walls. The walls were crowned with shaggy, thatch-grass roofs that came to a point at the top. There were no windows, so the interiors were dark and poorly aired. When in good repair, the houses were worth about $10 in local currency. The price was low because the structure had limited utility. Their small size made them good only for sleeping, for storing food, and as shelter from storm. Beyond that, people avoided them; villagers lived their lives outdoors, under the sky, away from their houses. When I came to Kalambayi, I did the same. For the first time in my life, I lived beyond the tyranny of walls.

Outside each house a large patch of grass was cleared, leaving a hard dirt surface that served as a kind of living-room floor. Here people spent most of their time when they weren't farming. Men relaxed on homemade chairs or woven reed mats. Women used hardwood poles to pound manioc in waist-high wooden mortars. Children wandered everywhere. Chickens scratched the earth. Dogs scratched themselves. The living room had no doors or windows, and the ceiling was blue and far overhead.

It wasn't long after I began roaming through this open outdoor scenery that I realized what a stranger the sky had always been to me. For twenty-two years it had been nothing more than an afterthought, something seen in joyless glimpses through the car and office-room windows of an urban-suburban world. But the sky was no stranger in Kalambayi. Under its reassuring spread, stretched huge across this African savanna, I spent my mornings and afternoons teaching village men how to raise fish.

We worked next to streams in grass-covered valleys beyond the reach of roads. We walked to these places and felt the sun on our skin, and when we didn't talk there was nothing to hear but the valley itself, its grass bending and moaning against an occasional wind. When we finished our work, we walked back to the villages and sat in outdoor living rooms next to $10 houses, rarely going inside and always hurrying back when we did.

Even when the sun went down and a velvety black replaced the blue above, no one in Kalambayi rushed indoors. Villagers sat outside and did what all people do living beyond the hypnotic glow of television: They talked and told stories. Most Kalambayans were capable storytellers, fond of the give and take of a good narrative offered inside a circle of chairs. "Mukendi," someone might begin above the chatter of crickets, "tell us again about the time you were bathing down at the creek and that pack of goats came and dragged away your clothes and you. . . ."

Once started, the telling would continue until another story or line of conversation took its place. The hours would pass this way before finally, sleepily, everyone wandered home to lay down for a while inside tiny houses.

Unfortunately, though, much of this outdoor storytelling art was lost on me when I first got to Kalambayi. I couldn't enjoy it nearly as much as the setting in which it was practiced because I didn't have the language skills to comprehend. I was satisfactorily conversant early on, but when people dropped the hyper-enunciated speech they used with me and talked freely among themselves, telling their tales, I usually got lost. It took about five months of advancing toward complete fluency in Tshiluba before I entered the world of characters and plot passing all around me.

As it happened, this higher level of Tshiluba came to me about the same time I was going through something of a crisis. I was running out of new work. I had made respectable progress during my first few months, persuading two dozen men to build ponds.

But around the beginning of my fifth month, before Ilunga and the other new farmers made their first harvests, the moderate flow of men joining the project abruptly and mysteriously fell to a trickle. Virtually no one was interested in starting ponds anymore. The slowdown continued and I started to panic. I started feeling like a real failure. My neighbor Lengos suggested I consult a sorcerer. Perhaps I had been cursed by a relative back in the States, he said. I gave his advice some thought, but turned it down, deciding to redouble my extension efforts instead.

I traveled from village to village doing everything I could think of to communicate the worth of the project. I gave speeches. I cornered men on paths. I drew little pictures in the dirt with sticks.

"This is what the fish looks like when you first put it in the pond," I would say, delicately sketching a baby fish the size of a matchstick. "Here's what it looks like after six months."

"That's a really big fish," the men would respond and then walk away, leaving me with the stick in my hand and defeat ringing in my ears. I rarely even reached the part about reproduction. I was a bomb.

After such failures I usually felt a sudden need to sit down and feel sorry for myself. I would repair to a chair outside the nearest house and pull myself together before attacking the next village. Men and women sitting in their outdoor parlors, perfect strangers most of them, were always happy to accommodate my intrusions. They gave me food and drink and a place to sulk even though they, too, refused to do fish work.

When my hosts were satisfied that I was comfortable, they would casually pick up the thread of whatever story they had set down to manage my arrival. Again, during my early months, I sat uncomprehending on such occasions. But as months passed the streaking nouns, verbs, and adjectives started to join hands to form storylines in my head. The yarn became intelligible.

When this happened, I discovered something. I listened and discovered that part of the reason I was failing as an extension agent had to do with history. My ear began to catch the voice of Kalambayi's past as it spoke in stories passed by oral tradition back and forth beneath the sky. The voice told of old suffering and violence. It told of slave raiders, and of a heroic, martyred chief. It also told of the *ndondo*, the sacred pit of heads that stubbornly haunts Kalambayi even now. It explained a great deal, this history. It explained why so many men wouldn't listen to me.

But my full understanding of Kalambayi's past came later. Before it I learned other important things. There were several reasons the project was foundering.

One afternoon in the village of Bajila Membila, I sketched a baby tilapia in the crusty dirt of a footpath and waited for my audience, Tshimbalanga Shambuyi, to walk away. But he didn't. Next I drew a full-grown fish and waited a second time. Again he stayed where he was. Excited, I sketched a school of baby fish swimming in a triangle below the adult, demonstrating how each stocking fish reproduced twice in six months.

Tshimbalanga stared at the sketch with the face of a man being told a bizarre and important secret. "I want to do it," he said. "I want to build two ponds."

"Really?" I half-shouted. "You want to raise fish? Two ponds? That's great! That's really great!" But talking to him further, I realized what he meant. He wanted to build two ponds *at the same time*. "Oh no, that's way too much work Tshimbalanga. You've got to start out with just one pond."

"No," he said adamantly. "I want two ponds. One for each boy."

To understand Tshimbalanga's arithmetic you have to understand his method of procreation. He tended to produce children by factors of two. In his fifty-five years he had sired not one, not two, but three sets of twins. The children from the first pair were grown men, working as diamond diggers in Mbuji Mayi. The children from the most recent pair were four-year-old girls, adorable, but sadly consigned to a life wandering cross-eyed about the house. They had been born mentally retarded after their mother got sick with malaria during pregnancy. The middle pair of twins were sixteen-year-old boys, bright-faced and healthy. But they, too, presented a problem, Tshimbalanga explained. He wanted to send them to a mission school in Mbuji Mayi, but he didn't have the money. Solution: twin fish ponds, one for each boy.

I acquiesced to Tshimbalanga's strategy, and he and his sons went to work, making steady progress as days went by. Elsewhere, however, the famine continued. In village after village, I got bland shrugs and disheartening refusals.

One factor keeping people away from the project, I knew, was the grim cycle of life in Kalambayi. To see it in action all you had to do was watch the bands of men and women coming back from their fields each day at noon. They moved as if in slow motion—faces drained, hoes at rest against bony shoulders, bodies limp and exhausted after just four or five hours of work. The poor diet and sickness endemic in each village bred chronic fatigue. Fatigue, in turn, bred reduced food production. Reduced food production, in turn, bred poor diet and sickness, closing the circle. Strapped to this grisly merry-go-round, who had the energy to lift and throw fifty thousand shovelfuls of dirt?

Another complicating factor was village philosophy. Why bother with ponds? A lot of people took a fatalistic view of the suffering, the child mortality, the disease, the hardship. These things weren't new. People had accepted them long ago as part of life. There was a saying: "In the beginning, the world was as man found it. The grass was already growing." *C'est la vie*, in other words. How can you change the grass? How can you change life? What man claims such power? Surely a few fish ponds won't make a difference.

And, finally, there was a third factor working against the project. It disturbed me more than the other two, and I learned about it somewhat by accident.

When I first started working with Tshimbalanga and his twin sons, something about my visits struck me as strange. There were never other people around. Usually when I went down to inspect ponds with farmers, at least a handful of their neighbors tagged along to marvel at my white skin and to examine the curious dikes we were building. But with Tshimbalanga this never happened. We were always alone. One day I asked him why.

"People just don't want to anger you," he said.

"Anger me? How would they anger me by coming to the ponds?"

He paused at this and stared at his feet as if he had just been caught stealing something.

"How would they anger me, Tshimbalanga," I repeated.

Stumbling for an answer, he said, "Oh, it's just . . . *udi mumanya mushindu wa bantu*. You know the way people are."

No, I didn't know the way people are. All I knew was that a discernible tone of subterfuge had crept into Tshimbalanga's voice. I pressed further and a confession spilled out.

"Everyone stays away," he said, "because I told them the ponds belong to you and you don't like people around."

"You what?"

"I told people the ponds are your ponds."

"You what?"

My body writhed with anger as he explained.

"When I began digging my ponds, some of my neighbors grew jealous. They accused me of thinking I was better than everyone else and trying to get ahead."

This was a fairly common phenomenon. It happened to fish farmers in other villages. What wasn't common was how Tshimbalanga handled it.

"The only thing I could think to do was to tell everyone the ponds weren't mine. I told them I worked for you, that the fish really belonged to the *mutoka* and that the profit was his."

Mutoka was the Tshiluba word for "white man." It was a rather unpleasant word, harsh-sounding, with the feel and roll of gringo. There were two other fish farmers in Tshimbalanga's village, and they later admitted to the same ruse. "They're the *mutoka*'s ponds," they had been telling everyone. "We dig them, but he gets the fish and pays us *petite* wages."

I was furious. I demanded the farmers put an end to this fiction. No one would want to practice fish culture if he thought all the fruits went to the funny white guy on the motorcycle.

Little did I know, however, that a large majority of Kalambayans already believed the white guy took all the profit. They had assumed this from the day I arrived. Tshimbalanga's lie was more a reminder to his neighbors than a revelation. To them and other villagers I was perceived not as an employee of the Zairian Department of Agriculture but as an enterprising foreign businessman come to construct ponds for his own benefit. At Ilunga's first harvest, which was still ahead at this point, the villagers helped themselves to the fish only after it became clear *I* wasn't going to take the catch as anticipated.

Following my startling conversation with Tshimbalanga, I confirmed the widespread suspicion of me by asking around. Three-quarters of the people I queried—market women, school children, even some of my closest neighbors in Lulenga— understood that I took the fish. "I thought you already knew that," Mbaya said when I went to him bearing what I thought was news.

No, it wasn't something I had already known. But I was starting to get the picture. Chief Ilunga, Bukasa, and the other farmers who had already joined the project were men given to leaps of faith. They had trusted me when I said the ponds were for their benefit. But having more or less exhausted this pool of risk-takers during my first few months, I now was running into the stone wall of a suspicious majority. Hence, the slowdown. Truly dumbfounding was the fact that, despite their distrust, people everywhere treated me with utmost generosity. They were glad to have me visit, glad to give me food. But the minute I opened my mouth about ponds, no one was interested.

Equipped with this new understanding, I continued roaming the villages with my drawing stick, now stating repeatedly that the fish weren't for me. Still, I had few takers. Villagers were too firmly convinced I took the harvests. Why else, they reasoned, had I traveled so far from my home to live in this hard-to-reach place? What possible motive could I have had except to take from them?

"I'm here to help you," I told them.

"Help us?" their skeptical eyes asked. "Why that makes no sense at all."

People were sure, whatever I said, that I had other plans. Their history permitted no other conclusion. For, although isolated and surrounded by rivers, Kalambayi had been visited before—and not just by Belgians seeking cotton. Several violent waves of foreigners had preceded me here. Each wave had come determined to take something, to leave the chiefdom looking different than how they found it. Why should I be any different?

The history of my predecessors' visits was stored and kept alive in the words of storytellers in every village. It was retold in outdoor living rooms, passed on below sun and stars. The story made people wary of me. It also made this rural chiefdom a tinderbox of long-accumulated grievances. Dry and brittle, those grievances had been waiting a long time for a flame to set them burning. In July, five and a half months after I arrived and one month into the fish-project slowdown, that flame materialized.

7

I HAD BEEN TOLD THERE MIGHT BE VIOLENCE BEFORE I EVER set foot in Kalambayi. Neil Jordan had warned me in Kinshasa, the Zairian capital. But he had been in a hurry at the time. He had a plane to catch and could only give me a summary of what had already happened.

"This close," Neil said, holding his thumb and index finger an inch apart as we drank tea next to a busy street. "They had clubs and machetes and they acted like they were ready to use them—really, to cut me up."

Neil had just finished two years working as a Peace Corps fisheries volunteer along the border between Kalambayi and Bena Nshimba. We crossed paths as he was on his way back to the States and I was on my way to start my assignment farther up the Lubilashi. Sitting under a grass *paillotte*, my duffel packed and ready, I listened as Neil told me what to expect in Kalambayi. There was a fierce power struggle going on in the chiefdom. Three men wanted to be paramount chief.

"Whatever you do, don't get involved with any of these guys," he said. "That was my biggest mistake."

Neil had lived in Katombe, a village near the confluence of the Lubilashi and Luvula Rivers. With three thousand inhabitants, Katombe was Kalambayi's largest and commercially most important village. While living there Neil had become close friends with Kalombo Luzadi, a man serving as head chief of Kalambayi while his brother, Kabuiya Nzala, the real chief, was away on business in Mbuji Mayi.

Serious political disputes had begun to pan-fry toward the end of Neil's stay. Members of Ngulungu, a village to the north, were dissatisfied with the leadership of brothers Kalombo and

Kabuiya. The Ngulungu men had started actively campaigning to have their native son, Kabemba Yambayamba, made chief. One day, a group of Kabemba's fanatical followers pulled Kalombo from his house and severely beat him with clubs. When Neil learned of this, he rushed to Kalombo's house and found the chief barely conscious, his clothes and face covered with blood. Neil left to get his motorcycle, intent on taking Kalombo to the Presbyterian mission hospital fifteen miles away. But when he came back, twenty of Kabemba's men were waiting for him, clubs and machetes drawn.

"They formed a circle around me," Neil said, "and kept crowding in closer and closer and grumbling about how if I tried to help Kalombo I might wind up like him. I mean these guys were serious. What could I do? I had to leave."

Neil quickly fled to Mbuji Mayi for safety. Kalombo, meanwhile, made it to the hospital on his own and his assailants later were arrested. Two weeks later Neil returned to the village, deciding it was okay to stay as long as he maintained a low profile. But when Peace Corps officials in Kinshasa caught word of what happened they made plans to withdraw from the area at the end of Neil's tour. Neil convinced the Peace Corps to send another volunteer—me—only after securing the tumbledown cotton warehouse in Lulenga, a rural village sixteen miles upriver from the area of greatest tension. This would be my house.

"The situation is still really shaky," Neil told me during our brief talk in Kinshasa. "All of these guys who want to be chief have a lot of followers and things might eventually blow up. But living out in the bush you should be okay. Just don't get involved, like I said."

This eleventh-hour briefing naturally disturbed me. It was the first I had heard of trouble in the area I had been assigned. Nowhere on my government application had I checked a box next to: "Is applicant willing to locate in war zone?" But eager to get to work and confident (naively) of the Peace Corps' judgment, I decided not to worry too much. Besides, it was quite possible Neil was exaggerating. Zaire's sprawling interior had a long history of spitting out foreigners wide-eyed with overblown reports of dark happenings. Forewarned and alert, but somewhat skeptical, I set off for Kalambayi.

When I arrived I found no evidence of intrigue. Virtually every villager I talked to said the situation was calm; the earlier political disputes had been resolved. Relieved, I settled into a work routine and thoughts of civil war retreated from my mind.

Living near Kalambayi's border, Neil had spent much of his time working in the neighboring chiefdom of Bena Nshimba and farther north in Bibanga. As a result, almost all of Kalambayi was unexplored for fish culture when I came in February 1985. I concentrated my efforts along the upper Lubilashi. In Neil's old downriver village, Katombe, I worked with only a handful of farmers, not wanting to spend too much time there given his experience. One of the men I worked with in Katombe was Kamangu Mpemba.

I visited Kamangu every Tuesday afternoon. He was a small, talkative man who taught *cinquième* students at the Catholic mission school. It wasn't uncommon to find him grading papers at his pond after class, his hands still lightly dusted with chalk. His own school of children, eight of them back at the house, had begun to outstrip his thin teacher's salary, and his pond was now his best hope.

And reason there was for hope. Kamangu did first-rate work, feeding his fish faithfully and fending off monitor lizards and other predators with slingshots he confiscated from classroom belligerents. For other thieves, the human kind, he had a different strategy. Although a religious man, Kamangu, like most villagers who professed Christianity, wandered from the path of orthodoxy in a pinch.

"God has allowed me to do this," he said one afternoon, pointing to a group of stick fetishes, called *buanga*, he had placed in the pond water. If so much as a drop of water touched a thief's hand, he explained, the fetishes would render the thief immediately and irrevocably insane. I wasn't in any danger, though. I could touch the water if I wanted to, he said. I refrained anyway, deciding that Kalambayi's fever-inducing parasites and teeth-cracking roads were enough. I didn't need anything else scrambling my brains.

Whether Kamangu's fetishes had anything to do with it or not, something was working. Weeks passed and his pond grew so dense with tilapia that I began to look forward to my visits with great anticipation. This was especially true by June, when project recruits elsewhere started disappearing, taking with them a lot of my hopes for fish culture in Kalambayi.

Because of the hour-long drive to Katombe, I usually stayed overnight on Tuesdays, sleeping on a straw bed in the backyard guest hut of Ilunga Clement, a fish farmer who lived near the marketplace. In the mornings I would buy supplies at the weekly market, the largest in Kalambayi.

So things progressed until June, when the chiefdom's wafer-thin layer of calm began to show holes and Neil's earlier warning gained credibility. Rumors of political machination and impending hostility spread as the three candidates for paramount chief began campaigning. It had been decided that a council of lower chiefs drawn from throughout the area would vote on the candidates in late August at the end of the three-month dry season. Clement told me that all three candidates claimed to be the rightful descendant of Kabongo Katombe, a powerful chief who had ruled Kalambayi one hundred years earlier.

On a Tuesday in early July, one of the candidates for chief, Kalala wa Tshijiba, held a rally in the Katombe market. I was in town visiting Kamangu, and benign curiosity led the two of us to attend. An extraordinarily skinny man given to making broad arm gestures as he spoke, Kalala stood on a crude stick platform and told the crowd of about five hundred people how he would transform Kalambayi into a paradise if elected.

"*Telejayi!*" he shouted, commanding the crowd to listen closely. "What you want and what I want are the same things. I'm one of you, and I'll work for those things. We'll have better schools. We'll have better roads. And I'll work to bring tractors to plow fields in every village."

The three promises received, respectively, scattered applause, shouts of approval, and a low-level rumble of cheers.

The speech went on for a few more minutes before Kalala noticed me standing toward the back of the crowd. When he did, I realized my mistake. I shouldn't have come. "See my power," he said, suddenly thrusting a finger at me. Everyone in the crowd turned around to look. The effect was like that of having a giant spotlight shined in my face. "It was I who brought Michel here to help develop Kalambayi."

It was a lie. Or at least I thought it was. Perhaps he had petitioned the government for an extension agent. I didn't know. Either way, though, there was little I could do about it now. The crowd was cheering Kalala's remark, and openly challenging his word would only involve me further in political controversy. The damage was done. Forgetting Neil's warning, I had been publicly linked to one of the candidates. I grabbed Kamangu's arm and we left the market.

I visited two more farmers that afternoon and later was walking back to Clement's house when I ran into Kabemba, the leader of the camp that had threatened Neil. He was with four of his followers. The men said they had been looking for me. The fact that none of them carried clubs or machetes eased my nervousness only slightly.

"I suppose you've been told all the lies about me," Kabemba began, mentioning he had heard I was at Kalala's earlier speech.

He was overweight and perspiring in a modified version of a Mao suit popular in Zaire. "You've probably decided to oppose me, too," he continued, "but I want to ask you for your endorsement anyway."

Was he asking or demanding? I couldn't tell. Feigning complete ignorance of the situation, I told Kabemba I had no interest whatsoever in local politics. My job was to do extension work, I said. He tried to discuss things further, but I quickly brought up the fact that I was in a hurry. I thanked the men for their trouble, bade them good day and made my way back up river to Lulenga, deciding not to spend the night at Clement's.

Perhaps it was stupid of me to return to Katombe the following Tuesday. Stories filtering into the bush all week held that the situation there had grown worse. Ardent supporters of Kabuiya, Kabemba, and Kalala were all in the village and supposedly on the verge of open conflict. But the most recent word was that the fighting wouldn't materialize. Government officials in Mbuji Mayi had sent messages warning all sides against violence. Encouraged by the latest news, I kept to my weekly schedule.

I arrived in Katombe and went directly to Kamangu's house. He told me that one of his children was sick with an intestinal parasite. To earn money for medicine, he wanted to net a few fish from his pond the next morning and sell them in the market. But there was a problem. Rumors had resurfaced of a possible showdown in the marketplace between the different political factions the next day, disrupting commerce. After talking it over, Kamangu and I persuaded each other it was safe to go ahead. He really needed the money. Besides, neither of us could bring ourselves to believe that large-scale fighting was about to break out. We had no way of knowing preparations were already being made.

That evening I went to Clement's guest hut and passed the strangest, most surreal night of my two years in Africa. At different spots near the empty marketplace, supporters of the three candidates for chief gathered to hold separate *bilumbu*.

These were meetings at which political grievances were aired, usually with great emotion. Each faction brought drums, and around midnight the booming, portentous rhythms began ripping through the village, each camp's beat apparently meant as a warning to the other two. Lying in bed, I started to worry. This was *definitely* unusual stuff. If those weren't war drums I was hearing, I decided, they were uncomfortably close cousins.

It was virtually impossible to sleep. After sessions lasting five or ten minutes, the drumming in one camp or another would stop, immediately giving way to primal screams. They were women's screams—high-pitched, oscillating yodels in the traditional style that communicated intense happiness, grief, or anger. The screams were followed, in turn, by the rapid, fiery voices of men speaking to the crowds, their words unintelligible in the distance. Together these sounds stabbed through the walls of my hut, leaving me in a state of genuine disbelief. The situation was beginning to take on all the clichéd markings of African intrigue snatched from a nineteenth-century explorer's notebook.

I lit a candle and tried to read, but my ears kept tuning in to the noise outside and my eyes wandered to the resident battalion of brown ants inside the hut. As if moving to the urgent drumbeat, the ants streamed hurriedly across the far wall, their line piercing the weird shadows created by my candle. In this same room three months earlier, I had awakened in the middle of the night, spitting and slapping, to these ants crawling across my face and chest.

Outside, the *bilumbu* went on without pause, their overlapping sessions creating a vague "Row Your Boat" of drums, screams, and speeches. I blew out the candle and managed to doze off, waking some time later to the sound of footsteps and voices near my hut. Small groups of men were roaming past the houses near the marketplace. The men spoke in hushed, hurried tones except for an occasional cry to someone farther away: "Hey, don't go over there. This way. Stay over here." These secretive movements continued throughout the night.

At one point, a man began pounding on my locked door, yelling for someone named Tshitoyi whom I had never heard of. I remained silent and the man went away.

The next morning it was quiet. The *bilumbu* groups had disbanded, leaving little trace of their activities. It was as if nothing had happened. I hurried to Kamangu's pond, where he had already prepared a net for catching the fish he needed. Despite the macabre goings on the night before, he said he wanted to press on with the plan. The drums and screams had been mere breastbeating, he said. I had reservations, but they were quickly forgotten in the success of the catch. With ease, we netted over fifty fish of encouraging size.

But good luck immediately gave way to bad. Carrying the fish back to the village we received devastating news. Kabemba's supporters had warned everyone in the village to stay away from the market that day in order to embarrass Chief Kabuiya, who had returned from Mbuji Mayi to personally manage the growing unrest. The ploy was a near-total success. By 10:00 a.m. only a fraction of the usual market-goers was buying and selling goods. Kamangu's wife left to sell as many fish as she could.

Startled by this latest turn, I went back to Clement's house to prepare to leave. Clement was standing outside. Judging by his tired and worried face he had gotten even less sleep than me the night before. We talked about the situation. Chief Kabuiya had just denounced Kabemba for his brazen market boycott and was threatening to have him arrested. It appeared there really was going to be a fight, Clement said. For safety, he was sending his family to stay with relatives in the bush. Men throughout the village were doing the same.

About thirty minutes later, Baba Mpiana, Clement's neighbor, arrived at the house. I was shocked and sickened by what I saw. Baba had been beaten. He walked slowly, his back hunched, one hand held to his swollen face. A supporter of Kabuiya, he had been jumped by some of Kabemba's men outside the village. They had taken his watch and pummeled him to the ground.

It was happening. The violence had begun.

"You need to leave quickly, Michel," Clement said. "Get your things and go."

I scarcely needed to be told. Given Neil's experience and my public encounters with two of the three candidates the week before, it wasn't unfounded alarm to consider myself in some degree of danger now that things were turning nasty. My mind quavered at the thought of a postage-stamp-size story buried in newspapers from London to Kuala Lumpur: AMERICAN DEVELOPMENT WORKER CLUBBED IN AFRICAN VILLAGE DISPUTE.

Hurrying, I mounted my motorcycle and pulled away, deciding at the last minute to make a brief stop at Kamangu's. Passing through the village, I saw growing signs of evacuation. Men and women moved rapidly across the road, fleeing in different directions, carrying children.

I reached Kamangu's hut and found his wife standing next to a basin of fish, her head hung despondently. She had sold only a handful of the catch in the market, not enough to buy medicine for her sick child. She had given up on the rest. The decision to harvest had been a huge mistake.

Kamangu, meanwhile, was inside, tending to his fourteen-year-old son. The boy had just been beaten by some of Kabemba's henchmen (they were now forcefully ejecting people from the market) and he was bleeding from one ear. When he heard me arrive, Kamangu came outside with a face so contorted with anxiety I hardly recognized him.

"What did I do, Michel?" he asked. "What did God see in my life to send this kind of suffering?"

I had no answer. Indeed, there was little I could tell him save to evacuate his family and possessions as fast as he could.

Reports of looting now were passing through the village. A lone gunshot had sounded in the distance. "But I'm not sure my son can make the walk," Kamangu said.

I wanted to stay and help, but I couldn't. I had to leave. Things were truly spinning out of control. Kamangu was rounding up his yard chickens and giving orders to his children when I pulled away. His face, sick with despair, stamped itself forever in my mind.

With hundreds of other people, I made my way out of Katombe, managing to avoid the roving gangs of men now turning the village upside down. I passed the last village hut and entered the bush, feeling with an intensity I never had before the sense of freedom and escape that comes from piloting a fast-moving motorcycle. All along the road to Lulenga I passed refugees, mostly women and children with confused, frightened looks. They were heading for relatives in the bush. Their poverty lay graphically summarized on their heads and backs: sacks of corn, pots and pans, wooden tables, farming implements, chickens, woven mats—virtually all their worldly possessions packed up in a rush of rumors and mounting beatings.

When I reached Lulenga, the villagers there besieged me, breathless for news of the situation. I told them everything I knew, adding that it wasn't altogether clear just what was happening. The next day, dozens more refugees streamed into the village bringing word that Katombe and the adjacent village of Bena Mbaya were deserted now except for combatants who were burning huts and fighting with spears and guns. At least one person had been killed and scores were wounded.

The fighting appeared to be confined to these two villages, but the threat of it spreading rose as, one by one, different village chiefs declared their allegiance to one candidate or another. For the first couple of days I considered leaving for Mbuji Mayi, but I finally decided to lie low and wait, working in rural villages where things remained relatively calm despite the swell of refugees. Besides, I reasoned, the government certainly would be sending troops soon to restore order.

Up to this point, I knew little about the nature of the conflict except that it was a power struggle. Three men aspired to a position only one could occupy. But like most aspects of life here, the situation was more complex than it seemed. Guiding events was a tangled thread of history previously obscure to me.

It was now mid July and my Tshiluba had improved such that I understood most everything being said around me. In the days following the outbreak of fighting, as news of growing brutality arrived, I sat in the outdoor parlors of numerous village houses—each dominated by talk of the conflict and its causes— and listened as the unhappy story of Kalambayi's past streamed out. Everywhere, the word *ndondo* surfaced, as in "They've all forgotten the *ndondo*" and "They should have known the *ndondo* would make this happen."

When I asked Lengos what the *ndondo* was, he suggested I visit Mbaya Daniel, the oldest man in Lulenga. We walked to the old man's house and found him busy managing the arrival of a half-dozen relatives who had just fled the fighting in Katombe. Daniel agreed to talk to us for a while, and we repaired to a spot under a papaya tree. There he told his story. It was a story that began one hundred years earlier with Chief Kabongo Katombe, the same chief whose legacy Clement had mentioned to me at the start of the unrest. According to Daniel, it was Chief Kabongo who had created the *ndondo* and it was the *ndondo* that was at the heart of the fighting now.

Around 1880, Daniel said, Kabongo Katombe became paramount chief of Kalambayi, having inherited the position from his father. To unite the chiefdom and solidify his power, the new chief summoned all the men of Kalambayi to his village of Bashia Kabuya and announced his intention of conducting a strange and powerful ceremony.

Kabongo told the men to spread out across the countryside and gather the bodies of every animal known to roam the land. Obeying, the men hunted antelope with bows and arrows. They set traps for birds. They plucked fish from rivers. After three days the men had collected many species. Kabongo then ordered his followers to dig a giant pit at the edge of the village. The men cut off the heads of the animals and placed the bodies in the pit. Next they placed the animal heads, one by one, in a huge clay pot in the center of the pit. The pot quickly filled with the heads of owls and chicken and goats, of wild pigs and antelope and chameleons.

But, Daniel continued, when all the heads had been deposited, there was still room for the head of the one animal that roamed the land that had not yet been sacrificed. Mutombe Tshitungula, a warrior captured in battle north of Kalambayi, was brought to the pit with his arms and legs bound. He lay prostrate inside the circle of men and screamed wildly before a machete blade sliced through his neck. His body was thrown into the pit and his head placed in the clay pot. The excavated dirt was then returned and the seed of a mango tree was planted on top to grow and stand as a testament to the ceremony.

This was the *ndondo*, Daniel said. When complete it gave Chief Kabongo the secret awareness and power of all living animals. It was understood that the spirit of that power was immortal and that any man who tried to take it away from Kabongo, or his sons after him, would die.

And this was what the warring factions in Katombe were currently fighting about. Although the *ndondo* site today was no longer carefully kept up, virtually everyone in Kalambayi believed it still had power and only one man could possess that power. The question now was who that man was. All three of the present candidates for chief claimed to be rightful inheritors.

I wanted to continue the history with Daniel but I couldn't. Lengos had warned me that at his age—close to ninety—he couldn't talk for long without getting tired. True to prediction, Daniel dismissed us after less than an hour, saying he wanted to tie up his goats and take a nap.

Meanwhile, four days had passed since I left the fighting in Katombe and news was still coming in. Savage exchanges continued, with prisoners being taken on all sides. Some prisoners were reportedly being tortured by having the blades of heated machetes applied to their chests and arms.

And in the outlying villages the refugee problem was growing worse than I had anticipated. I watched as village leaders in Ntita Konyukua almost came to blows during an argument over how to feed and shelter the surfeit of arrivals, many of whom were now sleeping under the eaves of houses or living in the bush along the Lubilashi.

A Peace Corps volunteer outside of Ngandajika learned of the conflict in Kalambayi and sent me a message encouraging me to leave at once. I wrote back saying that although there was a chance the growing tension in the rural areas would lead to more violence, I still felt safe to stay.

In the meantime, I visited other village elders in order to pursue the Kalambayan history Daniel had started. With minor variations, men in Kalula, Bena Ngoyi, Ntita Kalambayi and Ntita Konyukua confirmed what Daniel had said about the *ndondo*. They then took the story several steps further, casting more light on the present conflict.

It was the power of the *ndondo*, they said, that had permitted Chief Kabongo to manage several crises confronting the chiefdom toward the end of the nineteenth century. First, as the ceremonial mango tree branched and grew, Kabongo defended the chiefdom against Ngongo Luteta, a bucktoothed slave raider armed by Arabs along the upper Congo River. Luteta captured several hundred Kalambayans before Kabongo's fierce counterattacks persuaded him to slave elsewhere.

Ten years later, the chief fought another successful war, this time routing the rival chiefdom of Baluba Shankadi, which had tried to annex a large portion of eastern Kalambayi.

And then there was the matter of the new Belgian colonists. By the early 1890s the Europeans were rapidly consolidating their power to the region and pressuring Kabongo to submit to their authority. He resolutely refused. There was a standoff until 1913 when the chief was asked to appear at the Belgian headquarters in Kabinda. There he was told he had no choice but to give in. Kabongo, in turn, informed the Europeans that if they tried to take his power they would die. The *ndondo*, the sacred pit of heads, would kill them. The Europeans laughed.

Angry and defiant, Kabongo left Kabinda and headed home with his band of warriors. Almost immediately after reaching Kalambayi he began complaining of severe chest and stomach pains. A month later he died. Outraged, the people of Kalambayi rose up in insurrection. Kabongo had been poisoned, they claimed. The Belgians had put something in his food in Kabinda.

Kabongo's oldest son, Ngoyi, took over after the death and declared the land of Kalambayi off limits to foreigners, invoking the power of *ndondo*. But colonial troops attacked anyway, quickly defeating Ngoyi and subduing Kalambayi at last.

When I asked different elders why the *ndondo* hadn't killed the attacking Belgians, I got different responses. Some said it was the fault of Ngoyi, the old chief's successor. Had he fought harder and been better organized, the *ndondo* would have helped him vanquish the invaders. Others said the *ndondo* had in fact worked. The Belgians succeeded in taking Kalambayi, but all the soldiers and officers involved in the attack died within a few years of various illnesses and accidents brought on by the *ndondo*.

This, finally, was the life history of Chief Kabongo Katombe as told to me by elders and other villagers. It was a history that ended in war. Now, seventy-two years later, fighting had returned, waged in the name of the same fallen chief. A week had gone by since the shooting and beatings around the Katombe marketplace had begun, and the combatants continued to trade attacks. Meanwhile, government troops still hadn't arrived and refugees in the bush were running out of food.

Of all the stories told to me during those days of fighting, I had the greatest trouble believing—aside from the talk of the *ndondo*'s magic—the part about the poisoning of Chief Kabongo. Even for calculating Belgian agents trying to wipe out resistance to their authority, it sounded a little too creative and sinister.

Whether the poisoning happened or not, though, doesn't really matter. The Kalambayan people believe it. Every villager I talked to *knew* the chief had been killed by the Belgians. And they knew something else: Alive, Kabongo had stopped a slave raider and protected the chiefdom. Dead, he couldn't stop the harsh system of forced cotton cultivation—hardly distinguishable from slavery—that came later. Most Kalambayans still need time to get over that fact.

After talking to more elders, I learned that Kalala wa Tshijiba, part of the trio of leaders whose men were currently battling downriver, was the great grandson of Chief Kabongo. By right of ancestry, he had been allowed by Belgian and Zairian government officials to continue as head chief of Kalambayi for many years, although with circumscribed powers.

Then, in 1979, Kabuiya Nzala walked up to Kalala and said: "I don't care if you claim to be chief or not. You can no longer be the legitimate leader of our people. Your grandfather, Ngoyi, surrendered. He gave up his power and betrayed the *ndondo*. I now declare myself chief of Kalambayi."

Kabuiya had become a successful merchant in Mbuji Mayi and had used his wealth to bribe state officials into recognizing his claim. But when Kabuiya went to Kalala to assert his new authority, Kalala responded with a warning. "Go ahead," he said. "If you try to take power from me the *ndondo* will kill you."

So it was, six years later, that fighting broke out on that frantic market day in Katombe. Chief Kabuiya and his men fought to maintain power. Kalala and his men fought to recover power. And Kabemba, the most unscrupulous of the three, fought to gain new power. Their battles went on for days, involving more than two hundred men and leaving three dead, dozens wounded, and at least sixty houses torched.

It was two weeks before a truck-load of government troops finally arrived to restrain the combatants. The troops patrolled the ravaged villages, declaring a cease fire and imposing a curfew. But the cease fire had barely taken hold and all sides were still poised for more violence when something very strange happened. Chief Kabuiya, camped with his men outside Katombe, suddenly died. He hadn't been wounded in the fighting. He hadn't been seriously ill. Indeed, according to his men, he was outwardly healthy up to the last day. Then he died. A doctor in Mbuji Mayi later speculated it was a heart attack. But across Kalambayi, village men gathered in their outdoor compounds and talked about the same thing. "The *ndondo*," they said. "The *ndondo* killed Kabuiya."

The government troops stepped up their patrols after the death, expecting more fighting. But it never came. The death spooked combatants in each camp, joining exhaustion in putting an end to further attacks.

When it became clear the worst exchanges had ended, I decided it was safe to travel through the afflicted area to visit fish farmers in villages on the other side. When I reached Katombe, sight of the most serious violence, I saw a village empty and rent by fighting and looting. I stopped my motorcycle on the dirt road and turned off the engine and surveyed the scene. Row after row of houses stood as burned-out shells, their mud walls black and crumbling, their roofs gone. In the outdoor clearings there were no people nor belongings nor animals nor, it seemed, any hope of their quick return. In the air there lingered a smoky smell. And it was silent. That was the most unsettling thing. A leaden, eerie silence lay on the village—a frightful counterpoint to the screams and hysteria that had come before.

Perhaps the fighting had been inevitable, I considered later. So much had changed in the span of a few generations. So many uncertainties, recriminations, old scores to settle. "Who betrayed the lineage? Who are we now? Who is our leader?" Into this fragile, weakened chiefdom I had stepped to live and work. Tucked inside a struggling new country on a troubled continent, flailed by the forces of a confusing century, the chiefdom limped along still clinging to Africa's pre-violated past as a guide. It was a frustrating balancing act, one that had been seeking expression for a long time.

After Kabuiya's controversial death, officials in Mbuji Mayi dispatched a state agent to govern in Kalambayi until the competing factions could peacefully decide who was their real chief. An agreement still hadn't been reached a year and a half later when I left. During that time, no new violence erupted. Refugees went back to their villages and life returned to a nearly normal state, but nothing had been resolved. The fighting was simply over for now.

There was still the question of how I fit into all of this. I don't believe most Kalambayans lumped me into the same bitter pot that held memories of past invaders and their assault on the land and the lineage. I never taxed anyone or asked anyone to work against his will. I didn't carry a gun or a whip, and the sticks I picked up were used to draw fish in the dirt, nothing more. My aim was to teach tilapia culture, period.

Still, there dwelled in most peoples' eyes varying degrees of distrust when they saw me coming. I approached along paths and roads that had barely finished erasing the footprints of my predecessors. Villagers were uneasy with me. Slave raiders had taken their people. Belgians had taken their labor. Missionaries had taken their souls. And now, Michel, what is it you want? Fish? You say you want us to raise fish, is that it? Well, you'll excuse us if we don't come running, won't you?

I still had much to do to gain their confidence.

Some months later, after all the fighting had wound down, I decided to visit the *ndondo*, the pit of heads. I wanted to see for myself this strange place that shaped so much of Kalambayi's past and present. Tshimbalanga Shambuyi, the fish farmer in Bajila Membila, lived about a mile from Bashia Kabuya, the old village where the *ndondo* was said to be. When I asked Tshimbalanga to take me to the site, he stood up from his chair and motioned me to follow him. At a point outside the village he stopped and pointed to the west, across a valley.

"That's where it is," he said. "Beyond that ridge in a patch of bush by itself. The village of Bashia Kabuya has moved a few kilometers from that spot and the *ndondo* is alone now."

I was ready to walk to the place and began considering what paths to follow. But Tshimbalanga said that regardless of the path we took the *ndondo* would be hard to find.

"What about the mango tree?" I asked. "Can't we just look for the tree?"

"It died and fell about twenty years ago," he said, "and people are afraid to go there now."

I wanted to try anyway. But Tshimbalanga refused to take me. Because the *ndondo* was no longer carefully marked, he was concerned we might tread on its hallowed surface.

8

THE NASTY LITTLE CIVIL WAR HAD BARELY ENDED WHEN RAIN returned to Kalambayi. It came in late August, coaxing the earth out of the dry-season slumber it had been in for the past three months. The first few storms were tenuous affairs, and it wasn't until mid September that the rain hunkered down to a regimen of one or two substantial showers each week. When this happened, villagers grabbed their short-handled hoes and cleared fields and tilled the soil. They stuffed fistfuls of corn seed into their mouths and, cheeks bulging, walked up and down the furrows, delicately spitting kernels into holes their toes punched in the dirt.

After a few days, the corn sprouted. Beans and sweet potatoes and peanuts planted between the corn did the same. But while this was happening, while the new crops were growing taller, the existing food supply in the villages began to shrink. Dried manioc tubers, corn, and beans—harvested the previous June and stored in the attics of huts—decreased to such levels by October that villagers began carefully eyeballing their stocks and measuring daily consumption so as to have at least something to eat until the next harvest in December. The problem was one common to all subsistence people: making the food from one harvest last until the next.

The mealtime bowls of *fufu* began to dwindle noticeably in late October, and I sometimes came home from work hungry even after taking several midday meals with farmers. People tended to grow irritable at this time of year. They complained of headaches. They began to lose weight. Anyone whose last harvest had been reduced by thieves (monkeys, hippopotamuses, insects, disease) was particularly hard-hit. By November most people were hanging on, hungrily watching their crops and showing the strains of living life so tightly bound to the earth's rhythms.

Then, in mid November, a gift arrived. Some benevolent force looked down on the land and saw faintly protruding ribs and decided to provide the villages with *nsua*, the brownish termite larvae of the central-African savanna. The insects sprang to life inside man-tall mud castles scattered throughout the bush. Newly hatched, they crawled to their nests' edges, blinked their eyes at the world, and immediately demonstrated the limits of their little insect brains. They got ambushed. Hungry villagers went to the castles at night and lit dollops of flammable tree resin outside the nests' openings. In between the burning resin and the nests, they dug small pits. Within minutes, the intrigued larvae ambled out to inspect the light and ended up crawling on each others' backs, trying to raise themselves out of the pits.

Food. Lots of it. People munched the agreeable-tasting bugs by the handful. They stewed them in manioc leaves and fried them in oil. Just when food supplies had begun to reach distressing levels, the protein-rich larvae had arrived to carry everyone into the December harvest season.

In February, the cycle began again. People spit seeds into the soil. Crops rose and attic food stocks fell. By April, people complained of headaches again. But this time there was no sudden salvation. The termite larvae came only once a year, in November. In April, villagers were on their own. Families began rationing their food. They began eating less.

Aggravating this lean period was bad weather, the worst weather of the year. The wet-season rains were heaviest from early March to mid May. April was particularly bad. It rained for days on end in April, falling in clamorous bursts. Rainwater cut deep gullies in paths and roads. Palm trees assumed the classic storm posture— trunks bending, crowns thrashing. Thunder cracked in the sky. Small streams became creeks, creeks became rivers, the Lubilashi became a moving lake. From the flooded areas rose clouds of mosquitoes that buzzed into villages, spreading malarial fever.

It was the worst time of the year in Kalambayi. People crouched around fires inside their dark houses, under leaky roofs. They ate small meals. From time to time they went outside to check the sky and were chased back in by rain and wind that chilled them to their roots.

And there was death. Cruel, shameless, opportunistic death. This was its finest hour. It needed no stronger cues than these, hunger and foul weather, to begin vigorously attacking anyone whose grip on life was subject to dispute. It curled up in the laps of the very old. It lay uninvited on reed mats next to the newly born. It joined families inside huts and watched nagging coughs turn to advanced bronchitis and finally pneumonia. Back and forth through the rain it followed people with intestinal illnesses to outdoor latrines. "Go away, death," the nervous faces of the sick and elderly said. "The rain can't last forever. Harvest time is soon. Give us time."

But it didn't go away. Death took more villagers during this time of year than any other. The frail, the weak, the afflicted—many just couldn't make it. After each death, women members of surviving families took to the village paths, walking slowly, announcing their loss in the public manner of African custom. They filled the villages with a dark falsetto of song and wailing, of anguished screams and narrative. At night, funeral drums became a constant feature, their weird and surging sounds evoking macabre images like those in medieval paintings of lost souls plunging into nothingness.

During this season of heavy rains, the number of people dying in the villages made me shake. It wasn't just the cries. There were bodies. I saw bodies being buried in family compounds, a piece of wood or a stick cross placed at the head of each new mound. Nothing had prepared me for this. All my life death had been an abstraction, something that occurred infrequently, out of sight, in hospitals. It usually attacked relatives who were extremely old anyway, reducing the pain of the loss. But now I watched people bury their dead, of all ages, every day, all around me. I had seen thousands of murders on television before coming to Africa and had dined at a daily banquet of war and famine in the news. But to see death next door, to hear its attendant cries wafting through your windows, to see real-life people stop breathing and real-life survivors sob with sorrow—that is something else entirely.

Unable to work in the rain, I often spent entire days at home during this time of year. I wore sweaters and read books and played Dylan tapes, my shelter in bad times. But there was no escape. At least once each day a party of mourners from Lulenga or a nearby village would pass by my house, filling the interior with fresh cries of lament. Some days there were two or three deaths, and by late afternoon I would be looking in the mirror, pulling at my cheeks, examining my eyes. Do I look pale? Am I feeling all right? If I fall asleep, will I wake up again?

The rain, the wailing, the nightly drums—day after day it continued. The heavy wet season dragged on. By mid April, I grew fabulously depressed. One afternoon I thought, "That's it. No one else can die. The village is saturated. It can't absorb another blow." Then I heard the screams. They came from different ends of the village. Kalala Nsepi's eight-year-old son had just died of measles in a hut at the bottom of the hill. At about the same moment, at the other end of the village, seventy-year-old Mbuyi Katumba's cough grew so severe that his chest rattled one last time and he died.

The two families sent out mourning parties, each made up of five or six women walking slowly in single file lines. The women were wild with grief. I went to my window and watched. The rain had stopped. The two lines were coming from opposite directions, heading toward each other on the narrow path in front of my house. When the parties met there was a moment of uncertainty. The path wasn't wide enough for the women to pass. The two lead mourners stopped and awkwardly faced each other, tears streaming down their cheeks, arms outstretched, gesturing, saying, "Yes, us too. Us too." Both groups began stepping off the path on either side, and, as they passed, the women hugged each other one by one in a spontaneous dance of bereavement that left me shuddering. I didn't want to be in Africa at that moment. I didn't want to be there. I shut my door and all my windows, and still the screams reached my ears.

9

I first met Kanyenda Mushia in late December, three months before the wet-season rains took his brother's life. Although the dust from the summer fighting had pretty much settled by then, the slowdown in my work continued, crawling into its seventh month. Except for a few new farmers I picked up here and there, most villagers stayed away from the fish project, still convinced the *mutoka* had a hidden agenda.

Then Kanyenda came along. It was early morning and I was sitting outside Bukasa Dikumbi's house in Ntita Konyukua. Bukasa had just harvested his pond for the first time and twenty-two kilos of fish lay in a tin basin on the ground. While his wife prepared to go to market, he and I sat on chairs, looking at the fish and feeling fundamentally pleased with ourselves.

Kanyenda was Bukasa's neighbor. He came over, introduced himself, inspected the fish, and sat down next to me. Then he asked a question I didn't want to hear.

"How much of the fish do you take?" he said.

My good mood began to crumble.

"I don't take any," I said. "The fish aren't mine. They belong to Bukasa."

The answer didn't satisfy him. Kanyenda was forty-three years old and had an expressive face that suggested a complex, brooding personality. With his calloused fingers he made a steeple and rested his chin on it, eyeing me carefully, skeptically.

"Why don't you take any?" he asked.

"Because that's not my job," I said. "I have a salary. The government pays me to teach people how to raise fish. I don't need them myself."

He still wasn't satisfied.

"Wait five minutes and I'll prove it," I said.

Most of the men in Kalambayi, it turned out, were like Kanyenda Mushia. Their lack of trust in me required they have some kind of assurance before they subjected themselves to the body-battering process of digging a pond. They waited until Bukasa, Ilunga, and the other already established farmers began harvesting their ponds. Then they waited to make sure I didn't stuff my knapsack full of fish.

Presently, Bukasa's wife came out of the house, hoisted the basin of fish onto her head, and set off down the trail to market. I did nothing to stop her. As I watched her walk away, I felt Kanyenda watching me. When she was out of sight I turned to him. "There," I said. "She's gone. I've taken nothing."

His next words were barely believable.

"Will you teach me how to dig a pond?"

So used to rejection was I by then that the words seemed to come from an enormous, merciful choir with French horns and kettledrum. I went through a momentary struggle over how to respond without hysteria.

"Sure. Yes. I can do that. When do you want to start?"

"How about tomorrow morning?"

"Tomorrow's fine," I said. "I'll be here at 7:30."

Finally. After almost seven months, after feeling like a failure and bearing the image of another invader come to exploit, I was finally getting through to men like Kanyenda Mushia that I wasn't lying. I really didn't take the fish. As other project farmers began making their first harvests, scenes like the one with Kanyenda were repeated in villages throughout Kalambayi. Neighbors noticed that the wives of fish farmers had new *pagnes* a few days after harvests and children carried new notebooks to school. By January, two or three men were flagging me down every week. Two young guys from Nzaji walked twenty miles to my house. "Okay," they said. "We're ready to do it. We want ponds." Over the next six months, the number of project farmers nearly tripled to more than eighty, and I had all the work I could handle. I threw away my drawing stick and a hefty load of self-doubt, and settled down to do my job.

— — —

The day after that December morning when I met Kanyenda, it was raining. The wet season already had begun its gradual buildup to the heavy showers of March and April, forcing us to postpone the search for a pond site. When we finally set off two days later, Kanyenda led me to a valley near his house that proved suitable for fish culture. It was then that I learned two things about him. First, he had bad luck.

The pond site we found was excellent. The slope was just right and there was plenty of water from a hillside spring. The only problem was that right in the middle of the spot, towering menacingly sixty feet up from the grass, was a mammoth palm tree. It had to go, I told Kanyenda. Every bit of it. We staked a canal, measured out the pond, and he went to work destroying the tree, first felling the trunk and then assaulting the stump.

Many times while I was in Africa the hardships I saw forced me to rework my understanding of what hell must be like. For a long time after meeting Kanyenda, this was my vision: In hell, people are given worn out, village-vintage machetes and are forced to remove palm-tree stumps—roots and all—from the ground. The tree Kanyenda attacked was anchored to the earth by a dense tangle of thin roots, each one a small Hydra: cut it and six appeared below. The roots spread out for ten feet in every direction. For days he chopped and shoveled and pulled. And just think, I secretly mourned, all that's left after this is the digging.

The only consolation was that the same tree that provided all the roots also provided anesthesia. From the felled trunk, Kanyenda tapped gourds of palm wine that left him in incongruously serene moods for a man mired in so much grunt work. Which brings up the second thing I learned about him: He liked to drink. At the site each week I'd find him standing a bit woozily under a midmorning sun, machete or shovel in his hand, wine at his side. "I've saved a whole gourd for you," he'd say, pouring me generous servings until I stood woozily with him.

As I drank I would listen to Kanyenda talk. This usually required a high degree of concentration because he had a complicated, roundabout, folkwise way of saying just about everything.

One morning, sweating, covered with dirt and rocking perceptibly, Kanyenda said, "I've been thinking, Michel."

"Yes," I said.

"If a man chases two chickens at the same time he goes to bed hungry."

He paused and I prepared for one of his weekly riddles.

"On the other hand," he continued, "a man must wear two bracelets on his wrist to make noise when he walks."

He paused again, this time waiting for a response. Maybe it was the wine, but I wasn't following.

"Well?" he said. "What do you think?"

"About what?"

"About building a second pond after this one. Would it be too much work or not? Would it be like chasing two chickens or like wearing two bracelets?"

That was it. He had a second pond on his mind.

"Two ponds are fine," I said, grasping the point. "I guess it would be like wearing two bracelets. It *is* a lot more work, though."

"Yes," he said. "You're right. But I think I want to do it. I once built two houses in one dry season. *Two* of them. And these ponds—they're bracelets, Michel. I want to wear two of them and really make noise when I walk."

That's the way Kanyenda talked. Chickens and bracelets and sundry other proverbs found their way into his speech with affecting regularity. It gave him the air of a peripatetic sage, and I took to him right away, unable to resist a man who could drink palm wine, dislodge a tree trunk, and pull off so much imagery with such ease.

It wasn't hard to see why Kanyenda was drawn to the fish project. He had an enormous family: two wives and sixteen children. "They're my investment," he said of his kids, explaining that their great number would protect him in old age. "If you catch a child a grasshopper to eat today, he'll catch you another grasshopper tomorrow."

Investment or not, though, the huge brood constituted a present-tense economic nightmare. Despite his energy and intelligence, Kanyenda was unable to manage the empire, and his was among the poorest families I knew in Kalambayi. They lived in two huts of dubious stability, possessing little beyond a few blackened pots and pans, a splintered table, and a particularly small and ragged band of yard animals.

But what a family it was. Perhaps my rapidly blooming fondness for Kanyenda made me prejudiced, but I swear he had some of the most beautiful children I had ever seen. This was true right down to the youngest, three-year-old Kamangu, who decided from the start that I was his best friend and attached himself to my pant leg each time I arrived, blinking up at me with silver-dollar eyes. He wasn't afraid of my white exterior, I later learned, because Kanyenda had assured him that underneath I was black like everyone else.

For my part, I did most of my blinking at Misumba, Kanyenda's sixteen-year-old daughter. In the swirl of bodies and activity that greeted me each week in the family compound, she shone like a minor deity. Her combination of shy smile, tall frame, and girlish good looks gave her the strange quality of looking both younger and older than her age. She stirred in me something I recognized to be more than casual interest and Kanyenda picked up on it.

He was always making little remarks about how Misumba was of marrying age and how he was turning away suitors every day, waiting for the right man to come along. But she was too young for me and I told Kanyenda so in clear terms. Nonetheless, my playful flirtations with her each week drew me further into the family web, and Kanyenda took to calling me *muananyi mupiamupia*, "my new little son." With my own father and family a full hemisphere away, the name started to sound good.

Working with Kanyenda and being his friend weren't always easy, though. A problem kept getting in the way: his alcoholism. It took me a few weeks to fully recognize the evidence. He did more than drink palm wine at the pond. When he had money, he drank *tshitshampa* at the house. Lots of it. There were also periodic dark moods, times when he was distant and wholly unapproachable. These moods seemed to both precede and follow the really heavy drinking. He would miss work rendezvouses, and I'd have to hunt for him in the fields. There, I'd find him polite but aloof, making up some excuse for not working while signs of hangover and depression suffused his face.

All of this kept me off balance, wondering what was bothering this man. He was either hot or cold, up or down. It was as if the same intelligence that produced humor and proverbs in lighter moments also caused him to despair more deeply than other farmers the setbacks of village life. And there were always setbacks: always a child sick with fever or a virus attacking a cornfield or some expense that had to be met.

Making matters worse, I suspect, was the fact Kanyenda had once known a time when things were different.

"This hand," he told me one afternoon over a bottle of *tshitshampa*, turning his right hand back and forth in front of my face, "once held 300,000 zaires. Right here. This hand."

For ten years he had prospected for diamonds in Mbuji Mayi and one day he had struck it rich as few diggers ever do.

He happened upon a glinting, $3,000 rock that for two years kept his family in a tin-roofed house with plenty of money and plenty to eat. But the money didn't last. There were no more lucky finds after the big one, and Kanyenda eventually moved his family back to the village with nothing to show for all his work but a tormenting memory of poverty's opposite.

Whether all of this had something to do with his drinking I'm not sure. But the drinking was there. When the chance came, Kanyenda drank hard. He drank beyond the point when most other men stopped, beyond the point when, imbibing with him, I covered my glass and shook my head. And there were Mondays. On Monday afternoons he would visit the wine vendors in the Lulenga market, swigging and socializing with other men under the mimosa tree behind the *pange* stalls. He often grew blustery and abusive after some argument there and would totter to my house to sleep it off before heading home.

There were many other occasions when I saw Kanyenda drunk, but one stands out in my mind. It was late afternoon and I was heading home along an unpopulated stretch of trail between Lulenga and Ntita Konyukua. Up ahead a man came into view, walking alone, stumbling, arms limp and swinging. I drove closer and saw it was Kanyenda. He was muttering, drunk out of his mind, heading home in the opposite direction. I stopped and turned off the engine.

"Kanyenda, where have you been?"

He swayed in front of me, dull-eyed. There was grass in his hair from where he had fallen down. His eyes were puffy, apparently from crying. An argument with someone? A fight? A funeral? I didn't find out. Kanyenda couldn't talk. He tried but his words came out gnarled and breathy. Straining terribly, pressing his face close to mine, he tried again and again to tell me something that was clearly important to him. Perhaps it was an explanation of his condition or some proverb he hadn't told me yet that described perfectly in that vague flash of alcohol the tightly wound knot he seemed to carry inside of him so much of the time. Whatever it was, though, it didn't come out. His words made no sense.

Finally, frustrated, he waved his hand as if shooing me away and continued walking down the trail. I watched him go. Later that night I grew ashamed of myself for not having made sure he got home safely. The fact that he likely walked the entire two miles to his village by himself in such a condition made me shake. In my mind I saw him stumbling through that uninhabited stretch of bush, falling in the trail dirt, yelling and crying, uttering sounds that had no meaning. Then I saw him repeatedly picking himself up and going on, a maimed figure, staggering home against a late-afternoon sun.

Despite it all, progress on Kanyenda's pond continued steadily. After removing the palm tree stump, which took a full week, Kanyenda began the digging. He was digging a big pond—one so big, in fact, he had to enlist the help of his younger brother Kanyemesha. When the wine from the first palm tree ran out, the brothers tapped a second tree and shoveled and tottered through a few more weeks of work.

But the wet season was catching up to the men. It was late March now and the near-daily rain was slowing them down. It was slowing down everyone in Kalambayi. From the Lualu to the Luvula, people were spending more and more time sitting in their houses, eyeing their food supplies, waiting for the blows the heavy wet season would soon deliver.

One blow was aimed at Kanyenda. His older brother, Kabongo, was sick. He had been ill for several months and his condition was deteriorating rapidly with the poor weather. One morning I went with Kanyenda to the man's hut. The interior was dungeon-dark and unventilated, smelling of mildew and woodsmoke. He lay wrapped in a white sheet atop two worn antelope skins, and his cough was tremendous. In long sessions—wheezy, then gurgling, then rumbling—it slithered from his diseased chest, sending chills up my legs. I figured he had emphysema or something equally frightful. It was clear he would soon die if he didn't get medical help.

"What can I do?" Kanyenda asked when we left the house and I stated the obvious prognosis. Outside, large puddles of rainwater littered the ground from a storm the night before. The sky was gray and dense.

"Have you given him any medicine?" I asked.

"Yes, yes," he said. "We gave him aspirin and vitamins every day."

I shook my head.

"You know that's not enough. You've got to get him to a doctor. You've got to go to the mission hospital."

A look of shame and embarrassment crept onto Kanyenda's face. "*Teta katuena ne falanga to,*" he said. "We don't have any money."

There they were. Those five words: "We don't have any money." They were permanently stitched to the sleeve of serious illness in Kalambayi, speaking like an epitaph for 90 percent of the chiefdom's dead and dying. Twenty-five dollars might get you professional attention at the hospital at Bibanga, but $2 got you a packet of aspirin dug out from under the candles and bars of soap on a village merchant's roadside table.

I, too, was running low on funds at the time and could only buy a little tea for Kanyenda's brother to drink during his final days. A week later he died. Then something really mind-bending happened.

Right in the middle of the heavy rainy season, with his family's food supply already running dangerously low, Kanyenda threw an elaborate funeral feast. Custom demanded it. The death of an elder like Kabongo was a major event regardless of when it happened. Within hours, dozens of relatives and family friends arrived at Kanyenda's house to note the passing. As the oldest male in his family now, the ceremony was his responsibility.

To accommodate the crowd, Kanyenda slaughtered his only goat. He killed all his chickens. He sold a sack of manioc tubers stored in the attic and used the money to buy flour, tea, palm wine, *tshitshampa*, and cigarettes. It was truly absurd. The same man who hadn't had enough money to send his dying brother to the hospital was now aggressively destroying what little wealth he did have. When the family's liquid assets ran out, Kanyenda kept things going by borrowing from his neighbors and relatives, burying himself in debt.

The funeral was raucous and intense for the first two days. That's when most of the animals were eaten and most of the alcohol consumed. I stopped by on the second afternoon and sat outside with the men, drinking and smoking in a large circle of chairs. The women, including Kanyenda's two wives, one of whom was six months pregnant, stayed behind the other house, cooking under the eave and looking after the profusion of children.

At the head of the funeral, wearing a cheap pair of horn-rim sunglasses that made him look like Ray Charles, sat Kanyenda. Next to him was a group of musicians hired to play deep-booming funeral songs with tom-toms and xylophones. The music inspired a few drunken men to dance from time to time, their hips grinding suggestively to the fast and angry beat. But Kanyenda didn't dance. He remained seated, his face rigid, rising only occasionally to manage the distribution of *tshitshampa* or to welcome newly arrived visitors. God only knows where he got the sunglasses he wore. Perhaps from his diamond-digger cousin Mutombo, a raffish character who showed up from Mbuji Mayi wearing gaudy jewelry and a watch that chimed "Dixie" every hour on the hour, "Hey, I'm from the South," I told him the first time the watch went off, but he didn't understand.

Through it all, Kanyenda kept his drinking under control and his behavior remained calm. Too calm, I thought. I kept my eye on him, half-expecting at any moment a wild burst of protest from him as he watched, from behind his sunglasses, 90 percent of his wealth go up in a blaze of drinking and eating.

But the protest never came and I decided to keep an eye on myself instead. Watching the tragicomic consumption, unable to imagine how Kanyenda's family would survive afterward, I was on the verge of launching my own protest. The fact that I was participating in the demolition made things worse. Kanyemesha came over at one point and led me and five other men to a room where we ate *fufu* and a large plate of sumptuous goat meat cooked in palm oil—a fantastic luxury. When we finished we walked back outside, passing little Kamangu and the other children huddled under the eave, passing through the barren compound soaked with rain, hearing the squeal and cry of a nearby baby as we reached the circle of chairs where *tshitshampa* flowed and the group of musicians played on, charging Kanyenda 100 zaires a day for the service.

It really was almost too much to bear. I had great respect for the Kalambayan people and most of their traditional ways. But this custom of extravagant funerals was something I never quite learned to accept. It was one of those things here I eventually stopped trying to figure out for fear of losing my mind.

The funeral for Kanyenda's brother dragged on for two more weeks, even after there was little left to consume. The musicians went home, Mutombo and his chiming watch went back to Mbuji Mayi, and the crowd of mourners shrank to Kanyenda and his brothers huddled around a single bottle of palm wine. Finally the funeral petered out completely.

"Do you have a light?" I asked Kanyenda, pulling out a cigarette a few days later when I came to visit. He motioned one of his sons into the house. The child came back with a stick the size of his arm and still glowing from the cooking fire from which it had come. Even matches, at two cents a box, were an impossible expenditure. The family had been bled white.

I smoked and looked around the muddy compound. Devastation. There were no goats. No chickens. Kanyenda had even sold his dog. The only movement came from the sixteen children who roamed listlessly in torn clothes outside bleak houses. Worse, the family was almost completely out of food. Misumba and Kamangu and all the others were eating comically small bowls of *fufu* supplemented now and again by a papaya or a handful of palm nuts. And on top of everything, it was mid April. It was raining every day now.

After the funeral I began avoiding Kanyenda's house at mealtime, knowing that if I arrived while his family was eating he'd enthusiastically insist I help polish off what little they had left. He knew I was staying away, and I think it embarrassed him. A couple of times when he wasn't home I gave skewers of smoked fish to his wives and contrived some excuse for not staying to eat.

It was the second week of April before Kanyenda and Kanyemesha heroically dragged themselves to the unfinished fish pond and began working again. I tried to persuade them to wait until the rains had ended but they were almost done and wanted to get it over with. I will never understand how they did it. They worked for two weeks, in between heavy showers, attacking the earth with their weak bodies. When they had finished they called me for a technical assessment. I walked around the pond and observed that the dikes were narrower and less built-up than was usually desired. But when I looked at the diggers—both of them reading my mind and trying to look as exhausted as possible—I didn't have the heart to tell them to dig more. "Okay," I said, "fill it with water."

Now that the pond was done, Kanyenda had a problem. What was he going to put in it? He needed three hundred stocking fish, and at the going price of one zaire per fish, he could afford exactly zero. He was broke. All together the fish would cost $3. "Here," I said, putting the money in his hand during my weekly visit. "Pay me back when you harvest." He wrapped his fingers around the bills and launched into a thank you so drawn out I had to cut it off by changing the subject.

Kanyenda bought his stocking fish from Kayemba Lenga who, along with Bukasa Dikumbi, had begun raising fish early on in Ntita Konyukua and now had plenty of fingerlings to sell to the newly converted. Using gourds of water, Kanyenda transferred the fish to his pond, carefully pouring them into their new home. At last, he was a fish farmer.

For a while.

Three days later he showed up at my house carrying something wrapped in banana leaves. I knew Kanyenda's emotional shifts well enough by then to read in his eyes maximum darkness. He handed me the bundle. I opened it and found a half-dozen dead stocking fish. "They're dead," he said. "All three hundred of them. I found them dead and floating on the surface this morning."

The news pierced me like a lance. Dead? I couldn't believe it. This had never happened before. It wasn't supposed to happen. Tilapia were chosen for our government project because they were virtually indestructible, able to withstand wide changes in water temperature and acidity. Rarely did they suffer disease or die *en masse.*

When I inspected Kanyenda's pond the next day, I noticed that the problem wasn't just the tilapia. A half-dozen toads were dead, too.

"What did I do wrong?" Kanyenda groaned softly.

Obviously, there was something toxic in the water or in the soil or, most likely, in the material Kanyenda had put in his compost bins to fertilize the pond. Not having equipment to measure water or soil toxicity, I couldn't be sure. I told Kanyenda to drain the pond and to remove everything he had put in the compost bins (grass, ashes, goat manure, cotton seed). He would then have to refill the pond with fresh water, restock it, and wait to see what happened.

Restocking the pond brought up the odious subject of money again. Kanyenda needed three hundred more fish and I wasn't up to facing his sad eyes another time. I went to Kayemba, from whose pond the original stockers had come, and made a fairly baroque proposal. "Go to Kanyenda and tell him you'll loan him the new fish," I said. "I'll pay for them. Here's the money. But don't tell him. When he harvests his pond and pays back the money to you, thinking it really was a loan from you, you give the money to me. Okay?"

I had to explain the plan three times before Kayemba understood and agreed. The next day everything was set to go. Then something happened that we hadn't counted on. Kanyenda refused Kayemba's loan offer. "No," he said. "I can't restock yet. There's something I've got to do first."

The volcanic behavior I had expected at the funeral had finally arrived.

"What do you have to do?" I asked Kanyenda when I learned of his refusal.

"I'm being attacked by bad spirits, Michel."

"You're what?"

"It's true," he said. "My brother has died. My fish have died, and now I'm sure I'm being attacked by bad spirits."

"Bad spirits didn't kill your fish," I said, reminding him that further investigation had shown the cause of death to have been the DDT-contaminated cotton seed he had taken from the village warehouse and used as compost material. "It was the DDT."

"The spirits put the DDT on the cotton seed," he said.

Nice recovery, I thought.

"Oh, Kanyenda. Do you really believe that?"

"Yes."

135

"So what are you going to do?"
"I've got to see a sorcerer."

❦

Between early March and mid May, when the wet season peaked and life in the villages reached its nadir, the people of Kalambayi probably had every right to believe themselves persecuted by bad spirits. The rain and sickness and lean food supplies all smacked convincingly of punishment. Given everything else that had happened to him, Kanyenda had a particularly strong case. Hurrying, he went to talk things over with Kamangu Makasa.

Kamangu was one of the most powerful sorcerers in all the villages along the upper stretch of the Lubilashi. He lived alone on the outskirts of Ntita Konyukua in a squat, cone-shaped house completely covered with thatch and situated on sacred land. The house had the look of a cave and Kamangu the look of a cave dweller. He was humpbacked and ancient, at least eighty, and his face was covered with an amazing geography of wrinkles. The folds gathered under his eyes, across his forehead, along his neck—each presumably born of a different supernatural crisis. The interior of the house was packed with the accoutrements of his trade—animal skulls, skins, canes, masks, feathers, spears, drums, necklaces—all hanging from the ceiling and piled on the floor with the haphazard organization of a garage sale. Like the dozens of other sorcerers in Kalambayi, Kamangu was regularly approached by villagers seeking help with everything from curing illnesses to ensuring good corn harvests to bringing fertility to barren women.

Sitting inside his grass cave, twirling the ends of a white flowing beard, Kamangu listened to Kanyenda's story. It was a story dominated by the commonly held belief in Kalambayi that death was never accidental. Except in the case of the relatively old, death always had something to do with supernatural forces. If a villager died of tuberculosis, he had been punished, perhaps, for thievery. If hepatitis took his life, it was the curse of a disgruntled relative. If the leader of the chiefdom died in the midst of a civil war, the *ndondo* was the cause. Only people who had reached an age roughly in the mid fifties died of causes having to do with old age.

"That's why I've come," Kanyenda told Kamangu. He explained his case. His brother, Kabongo, had been about fifty-five when he died. (No one, not even Kabongo, had known the exact age.) Because this fell on the cusp of acceptable old age, there had been no suspicion of black magic at the time. But when the three hundred tilapia died, all of them spry babies, the pattern became clear to Kanyenda. His brother's death *was* the result of a curse, and the fish massacre was a continuation of that curse.

Kamangu agreed. "Make a *mukishi*," he said. "I recognize your problem. You've failed to protect your family with the proper charms and now your ancestors are punishing you for your irresponsibility. Make a *mukishi*."

Kanyenda made a *mukishi*. In the middle of his compound he built a waist-high stick platform. On top of the platform he placed a two-foot-tall, wood-carved bust with a face twisted and menacing like someone who had just stepped on a rusty nail. Real bogeyman stuff. This was a *mukishi*. It was a powerful fetish doll.

Since arriving in Kalambayi, I had seen all manner of charms and talismans born of the thick pall of superstition that hung over every village. There was Chief Ilunga's leather necklace meant to keep him strong and wise. There were the special sticks in Kamangu Mpemba's pond that made thieves go crazy. There were the beads hanging from Kazadi Manda's roof that kept away *tumiyambi*, the tiny invisible men who wandered through villages at night sprinkling measles on sleeping children. But never had I seen anything like this thing Kanyenda put together. Given the gravity of his situation, he made his fetish bigger and better than any other in Kalambayi.

When complete, the *mukishi* took on a life of its own, actively protecting the compound against misfortune. To keep its spirit alert and savage, Kanyenda began pelting its face every day with whatever sludge happened to be on hand—mud, rotten fruit, ashes, flour. The process was something of an art form. One day I watched him pour a bucket of bath water over the *mukishi's* head while telling it that its mother was a prostitute. The abuse girded the fetish for battle. It made it ready day and night to slay whatever spirits tried to attack the family.

When the fetish's face was sufficiently caked with refuse, Kanyenda walked to Kayemba's house and finally accepted the loan of fish, secure in the knowledge that he was insulated against further disaster. He had already emptied his pond of the suspect compost material and filled it with fresh water. He stocked the pond, spread a bundle of papaya leaves over the surface, and waited for the fish to start eating. Then he walked home.

It wasn't Kanyenda's *mukishi* that finally brought an end to the wet-season rains. The rains quit every year in mid May. Still, it was tempting to allow myself some notion of cause and effect. A week after the *mukishi* was built, the world changed. The rain stopped. The days became bright and clear, and people began harvesting their crops. And there was the wind, the wonderful dry-season wind—warm and soothing, bending the savanna grass like the caress of a lover's hand. When you stood still you could hear it hissing and blowing across Africa, sweeping away the anxiety and hunger of the past two months.

And after the *mukishi*, Kanyenda's fish lived. They were still happily munching papaya leaves when he returned the next day. The third day came, then the fourth, and still the fish exuded nothing but good health. It was over. Kanyenda was a fish farmer for good this time.

A few weeks later, when he had only barely begun to recover from his brother's funeral and the hard setbacks of the wet season, Kanyenda cornered me and dragged me to his house with the intention of making up for all the weeks he had been unable to feed me. I found him on a trail just outside his village, waving his arms and practically doing somersaults as I approached on my motorcycle.

"We have to go to my house," he said when I stopped.

"Why?" I asked. "I'm on my way to look at ponds in Bena Ngoyi."

"I have to show you something."

"What?"

"No, you have to come see yourself."

I shrugged and he got on the back of the motorcycle. When we got to his compound, he led me into one of his houses. Inside, his wife held a ten-hour-old baby boy sucking hungrily at her breast.

"This baby is you," Kanyenda said. "This is my son Michel."

Wordlessly, I stared at the child. Like most babies in Kalambayi, it had been born seriously underweight, its body frail and weak. Still, it was gorgeous—tiny fingers, tiny toes, eyes not yet open on a fussy face. I turned to Kanyenda. He was barefoot and dressed in the rags he wore to farm in. Gaping holes revealed his dark brown body, skinny as ever. "I've named my son after you," he said, his face tap-dancing with pride.

I didn't know what to say. I bubbled and smiled and kept mumbling something about how honored I was until Kanyenda helped me out of the house and into a chair outside. "You must stay with us today," he said. "We must share this happiness. I've named my son after you and that means you've entered my family today just as he has. From now on, my wives are your mothers and my children are your brothers and sisters. And I'm truly your father now, and you're my son. This is our custom."

Kanyenda went back into the house to discuss something with Misumba. I remained outside in the chair, feeling flattered to my boots. But the joy racing inside my veins quickly began to dissolve as I looked around the compound. It was as dreary, as barren, as disfigured by poverty as ever, and it sent crashing through me all the love-hate emotional cargo that accompanies new life in a poor community.

There was room for only a small bit of optimism. In the far corner of the compound, about fifteen feet from the *mukishi* stand, a white-feathered chicken pecked at the ground. Kanyenda had not lost everything during the funeral after all. A single chicken remained. At least it was something. But soon I noticed the chicken was moving in a curiously resolute way. It followed a series of corn kernels being tossed, one by one, from behind the door of one of Kanyenda's houses. Each kernel landed closer and closer to the door until finally the chicken entered and the door slammed shut and there was a squawk.

An hour later Kanyenda called me into the house. In the front room two bowls sat on a small table. One bowl contained *fufu* and the other a seasoned, steaming pile of boiled chicken parts. Every bit of the chicken was there—the wings, the drumsticks, the organs, everything. I immediately began protesting. "No Kanyenda. I can't eat this. I can't accept it. It's too much." But I knew what was going on. It was another custom. One just as incomprehensible as the funeral feasts. A whole chicken was always prepared for the person after whom a child was named. The fact that the rest of the family hadn't tasted fresh meat for weeks didn't matter. This chicken was all mine. Kanyenda had spared its life during the funeral for this purpose alone. "Sit and eat," he said. "I'm your father now and you can't disobey me."

He left the house, leaving me alone with my meal. I ate and felt honored and guilty and happy and angry. A new child had been born. He had my name. Kanyenda said he *was* me. I thought about that for a long time and it almost made me cry.

10

THERE WAS A MAGNIFICENT GRANDFATHER TREE IN THE VILLAGE of Ntita Konyukua whose branches spread out in all directions, casting a languorous pool of shade over one end of the village. The tree was so big that, in addition to all the huts built under its crown, children had found enough room beneath it to line off a miniature soccer field. One afternoon, the village men and I chased the children off the field and set up a circle of homemade chairs. There, near the midfield stripe, we held a ceremony to keep bad bush spirits from foiling the dry-season hunting campaign.

Mukalenga Kazadi, the dour, craggy-faced chief of Ntita Konyukua, began the meeting with a speech asking the ancestors for good luck during the six-week hunting season, which would begin the next day. A few more speeches followed and then all order broke down as the gathering settled into its true function: a chance for the men to drink bottles of *tshitshampa* and tell hunting stories. Shouts and peals of laughter floated up to the canopy of branches each time a bush pig or antelope was killed and re-killed in the soccer-field dirt. Eventually, there was much arguing. Men challenged each others' stories, and booze-soaked minds issued sentences that teetered on the brink of nonsense. At one point, I went to urinate in the bush and almost tripped over Kanyemesha, who had passed out on a trail. I came back and was assaulted by Kanyenda's whiskey breath. "Have you seen my brother?"

Because I had no hunting stories of my own to tell, I spent most of my time listening. I vicariously participated in the dramatic chases being described all around me, unaware that the stories were a preview of my own experience. In two weeks, I, too, would be a hunter with a story. I would be able to tell how, with a spear in my hand, a lump in my throat, and second thoughts pounding behind my forehead, I confronted an angry, charging bush pig.

─── ✦ ───

The dry season in Kalambayi was more than a time of year; it was also a state of mind. There were no rainy days, no cultivation to be done, and the June harvest meant there was plenty of food. The pace of life, never rushed to begin with, slowed down even more until a dreamy consciousness seemed to prevail. People were happy and relaxed. The only problem was the mornings, which were uncomfortably cool at this time of year. Each dawn, villagers built outdoor fires and huddled around them in clothes too tattered and thin for the chill. This discomfort was long forgotten by noon, however, when the warm dry-season wind murmured in the palm fronds and the annual swarms of white butterflies danced across the land like clouds of erratic snowflakes.

August and September marked the culmination of the dry season. These were the hunting months. After spending June and July leisurely engaged in domestic work—building houses, making tools, weaving baskets—the village men were by August ready to throw their spears. They set fire to the bush, destroying the cover of animals lurking there and making kills easier. The men of Ntita Konyukua had a reputation for being the most skilled hunters in all of Kalambayi. One Saturday in early September, I joined them on one of their forays.

When I arrived in the village at 10:00 a.m., my first goal was to find a spear. I went to Kanyenda's house, but his wife said he was feeding his fish. He had left instructions for me to meet him at his pond, which was in the valley where that day's hunt was planned. I walked next door to Mutombo Mukendi's house, but he was still in Mbuji Mayi prospecting for diamonds, a common dry-season employment for village men. I decided to try Kazadi Manda.

Moving along the trail to Kazadi's house, I was struck by the sense of excitement that surged and swirled through the village. Outside their huts, men were preparing for the hunt. They discussed strategy, sharpened their spears, cleaned their muzzle-loading muskets, and called their dogs. Other men from the nearby villages of Bena Ngoyi and Konyukua Mutombo were, like me, arriving for the hunt on trails at either end of the village. To the west, above the trees, I could see faint wisps of smoke rising into the sky. The bush was already beginning to burn. I had to hurry.

I reached Kazadi's house and found him ill with a mild case of malaria. He would not be hunting, he said, and I was welcome to take his spear. Typical of the style in Kalambayi, Kazadi's spear consisted of a two-foot-long metal bar lashed to the end of a carved-wood shaft. The spear tip was sharpened into a deadly point. Because my previous experience with spears was limited to gigging toads along pond banks, Kazadi offered me brief instruction in the science of spear-throwing. I practiced on a ripe papaya lying on the ground and missed five times from ten paces. Prodded by the snickers of children watching near the house, I resolved to skewer the fruit at least once before leaving. After ten more throws, I hit the papaya.

"Okay," I told Kazadi. "I think I'm ready."

Spear in hand, I walked farther down the village trail to Kayemba's house. I found Kayemba and his neighbor, Katembua Ndaya, just as they were about to leave for the bush. Both men were armed—Kayemba with a spear, Katembua with a musket and his father's schizophrenic, wire-haired cur named Khadafy. The dog's moniker, gleaned from shortwave radio reports reaching the villages, was well earned. Although endowed with the intelligence of a bowl of *fufu*, Khadafy was a courageous hunting dog. He proved this by dutifully hurling himself at the noisy, single-cylinder antelope I rode past his house several times a week.

I joined Kayemba and Katembua, and we took off for the hunt. As we walked through the last stretch of village houses, I immediately noticed a pronounced change in the way villagers greeted me. It wasn't the sight of a spear per se that caused the change. Most Kalambayan men carried spears all the time, ready to chase bush animals whenever the chance arose. What was suddenly upsetting to the people I passed on the trail was the fact that, for the first time in their village, a spear was in *my* hands; the untutored foreigner was carrying a weapon and he looked as if he meant to use it. People who normally would have greeted me warmly, glanced at the spear, then at me, and then stepped quickly off the trail as if I were slinging around a loaded shotgun with the safety off. Their anxiety was compounded by the fact that I insisted on holding the spear improperly. My immediate tendency was to grip it around the middle and carry it parallel to the ground like a fishing rod.

"No, no, no," Kayemba admonished me. "This way." He turned the spear perpendicular to the ground. "Hold it upright so you don't stab anyone as you walk."

"Oh, yes, of course," I said.

Kayemba's warning and the apprehension of people along the trail awakened me to the seriousness of what I was doing. A spear is a spear, I told myself. It's sharp and it can kill people as easily as it kills animals. This was my first time hunting in Kalambayi and I had to be careful. We weren't on our way to play games.

We passed the final village hut and entered the bush. The savanna grass immediately surrounded us, rising up on both sides of the narrow path in ten-foot-tall walls, dense and brittle and dry. After a few minutes, we came to a fork in the trail where we met four men from Bena Ngoyi coming toward us from the right branch. They carried spears and had with them a dog. The men looked nervous. "Hold your spear the right way, Michel," one said in a scolding voice. I looked around. Sure enough, everyone's spear was in the correct, upright position but mine, which was horizontal. "Yes, yes. Okay. I'm sorry," I said. The men laughed, uneasily.

We took the left branch of the fork and followed the trail along a ridge that formed the southern edge of the horseshoe-shaped valley we were about to hunt. At different points along the trail, we passed men carrying straw torches. The men used their feet to mat down a three- to four-foot-wide area of grass all along the left side of the trail. Then they set the grass ablaze with their torches, careful to keep the fire from spreading to the right side of the trail and so burning out of control, ruining hunting in other valleys.

Kayemba and I left Katembua and continued along the trail for another ten minutes until we came to a point where the fire had already burned about two hundred feet down the hill. From this clearing it was possible to view the entire valley and so comprehend the hunting technique. At more-or-less evenly spaced points along the periphery of this one-mile-wide, two-mile-long section of the valley, columns of smoke boiled up from the bush. Men had spread out along the ridgetops to form a giant oval around the hunting area, and now they were simultaneously burning the grass with their torches. Beneath the smoke, I could see orange flames flickering and spreading out in sinuous lines that eventually would join together to form a ring of fire around the valley. The ring would burn and constrict until it reached the valley floor, where a narrow forest grew nourished by a hidden stream. The forest, which began at the head of the valley and ran unbroken along the valley floor, was about 150 feet wide. It was thick with trees and green undergrowth that would not burn.

The logic was simple. The ring of fire would trap whatever bush animals happened to be in the valley at the time of the burning, forcing them to take refuge in the forest. As the fire burned out, a second ring—a ring of men—would tighten around the forest. It was eleven o'clock now and the hunting party had grown to about one hundred men, all of whom, like Kayemba and I, had taken up positions along the valley rim. Soon we would work our way down the slopes, careful not to let any animals escape through possible gaps in the fire. When the fire finished burning, the hunt would be a matter of flushing the animals out of the forest with dogs and killing them with spears or guns. Kills might include any number of species, including wild pigs, impalas, waterbucks, bushbucks, duikers, porcupines, and various species of bush rats.

By noon, the fire had burned most of the valley grass. Kayemba and I left the ridgetop and walked diagonally across the hillside toward Kanyenda Mushia's pond, which was on the valley floor next to the strip of forest. Moving down into the torched valley was like walking into another room. The land had been transformed. Where thirty minutes before grass had covered the ground with impossible density, there was now a moonscape. The valley was naked and unprotected, its surface covered by a layer of gray-black ashes that rose up in small, smoky clouds under our feet.

Kanyenda and Kanyemesha were sitting by the pond when we arrived. They had been feeding their fish when the fire started and had watched the wall of flames move toward them and pass without burning the dike's green, canal-fed grass. I walked around the pond and was about to comment on how well the fish were growing when Kanyenda turned to Kayemba and said, "Hasn't anyone shown Michel how to carry a spear yet?" Again I was blissfully walking around with my spear at an irresponsible angle. I apologized. Too many fishing trips in my past.

We heard the hollow whistling of a *kashiba*, a small wooden flute the hunters used to send messages. Kanyenda listened to the series of changing, high-pitched notes. He translated for me: "Chief Kazadi says the fire has finished burning, and he wants everyone to move to the head of the valley."

By now, the ring of hunters had descended to the valley floor and had closed in on both sides of the forest. Any animals that had been in the valley that morning were now hiding in the forest, where they would stay until forced out. The hunting party began moving to the start of the valley to concentrate its forces.

After a thirty-minute walk along the edge of the valley-bottom forest, Kanyenda, Kanyemesha, Kayemba, and I joined about fifty other hunters at the head of the valley. On the other side of the forest's tangle of trees and vines, an equally large group of hunters was gathering out of view. Chief Kazadi used his *kashiba* to tell both sides to prepare for the hunt. The chief had painted tiny white teardrops on the outside corners of his eyes, a sign of sorrow and respect for the village ancestors.

Among the hunters were four men whose job it was to enter the forest with the party's cadre of eleven dogs. These dog handlers used machetes to hack their way through the forest undergrowth. They walked behind the dogs, directing them through the forest and yelling instructions, ready to alert the hunting party when the dogs' behavior indicated an animal was near. Meanwhile, we on the outside spread out in two lines, one on each side of the forest, about fifteen feet from the trees. We stood five feet apart, armed with spears and guns, prepared to kill whatever animals the dogs chased out. The entire operation—dog handlers in the forest, armed hunters on the outside—moved slowly down the valley, section by section, guided by the flute sounds of a chief who cried symbolic tears.

I took my place in line next to Kanyenda on the south side of the forest. With our spears at our sides, we stared at the leafy green wall and listened as the dogs and their handlers moved about, their actions hidden from us. We heard water splashing and leaves slapping and sticks snapping as the dogs rooted intently through the undergrowth.

After about ten minutes of searching through the first stretch of forest, the dogs turned up nothing, and the two lines of hunters shifted two hundred feet down the valley. The dogs entered a new section of forest. Again, no animal was found. Again, we moved two hundred feet down the valley.

Soon, the hunt's initial excitement began to subside some and we settled into the long, dreary slog that is the near-universal hallmark of hunting. As the dogs searched, we stood leaning against our spears, relaxing and telling jokes like bored sentries trying to pass an uneventful night.

Then a single word rocketed from the forest:

"*Nyama!*"

We stopped talking. Everyone listened.

"*Nyama! Nyama!*"

It was the dog handlers. They were yelling from inside the forest. Our line of hunters snapped to attention. Men sitting down scrambled to their feet. Everyone assumed his place, raising his weapon.

"*Nyama! Nyama! Nyama!*"

The word was Tshiluba for "animal." The dogs had found something. The commotion inside the forest rose sharply. "*Kuata,*" the handlers yelled, instructing the dogs to give chase. "*Kuata nyama!*"

The moment of action had come. A kill was near. I manned my spot in line and looked to my left and right at the long string of hunters on either side of me. The party had turned deadly serious. The men with spears drew them back, their stances Zeus-like, their arms ready to hurl lightning bolts. I did my best to effect the same posture. About every tenth man held a musket, cocked and pointed at the forest.

"*Nyama! Nyama!*"

The handlers were screaming louder now. The animal, whatever it was, was moving around and making a lot of noise.

Soon the dogs would force it out of the forest and into the waiting phalanx of armed men. For a man to get a kill in this form of hunting is purely a matter of chance. He has to be standing, spear or gun ready, at the exact point where the animal chooses to make its exit.

The dogs continued their fierce barking. Finally, the animal burst out of the trees . . .

. . . but on the other side of the forest, away from my party of men. Through the trees, we heard muffled sounds. Men were shouting. A gun went off. As if listening to an important but poorly tuned-in radio broadcast, we strained to hear the action: "I got it. I got it," someone yelled on the other side. "A pig," someone else yelled. A bush pig had run out of the trees and Mukenga Muembo had killed it with his gun. We heard rounds of congratulations being made. We heard laughter and excited talking.

On our side we were pleased that an animal had been killed, but disappointment ran through the line. The pig had chosen the other side of the forest. Bad luck for us. The hunt moved on.

Although it had been some distance away, the gun blast that killed the pig had startled me. As I moved down the valley, I now felt my already healthy fear of guns grow rapidly. Six men on our side of the forest had muskets and I didn't want to be anywhere near them. On a group hunt such as this, with armed men standing close together and wild animals bolting out of the forest, it seemed quite possible that, in the heat and confusion of battle, a gun carrier could turn and accidentally blow a hole in the man next to him. What made this thought particularly mortifying was the fact that the locally made, Civil War–quality muskets were loaded not with bullets or shotgun shells, but with a mixture of rocks, nails, broken glass, and homemade lead balls—the ammunition of resourceful villagers. Now, every time I saw a man with a musket, I felt a rumbling fear. It was a fear familiar to me while I lived in Kalambayi. The fear said: If you get hurt—seriously hurt—in this isolated region, your chances of survival begin to take on the nature of a crapshoot.

It was now around three o'clock. We had been hunting for more than two hours and the dogs had turned up nothing since the first pig. One of Chief Kazadi's flute messages fluttered down our line. We shifted again. The haze of smoke from the morning fire had dissipated from the sky, allowing the equatorial sun to pelt down in full force. Rivulets of sweat rolled down my temples. My shoes and pants were growing black from the ashes along the ground.

Standing in our line, five feet between each hunter, we listened as the dog handlers moved through another stretch of forest. We seemed to be moving down the valley with glacial speed. Eventually, the sound of the dogs in the forest became a background noise, and, hot and dirty, I grew aware of how profoundly boring all of this was becoming. The sunshine patriot in me began entertaining notions of heading home. The fish weren't biting.

Apparently reading my thoughts, Kanyenda suggested we cross through the forest and try our luck with the hunters on the other side. He said there was a trail a short distance down the valley, beyond our line of hunters. I led the way, with Kanyenda, Kayemba, and Kanyemesha some distance behind me.

As I passed the last man in the line of hunters, I stopped abruptly. There it was. It came out of the forest, unannounced, just down the valley. It bounded silently, weightlessly, seventy-five feet in front of me—an impala. Taken completely by surprise, I could only watch as it moved. My eyes photographed the animal: dark copper skin, black stripes across the hind, delicately spiraling horns.

In an instant, the impala was past me and streaking up the barren valley slope, escaping. Several men in the line behind me had seen the animal, too. One threw his spear, belatedly, and yelled something I don't remember. Two other men ran after the impala with their spears cocked. But in no time the animal was up the hill, over the ridge, gone. Hopelessly out of range, the men threw their spears anyway, as if spitting in anger. Just then, a dog came out of the forest, sprinting after the animal's scent. The hunters called the dog back and showered it with insults. More bad luck. The impala had barely missed our line. The dogs had chased it out too quickly. There had been no warning.

"I was watching it," I told Kanyenda and the others when they ran up and asked me why I hadn't thrown my spear. In truth, the impala had been just out of spear range. Still, I should have tried. Idly standing by and watching as an animal passes before you is a form of madness, the men said. I apologized. "It's just that I've never seen an animal like that before," I told them. They were unimpressed, and suggested I shape up. I promised I would. Seeing the impala had renewed my flagging spirit and I was ready to press on.

Kanyenda, Kanyemesha, Kayemba, and I stuck to our decision to traverse the forest. A few hundred feet down the valley, ahead of the hunting party, we found a path that penetrated the wall of trees and led into the forest's sanctuary of greenery. Inside, the expansive crowns of palm, mimosa, and mahogany trees welcomed us with soothing shade. Here and there, bars of sunlight passed through gaps in the canopy, traveling down to scatter yellow-white patches of light across the understory of shorter trees, bushes, and vines. Heart-shaped taro leaves grew copiously on both sides of the footpath, their lush green color a striking contrast to the scorched valley outside.

At the center of the forest we came to a small stream that moved slowly, almost imperceptibly, past taro-covered banks. We stopped and splashed water on our faces and over our heads. After a brief rest, we crossed the stream and followed the forest path until the trees ended and we were tossed back out into the harsh, sprawling landscape of burnt savanna. In the sudden glare we had to squint our eyes.

We saw the other hunting party just up the valley and headed that way. Barely ten minutes after we reached the men and took up places near the center of the line, the word came out:

"*Nyama!*"

The dogs had found another animal. The handlers were yelling.

"*Nyama! Nyama!*"

The line of hunters made ready. Spears went up. Guns were aimed. Everyone listened. There seemed to be considerably less thrashing and rustling in the forest this time. A few seconds later we learned why: The animal wasn't a pig. It was a small porcupine. And, to our chagrin, it emerged on the other side of the forest, the side we had just left. Kanyenda and I looked at each other and rolled our eyes. The porcupine was quickly speared. Again, we listened to distant congratulations.

Up the hill, behind the line of hunters we had just joined, I saw a strange sight. The 150-pound pig Mukenga Muembo had shot earlier on this side of the forest was sitting five feet off the ground, its dun-colored, bristle-haired body wedged between the forked branches of a scrub tree. Every time the hunt shifted down the valley, Mukenga carried the pig and placed it in a tree like this, out of the reach of dogs who occasionally strayed out of the forest.

Presently, two dogs stood below the pig. With their hind legs on the ground and their front paws against the trunk, they lapped furiously at blood dripping from wounds on the animal's neck. The process was something like trying to catch raindrops on one's tongue. Most of the blood landed on the dogs' faces. After a while, the dogs returned to the ground and vigorously licked each others' blood-flecked faces. This ended when a nearby hunter kicked one of the dogs in the ribs and ordered the pair back into the forest.

The hunting party had shifted down the valley twice since the kill of the porcupine. I manned my spot in line and noted that it was getting better as the afternoon wore on. And I was getting restless again. Nothing was happening. I looked down at my spear. It looked back. "Who are you trying to kid?" it seemed to say. Weariness filled my body as I listened to the dogs. They were still searching, sniffing, rummaging through the forest. Where did they get their energy? I wondered.

Now, suddenly, the dogs were barking. They were barking frantically. Inside the trees something big was going on. The handlers' shouts rang out.

"*Nyama! Nyama!*"

Our line went on alert.

"*Nyama! Nyama!*"

We raised our spears.

"*Nyama! Nyama!*"

Musket hammers went back.

"There's something here," a handler yelled out. "There's something here."

We hardly needed to be told. The sound of activity inside the forest was loud, much louder than before the first two kills. And this time it was clear that the animal was on *our* side. Through the trees, a noise like someone running through autumn leaves gushed out. The noise grew louder and louder. And louder, still. It grew so loud that I realized something: It couldn't possibly be coming from a single pig or antelope or porcupine. Either there were several animals running around in this stretch of forest or something else was making the sound. I felt a stab of fear. The rustling and thrashing went on. Apprehension triggered my imagination. Could it be an elephant?

"No, no, no," my common sense countered. "Calm down." The idea of elephants hiding in the forest was outrageous. I had been assured that the last of these animals had been driven out of Kalambayi several years earlier. Very well then, I thought. It wasn't an elephant. But what was it? What was making all the noise? Standing so close to the forest, thinking these thoughts,

I began to feel quite vulnerable. I sensed somehow that a giant fist was approaching from behind that leafy curtain, and I was leaning into it. The commotion in the forest continued. The fist was getting closer.

On reflex, I began to take backward steps. Elephants or no elephants, I didn't want to get trampled when the animals came charging out. Twenty feet up the slope, I stopped. To my left and right, I noticed other men doing the same. I stood stock-still, spear raised, and listened to the sound of leaves slapping, of branches shattering, of something coming, coming, coming toward our line. Blood pounded through my body.

Unlike me, Kanyenda didn't retreat an inch from his position. He stood to my right, thirty feet down the hill, just a few feet from the forest wall. He held his spear—his lightning bolt—and waited. Suddenly, in addition to the forest sounds, there was movement. I saw a small tree shake. I saw leaves move.

Then the pig appeared. It burst out of the forest in a full sprint to Kanyenda's left. It almost ran into him. In a quick, sidearm motion, Kanyenda threw his spear into the pig's shoulder, driving the tip several inches deep where it held. But the pig didn't fall. It didn't stumble. It let go a high-pitched, panicked squeal, and, nostrils flaring, legs churning, spear hanging out of its side, charged on. It was coming straight at me. It was a very large pig.

To my left, fifteen feet away, Katembua Muamba threw his spear into the pig's other side. It held too. But again the pig didn't slow down. With spears protruding from both sides of its body, it kept running up the hill, closer and closer, grunting and squealing—toward me. There was no one behind me. I was the last obstacle between the pig and escape.

I had never really expected this to happen. I had never expected the moment to come when all eyes in the hunting party turned to *my* arm and to *my* spear—everyone counting on me, a randomly selected link in the chain, to act. I had joined the hunt in the spirit of a spectator. Using my spear, I suddenly realized, had never really been my goal.

But then, why not me? Why not me the one who kills the pig? I had earned the chance as much as anyone. I had endured the heat and the boredom, the smoke in my eyes and the ashes on my clothes. Through all the walking and stopping I had remained loyal, and now a wild pig approached.

But as the pig moved closer and closer, right in front of me, I felt the ache of inexperience break out all over my body. I had a spear in my hand, but I wasn't a hunter like the men around me. I was an imposter. I had faked my way into a difficult situation and now the next move wasn't clear to me. Just how was I going to bring this animal to the ground? Surely the pig, charging up the hill, read my hesitation. Surely it saw by the way I held my spear that I was a confused, papaya-class amateur. It needn't charge with such vehemence. It needn't act so convincingly like it was ready to knock me down and plant a hoof in my forehead.

Before the pig could barrel into my knees, I stepped out of the way, to the right. In the same motion, I turned and threw my spear.

I missed. I was standing so close to the pig I could have almost touched it. Still, I missed. The spear flew low, under the animal, and skidded into ashes on the ground. The pig raced by. I turned and watched it run up the denuded slope, the spears hanging from both sides of its body bouncing with every stride. As I watched, I saw about twenty more spears sail into my frame of vision, thrown by hunters on both sides of me. The spears landed all around the animal, but none connected. Then Kanyemesha entered the frame. Machete drawn, he sprinted up the hill after the wounded animal. Four other men ran behind him.

"My spear was first!" Kanyenda yelled. "My spear was first!" He had run to my side and was jumping up and down in excitement. If the pig were captured Kanyenda would get credit for the kill and the largest share of the meat.

For my part, all I could think about was my utter incompetence. "I can't believe I missed," I muttered to Kanyenda. "It was right there."

Just then, from inside the forest: "*Nyama! Nyama! Nyama!*"

The dog handlers were yelling again.

Another animal.

Kanyenda and I turned around just in time to see a second pig blast out of the forest at the same spot as the first one. It was racing straight toward us. The hunting party wasn't ready for this second charge. Most of the men standing nearby had thrown their spears at the first pig.

As soon as we saw the second charge, Kanyenda and I bent over. With our eyes riveted to the oncoming pig, we began fumbling frantically along the ground for my spear. Before either of us could find it and wrestle it from the other, the earth shook. There was an explosion. It fractured my ears. A cloud of gray-white smoke filled the air, carrying with it the heavy smell of sulfur. At the same moment, Kanyenda and I saw the charging pig drop to the ground twenty feet in front of us, its face having collided with a spray of rocks and glass and nails right before our eyes. I immediately turned and saw Katemba Pascal standing next to me, his just-fired musket still pointed at the dead pig. The gun had exploded three feet from my head. Panic galloped through my body.

"*Nyama! Nyama! Nyama!*"

When the third pig came out of the forest, there was calamity in our ranks. We were unarmed. The nearest gun had been fired, all ammunition spent. I still hadn't found my spear and had given up trying. I just watched the pig. It was coming toward me, running and snorting, wildly determined to escape. Before it reached me, two hunters appeared from nowhere. They jumped between me and the animal. Without spears, completely unarmed, the men began yelling and flailing their arms, trying to scare the pig back into the forest. The Maginot Line was breaking up.

"Nyama! Nyama! Nyama!"

A fourth pig barreled out of the trees. All semblance of organization dissolved. The enemy had reached the trenches and was jumping in. The fighting was grisly, *mano a mano*. Kill the bastards any way you can. Throw them back. Do something. Do anything. Pigs ran everywhere. We had been tricked, outmaneuvered. Our ammunition was gone. Cries went out for reinforcements. Still-armed men from the outer sections of the line rushed toward the besieged center. But in the congestion of bodies, they couldn't take aim with their spears and guns. And the dogs! The dogs were spilling out of the forest now, barking and biting, compounding the confusion.

In the middle of this maelstrom of men and pigs and dogs and weapons, I stood motionless, paralyzed by a fear of catching a spear or musketshot in some critical region of my body. I remember watching a blur of figures move around me. I heard men shouting, pigs squealing, dogs snarling. Machetes flashed. Burnt gunpowder seared my nose, and my ears were still ringing from the last blast. On all sides, men were trying to take aim at pigs running here and there. As they did, my ribs began to feel ridiculously fragile, like sticks ready to splinter and yield, exposing parts of me that weren't replaceable. Please let it end soon, I thought. No more pigs. Let there be no more pigs.

The men who had jumped in front of the third pig had forced it to turn and run down the line of hunters to the right. It dodged people and weapons for a short distance before heading the opposite way, down the left side of the line, where it was finally speared. The fourth pig had run out, seen the bedlam, and circled back into the forest. Seconds later, it emerged again, trailed this time by the pack of frenzied dogs. Again it managed to circle back into the forest. When it emerged a third time, it was knocked down, speared, macheted, killed.

Then it was over. The dog handlers stopped hammering us with their chant of "*nyama*." The forest had nothing left to throw at us. Three animals lay dead, and another was wounded and in flight. Spears littered the ground. The episode had lasted no more than two minutes. At first, the nerve synapses crackling in my body refused to believe the attack had ended. I waited for another animal to rush toward us, another projectile to sail past my ear, another gun blast to rock my brain. But it really was over. And, to my utter amazement, not a single man or dog had been injured.

In the aftermath, the hunters and I walked around, stunned, searching for our spears, inspecting the kills, looking at one another wide-eyed as if saying, "Did you *see* that?" The men from the hunting party on the other side of the forest came over and each man on our side began giving his version of what happened. Even these seasoned, life-long hunters seemed to think it had been an exceptionally woolly affair. Kanyenda, always the animated raconteur, drew an especially large crowd of listeners. Before the day was over, he would repeat the blow-by-blow yarn a dozen times, calling me over during each presentation to recount my supporting role. "Michel, tell them how that pig almost ate your knees, and how you didn't run away like we all expected you to."

While we stood calming ourselves and congratulating one another, Kanyemesha appeared in the distance along the ridge. He moved with halting steps down the valley slope toward us, laboring under the weight of his brother's dead pig. The animal had gone a quarter mile beyond the ridge before tiring. Kanyemesha carried it on his shoulders, the belly against the back of his neck and the legs hanging across his chest. The pig's thick wiry bristles were covered with blood in several places. As I watched Kanyemesha approach, I began to wonder how many times this valley had played host to such a scene. Barefoot, pig on his shoulders, body covered with sweat, machete tucked under his crude hunting belt, Kanyemesha looked positively ancient. When he reached the valley floor, he placed the pig in a scrub tree. Dogs gathered below to catch falling drops of blood on their tongues.

The rest of the hunt was somewhat anticlimactic. We continued down the valley, killing another pig and an antelope (my spear wasn't involved). But these were trifles compared with the mad heroism of slaying four pigs at the same time. We basked in the afterglow of that victory for the rest of the day and nothing else was quite as important.

At about five o'clock, Chief Kazadi played his flute one last time, sending the message that the hunt was over. We were tired. It was time to go home. All the large kills—six pigs and an antelope—were placed side by side on the ground and butchered with machetes. The division was a complex process. From his pig, Kanyenda got a front leg, a back leg, the ribs, the back, and the organs. The rest was divided among Katembua Muamba (second to spear the pig), the dog handlers, Chief Kazadi, and a handful of elders. Had my spear connected I would have gotten half the pig's head, Kanyenda informed me. I was almost glad I missed.

Butchering over, we skewered large pieces of meat with our spears and carried the prizes over our shoulders the way hobos carry their bundles. We left the valley together, men and dogs, and headed back to the village where word of our success had already arrived. In Kalambayi, any hunt that produced two or three large kills was considered a success. Five kills was rare. Thus, it was an atmosphere of complete jubilation that greeted us as we entered the village of Ntita Konyukua, seven kills to our credit. Women and children stood outside huts and along the main path, yodeling and clapping as we walked by. Several women had painted their faces white and were dancing in celebration. Like victors home from war, we swaggered past the welcoming crowd, soaking up praise, fresh meat hanging from our spears.

Kanyenda and I stopped at Kazadi Manda's house to return his spear. I began telling Kazadi about how great the hunt was and how I had thrown my spear. But he quickly raised his hand, signaling me to stop.

"I already know all this," he said rather mysteriously. "I knew the hunt would be successful this morning before it began."

"How did you know?" I asked.

"I had a dream last night," he said. "I dreamed I was in Kinshasa, riding around in the back of a taxi, and the taxi had no radio."

He stopped.

"So?" I said.

"The taxi had no radio," he said. "Don't you see? It was a sign that the hunt would be successful."

"Hmmm, yes," I said. "I think I see now."

I let the subject drop. I didn't tell Kazadi I thought his vision was a bit flimsy, nor did I ask how it was that a man who had never been to Kinshasa nor stepped inside a taxi could have had such a dream. As it turned out, however, Kazadi's wasn't the only dream we heard about when we returned from the hunt. The village was full of people claiming to have had prophetic visions of success the night before. Some of the dreams were quite complex and all involved odd symbols. It was a little spooky.

The first thing Kanyenda did when we reached his compound was walk over to the *mukishi* stand, gather a handful of dirt, and throw it square in the fetish's face. It was his way of rewarding the thing for an obviously effective day of work. Meanwhile, I stretched out in a chair, an act my body had been calling for since early afternoon. I watched Kanyenda move from the *mukishi* stand to the mound of pig meat we had carried home. He and Kanyemesha cut the meat into smaller pieces and then began giving it away. Members of their extended family poured into the compound, and just like at a fish harvest no one walked away empty-handed. The scene was being repeated throughout the village. By late evening, when all seven kills had been divided and redivided, almost everyone in the village would have tasted the rare and relished flavor of fresh bush meat.

When the brothers finished distributing the meat, they settled into chairs. It was time for a fête. I bought two bottles of *tshitshampa*, and we sat around—me, Kanyenda, Kanyemesha, Kayemba, and various friends and neighbors—in Kanyenda's compound. We drank and talked about the day's experience. Soon, the sun set and darkness settled on the village. As we talked, we smelled the aroma of pig meat cooking in palm oil. We heard the evening clatter of insects drifting down from nearby trees. Above, a million stars blinked on in an ink-blue sky. We ate ferociously when Kanyenda's wives brought out the food. After the meal, a few men smoked tobacco from calabash pipes. The tobacco burned vigorously in the darkness, casting an orange Halloween glow on the men's faces.

Moved by a feeling of thanksgiving, I, too, made a pilgrimage to the *mukishi* before the night was over. I held a glass of *tshitshampa* over the fetish's head and inventoried my blessings. I was thankful for the success of the hunt. Thankful that I had not been injured. Thankful for the men around me— my friends, these peasant farmers, these bush hunters. The pell-mell excitement and glory of the day's expedition had tightened the ties binding our lives. Now, our stomachs full and our bodies reclined in sweet fatigue, we talked and laughed in the calm night air. It was a rare triumph, a moment I wanted to lift with both arms and carry away, pure and glistening, as a counterbalance to the other, less happy times. I poured the *tshitshampa* over the *mukishi*'s head and watched as the liquid streamed down its face, down its neck, finally dripping to the ground.

11

YET EVEN AS MY VILLAGE FRIENDSHIPS IMPROVED, MADE deeper by the hunt and other experiences, the lonely times in Kalambayi never left me. There were a lot of them, times when I felt utterly by myself and close to bursting from the pressure of uncommunicated feelings.

The big disaster was a good example. It happened on a day when I was out of touch with the world, spending the night in a downriver village without my shortwave radio. I got home the next afternoon, turned on the radio, and caught the upper-class tone of a BBC reporter in mid-report. "Political fallout from the *Challenger* disaster. . . ."

I stood up and sat back down and stood up again. I stared at the radio, mouth agape, until the report ended. Then I ran to my door and looked out, searching for someone, anyone, with whom to share the news. All I saw, though, were women loaded down with manioc like burros and dirty children eating sugarcane outside boxlike houses. My neighbor Mbuyi sat on a woven mat, gazing unintelligently into the air, his eyes white with cataracts. I went back to my chair and nearly exploded like the spacecraft, streaking and whistling. With whom could I discuss the space shuttle, much less more subtle matters like the frustrations, longings, and loneliness that called on me in this remote place?

Even with Mbaya, with whom I could discuss many of my thoughts, there were limits.

"What village are you from in *Amerika?*" he asked me one day.

I got out the small world map I had brought from home and pointed to my village—Atlanta. He seemed unimpressed.

"Don't you see how far away it is?" I asked. "If it were all land it would take a man six hundred days to walk there."

Still, he showed little reaction. Then it occurred to me why. "Where's Zaire on this map?" I asked him. He stared at the paper with a look of pained incomprehension.

"Where's Africa?" I said. Nothing. "Okay, just show me an ocean." He couldn't. To him and the rest of the people of Kalambayi, I had emerged from a mysterious mist beyond the known universe and there was little point discussing matters there.

This situation made the arrival of American visitors to Kalambayi occasions for serious celebration. Volunteers from different parts of the region visited from time to time, bringing with them a cultural likeness that supplied therapy and release. I also enjoyed visits from my Zairian boss, Lukusa Mandako. He was the regional *coordinateur* of the fish project. After tossing me from his Land Rover that first day, he returned every few months to check on the progress of the project. Owing to his university education and loquaciousness, conversations with Lukusa strayed easily from village affairs and into the realms of world events, development theory, and sports.

The fish farmers liked Lukusa, too, although for different reasons. As a Muluba raised in a poor village like them, he connected with the men at a level I couldn't reach. His counsel was delivered in perfectly accented Tshiluba, reinforcing what I told the farmers every day: stock the ponds properly, feed the fish faithfully, and harvest on time.

Lukusa's closing speeches at fish farmers meetings were particularly effective. "Zaire is a poor country," he would say, starting out slow like a skilled gospel preacher before moving on to real acrobatics. "We're a poor country but we're developing. Don't despair. Be proud that you're a farmer. Be proud that you live in a village and that you raise fish. With you, the small farmer, we'll build a new and better Zaire. With you we'll build a new and better tomorrow. Be proud! Be proud!"

The speeches always brought the farmers to their feet, clapping their hands, sure that with enough dedication they could feed the whole world. By the time he climbed into his Land Rover to leave, Lukusa had accomplished his mission. He had everyone feeling good about the project and pumped to the hairline with hope. Everyone but me, that is. As hard as I tried, I couldn't contemplate the country's future with as much optimism as the other men. When I looked ahead I saw an ominous problem ready to sabotage everything. It was a problem that disturbed me as much as any other in Kalambayi. The problem was children. The chiefdom was drowning in them. But like the explosion of a space vehicle on its way to orbit the Earth, this was something I couldn't possibly get the fish farmers to understand.

〜

I was riding home from work one afternoon in a light rain when, not far from my house, it started coming down in torrents. I pulled up to Mbaya's hut and took cover. Under the cave, he greeted me with unsmiling seriousness.

"*Coordinateur* Lukusa is dead," he announced.

"What?" I said, disbelieving, thinking it was a bad joke. "Lukusa? Who told you that?"

"It came over the 4:00 p.m. radio report from Mbuji Mayi. He's dead. He died this morning."

It wasn't a joke. The head of the fish project had passed on. It happened in Kabinda while Lukusa was visiting fish farmers at the post of Emily Arnaiz, a volunteer to the east in Kabinda. I saw Emily two months later in Mbuji Mayi and she told me the story. Lukusa had arrived complaining of a sore throat and the flu, but had insisted on visiting farmers anyway. After two days his throat got worse and he had trouble swallowing. Then his jaw locked up.

"It was crazy," Emily said. "At the end of the day he stood up to give his rah-rah speech—you know the way he does—but his jaw was clamped shut and he sounded really weird, like a ventriloquist."

That night, Emily and another volunteer, Paul Baglione, took Lukusa to a nearby Catholic mission hospital. They put him on a bed under a bare lightbulb, and he later went into convulsions so severe that he fell off the bed and landed on the concrete floor with a thud. A doctor ordered him kept on the floor, where he died, before dawn, of tetanus.

Emily and Paul reported the death to the head of the local government later that day. It was then that they began to get an idea of what had happened. The government official examined Lukusa's identity card and gasped when he reached the section reserved for the names of closest relatives. "*Pas d'enfants*," he said, pointing to the card. "There are no children here. Lukusa didn't have any children. *Pas d'enfants*."

It was true. At the age of thirty-six, after going through three wives, Lukusa Mandako had not sired a single child. Despite his rise out of poverty and successful government career, this made him a near-absolute failure by all standards in Zairian society. It later came out that Lukusa had tried everything to cure his sterility—various medicines, diets, visits to Western doctors, visits to village healers. Nothing had worked. Two weeks before his trip to Kabinda he had bought a liquid concoction from a village healer, and his wife had given him multiple injections with a syringe. But the needle, it turned out, was dirty, and Lukusa died because of it. He died without children. *Pas d'enfants*.

When the Kalambayi fish farmers learned of Lukusa's sterility, their respect for him plummeted with dismaying speed. They hadn't known that their chief, their mentor, with all his inspiring words and bravado, was childless. Informed, they began spreading talk of shame and dishonor through the project. How upsetting, they said, to discover only at the end what kind of person he was. I was shocked by their reaction. It smacked of betrayal. I endeavored to come to Lukusa's defense.

"It doesn't make him a bad man just because he didn't have any children," I told Kayemba, who was particularly adamant about Lukusa's shortcoming. "Look around. Aren't there enough children here already? What does it matter that Lukusa didn't have some of his own?"

"I never said Lukusa was a bad man," Kayemba answered. "He *wasn't* a bad man. In fact, he wasn't a man at all. That's the point. You *can't* be a man without children. You can't be human."

Kayemba was speaking from the sacred core of his understanding of life. It was a core that had bedeviled me since the day I arrived in Kalambayi. Lukusa wasn't human because, in Africa, children are the central, insuperable, all-important fact. They roam everywhere, five to every parent, and producing them is the first goal in every man and woman's life. I had tried for some time to suggest to farmers that perhaps this crush of offspring wasn't in their best interest, but I had gotten nowhere. Now Kayemba saw in my defense of Lukusa a disturbing revelation. The *coordinateur* had foundered utterly in the most important aspect of life, he reminded me. To defend him could only mean I hated children.

Kayemba was wrong, of course, and I told him so. I didn't hate children. I just hated what they did to family incomes. I hated what they did to the fish project. Their large numbers made every pond harvest an airplane ride of emotions. The harvests went like this: Draining the pond at dawn and gathering the fish provided the heady, early-morning takeoff for the farmers and me. Next, walking out of the valley, muddy and happy and carrying the results, we soared to peak altitude. But then came the crash landing. Back at the house, the money from the sale disappeared into a raging fire of children's needs that included clothes, medicines, and school fees. The money was gone before all accounts were settled. Six kids went to school, two stayed home. Five got new shirts, three made do another three months.

From the start, I found myself wondering why each farmer found it necessary to have so many children. If parents had only five kids instead of ten, wasn't it clear that each child would get a greater share of the family food and wealth, and so be healthier? Having failed, as I said, to press this reasoning on a few farmers, I concluded that what I needed were visual aids to help me make my point. A few months after Lukusa's death, I procured from the Peace Corps a collection of watercolor illustrations bound in a flip-chart fashion. The illustrations were designed to help extension agents explain the government fish project to villagers.

When the flip chart arrived, I invited all the fish farmers along the upper Lubilashi to a meeting outside the schoolhouse in Ntita Konyukua. By three o'clock, most of the men had arrived—Bukasa, Kanyenda, Chief Ilunga, Kayemba, and about twenty others. They sat under a palm-branch pavilion and drank a requisite, pre-meeting gourd of palm wine while a dry afternoon wind blew soothingly across the schoolhouse yard. I could tell this was a big event because everyone was wearing shoes, some for the first time I could remember, having borrowed them from relatives.

While I was setting up the flip chart and searching for a stick pointer, something predictable began to happen: The village children came. And came and came. Soon they sat ten-deep in a ring around the pavilion, representing all ages, twittering and giggling and running about. So many children were there in every village that at the slightest spectacle—a soccer game, a heated argument, a fallen tree blocking the road—they appeared in droves this way, attaching themselves like barnacles to whatever was happening.

I finished setting up the flip chart and opened it to the first illustration. It showed a village man with his four children, all of them underfed and dressed in ragged clothes outside a beleaguered mud hut. I turned from the chart and briefly surveyed the children sitting around the pavilion. With their runny noses and herniated navels, their scabby heads and festering skin abscesses, 90 percent of them could have served as models for the illustration.

Standing before the farmers, I pointed to the flip-chart picture and asked rhetorically, "What do these children need?"

"Fish ponds," the men answered in unison.

"Yes," I said. "Fish ponds."

I began flipping through the pictures. Each one illustrated a different aspect of fish culture, showing the village man of the series digging his pond, stocking it, feeding his fish, and so forth. I asked technical questions as I went.

By the last page, the man impoverished in the first illustration had harvested his fish and now stood with his four children, all of them better dressed and fed.

"So things have improved for this family," I said. "One fish pond has allowed four children to live better lives. But what happens if this man's wife has four more children?" I flipped back to the malnourished kids in the opening picture. "Things start to look like they did in the beginning, don't they?"

"No they don't," answered Kayemba from the back. "If you have four more children, all you have to do is dig another pond."

"All right," I said, "you could do that. But what if there were no more children and you still dug a second pond? Then you would have two ponds for four children. It's a better situation, don't you think?"

"No, then you would have too many fish," he said.

"*Too* many fish?" I asked, baffled by the response. "How is it possible to have too many fish? That's like saying you could have too much money. You're always complaining that you don't have any money, Kayemba. Do you think you could ever have too much of it?"

"Yes, if I had a lot of money and I didn't use it to have as many children as I could, then I would have too much. It's the same with ponds. If one pond allows me to help four children, then two ponds allows me to help eight. Why would I have only four children when I could have eight?"

"Because if you have more ponds and fewer children then you have more money and food for each child."

"No, you need as many children as you can rear," interjected Kalombo.

"Why?"

"Because they help you with the work around the house and in the fields."

"They also give you more work," I said. "You have to feed them and send them to school."

By this point, Kanyenda was growing hugely annoyed with my line of arguing. He cleared his throat, threw back his shoulders and trotted out his favorite argument. "*Kuatshila muana mpasu lelu, ne yeye ne a kukuatshila mukuabo malaba*." It was the grasshopper proverb. "Catch a child a grasshopper to eat today and he'll catch you another grasshopper tomorrow." Everyone grinned widely at this, apparently agreeing that Kanyenda had delivered a definitive, double-barrel blow to my argument.

"But one well-fed, well-educated, strong son is going to catch you a lot more grasshoppers than three weak ones," I countered.

I was proud of myself, thinking I had come up with a reasonably persuasive response. But I could tell by the farmers' faces that we were still a million miles away on this issue. "Isn't there anyone who sees anything good about keeping families small?" I asked.

I looked around. The ring of children circling the pavilion had thickened. Every child from five miles around must have been there. In the center were the farmers, looking awkward and uncomfortable in their shoes, their moods serious despite the wine they drank. No one raised a hand. Indeed, just my talking about family planning was producing the same look of shock on their faces that had been there when I tried to defend Lukusa's honor.

The awful realization rose in my mind like a just released balloon: A lot of changes were possible in this society, but the social imperative to produce enormous families wasn't even negotiable. I might as well have been speaking Russian under that crude stick pavilion. At that moment I abandoned for good my small effort toward promoting zero population growth, toward helping stave off the ten billion people projected to inhabit—and greatly tax—the planet by the end of the next century. If the world's population is ever going to stabilize, it won't begin here, not among these tattered African villages.

Everyone at the farmers gathering heaved a sigh of relief when I finally dropped the preposterous subject of family planning. The meeting continued for another hour, ending with a flourish of palm wine and *tshitshampa* and discussions on how to raise as many fish as possible so everyone could raise as many children as possible too.

It wasn't until my second year in Kalambayi, when I became a fish farmer myself, that my Western notions began to soften and I started to think more like village parents when it came to the subject of children. I had wanted a pond of my own for a long time, and when Mupeta Mudinda, the Lulenga schoolteacher, moved to Mbuji Mayi, I bought his. This presented a problem, however. Working sixty hours a week as an extension agent left little time for feeding my own fish. What I needed, I decided, was a child to help me with the work.

I went to Mutombo Mulengela, my closest neighbor, and from his ten kids recruited Miteo, a smart, twelve-year-old boy with a gap-tooth smile. Like virtually every kid in the area,

Miteo was small and frail and looked about three years younger than his age. I knew him fairly well because each night he and his brothers slept atop the cotton in the warehouse. His face brightened when I offered him fifteen cents a week to help with the pond. "I would like that very much," he said.

Most afternoons, Miteo would gather bundles of papaya leaves in the village and we would go down to the pond together before sunset. I took advantage of the arrangement to teach him the basics of tilapia culture. But being a child he tended to look at things differently than the adults I worked with. He posed questions that from time to time just plain stumped me.

One day, fixing me with his narrow, brown face, Miteo asked, "Michel, do fish ever sleep?"

"Hmmm," I said, not really sure if they did or not, but deciding to fake it. "Well, yes, fish do sleep."

"But you told me earlier that they have to keep moving in order to breathe."

"Yes, that's right."

"So how do they sleep if they're always swimming. Don't they bump into each other?"

His twelve-year-old eyes were watching me, waiting for something wise and sophisticated to issue from my lips.

"I don't know, Miteo, they just do. Now add some more leaves and be quiet."

The answer was neither wise nor sophisticated, of course, but at least it saved me until the next day and the next knotted question.

These awkward episodes notwithstanding, Miteo and I grew to be good friends through our work relationship. Soon he and his brothers and sisters took to playing and hanging out outside my house, feeling they could now make special claims on me. Many afternoons after work I would play with them. The children would run up to me yelling "swing me, swing me," beseeching me to employ my skill for holding a child by the wrists and swinging him 'round and 'round, feet aloft. When, after swinging five subjects, I would grow cross-eyed with dizziness, I would pause to teach a few children the high art of juggling mangoes, and they would teach me how to play jacks with stones or how to make a pet of a giant beetle by tying a string around its leg and letting it fly in circles on its leash.

These play sessions never lasted more than thirty minutes, however, because an enormous wave of other children would quickly arrive. Just like at the fish farmers meeting, the children seemed to emanate from nowhere, popping out from behind cornstalks, dropping from trees, emerging from thin air. They came and came, dozens of them, until there were more than I could count. "Swing me! Swing me!" they would roar simultaneously, standing together in my yard as if part of a clamorous crowd scene in some epic motion picture.

With tiny hands pulling me in every direction, I would start backing up to my door, answering, "I can't swing you all. I'm sorry. Go home. Go away. I can't swing you all."

The children would follow me to the door, continuing their cries until I slipped inside and disappeared, my face flushed with panic.

Many times after the crowds had dispersed and the sun had gone down, only Mulumba, Miteo's dimple-faced, three-year-old brother, would come back to visit me, calming me after the earlier mayhem. He'd stick his head under the curtain drawn across my door and peek into my lantern-lit sitting room. "Michel," he'd say, "*ndeja mutoto wanyi*. Show me my star, Michel."

This was a game we played, although Mulumba didn't know it was a game. I would pick him up, put him on my shoulders, and walk to the center of my yard. There, below the African night sky, with the village houses tranquil and still all around us, I would pick a star, a random star from the millions above.

"There, Mulumba," I would say, pointing. "There it is. That bright one. That's your star. That's the one named after you. It's all yours and no one else's."

He would giggle wildly at this. They were little three-year-old giggles that rippled down my shoulders all the way to my feet, filling me with the same innocent joy and wonder, making me feel anew the precious value of every Kalambayan child in this difficult place. Mulumba had a stake in the universe. He was somebody. His star proved it.

The work arrangement with Miteo progressed nicely, meanwhile. A month went by and he began feeding the fish on his own while Mbaya and I added compost material once a week. It was a good system, but everything depended on Miteo. *I* was dependent on Miteo. Then he got sick.

It started with complaints of fatigue and headaches. At the ponds, I noticed he was gathering fewer leaves and asking fewer questions. Three days later I came home and found him lying on an antelope-skin cot outside his family hut. His father described his condition: no appetite, blurred vision, stiff joints, vomiting, listlessness. I now recognized the symptoms. I had seen them in other children. Miteo had meningitis.

For days his health got worse. I visited every afternoon and his mother would shake her head, grimacing an answer: no change. On each visit, I would squat next to Miteo and take his hand, my questions about how he was feeling eliciting brave smiles but few words.

It was then, going back to my house, knowing that Miteo was dying right outside my window, knowing that I was losing a friend, knowing, too, that my fish needed feeding and I had to find another child to help me—it was then that I began to better appreciate the one answer at the fish-farmers meeting that had given me greatest pause during our debate over limiting family size. The answer had come from Kazadi Manda after I had tried everything to get the men to see my point of view.

"But don't you see?" Kazadi had said, averting his eyes from mine. "The children die."

The words had pricked me, and I had averted my eyes too. Yes, the children die. In all my years prior to going to Africa, I attended a total of four funerals. In two years in Kalambayi, I attended, at least briefly, close to two hundred. Three-quarters of them were for children. I estimated that one third of all the sons and daughters in the area died before the age of five. Some farmers I worked with had lost five or six kids.

Still, nothing brought this ghastly reality home to me more than Miteo's condition. I needed him and cared for him, and now he was dying. Watching his body wither away, I understood as I never had before the deep fear shared by all parents in Kalambayi. There were many reasons why parents refused to limit family sizes, but the biggest was the fear that death would do it for them.

Without adequate medical care and improved living standards, only armed force would get these adults to change. The practice of having huge families was an insurance policy. It was something parents knew to be in their best interest. The fact that the insurance policy helped undermine improvements that might permit parents to have fewer children is one of the cruel paradoxes of the developing world.

As for Miteo, two weeks went by and it grew increasingly likely we would be burying him like the hundreds of other children. His sickness was strangling him. His neck grew stiff, he stopped eating altogether, and he could no longer muster smiles when I visited. Then, for a week, his condition hovered in a stasis, neither improving nor getting worse. I had begun trying to figure out a way to get him to Bibanga, paying to have him hospitalized there, when he finally turned the corner and started getting better. The recovery came slowly, a little each day. His younger brother Ditu helped me with the fish pond until eventually Miteo regained most of his strength. He didn't die. He had dropped out of school and looked even frailer and weaker than before, but he didn't die.

———

Miteo's recovery was truly astonishing given the severity of his sickness. Yet there it was: After two months he was passing his time outside my house again, feeding the fish in the afternoons. In the meantime, my relationship with him and my play sessions with the local children rekindled a question in the minds of most adults in my village. Why, they wondered, when I was approaching my mid twenties and apparently attached to children, did I live alone, without a wife and without children of my own? Of all my peculiarities, this was the reigning champion. It made people feel sorry for me and it had caused my neighbors to whisper to the village chief soon after I came to live in the village. Please, they told the chief, you have to *do something*. That's when he appeared outside my house with his four eligible daughters, determined I take one. But I wouldn't cooperate.

"You mean you *want* to live this way?" he said after we talked inside. "You want to live without a wife and children?"

"Well, yes," I confessed. "I do for now."

At this he threw up his hands and walked out with the crumpled look of a failed parent. I suspect that most of the people in the village privately wept for me that night, certain I was impotent. But I was a foreigner and relatively young and there was still a small chance I lived alone for reasons other than sexual competence. As a result, I wasn't openly scorned for my childlessness.

The other childless adults in Kalambayi weren't as lucky. Again, so important were children to the family economic unit, so much were they a source of pride for men and a badge of fertility for women, that those people without them, those people barren or sterile like Lukusa Mandako, simply weren't human. They were shunned mercilessly. *Pas d'enfants.* You might as well have said they were lepers.

With all the public shame heaped on them, it wasn't long after I moved to Lulenga that I learned who the village's childless people were. One was Kamuena Ndala, a handsome river ferryman with many talents. Kamuena was intelligent, played guitar, and was known for having pulled one of the biggest catfish out of the Lubilashi that anyone could remember. But nowhere among his skills was the ability to father children. He and his wife Kabanga had been married several years. Now in their late twenties, they had no children and were ostracized accordingly. Like Lukusa, they tried everything. Finally, they tried the ritual chicken ceremony of the Bena Lupemba Church, which involved sacrificing a chicken to God and pleading for His intercession.

The sacrifice worked. Or at least partially. Kabanga conceived a few months after the ceremony. But the pregnancy went badly. Nine months later, in the middle of the night, she went into labor and Kamuena came pounding at my door. The noise woke me and my guest John Dodier, a volunteer from Ngandajika who had battled Kalambayi's mud-snarled roads that day in his Land Rover, bringing me supplies.

The pounding outside continued. I lit a lantern and opened the door. Dim images hovered in the night heat: There was Kamuena standing before me with his staring eyes and hollow cheeks. A bicycle was behind him. Three men were behind the bicycle, carrying his wife.

"The baby," Kamuena began, gesturing behind him, "is stuck. We can't free it. It's halfway in and halfway out. It's already dead and my wife is bleeding badly. She's about to die. The baby's stuck between her legs. You've got to drive her to a doctor."

The men in the distance were Kamuena's brothers. They were taking Kabanga to see a village healer who, for reasons of superstition, would examine the women only in his own hut.

"If the healer fails," Kamuena said, "we'll be back."

I shuddered and my stomach fell at the thought of the woman's condition. I assured Kamuena we would drive the Land Rover if needed. The entourage then moved down the hill and John and I waited, unable to imagine making the violent, bouncing, five-hour trip to Bibanga with a tormented woman bleeding to death in back. I went outside to get the Land Rover ready, cleaning the truck bed and putting down a reed mat.

We waited for more than an hour on my doorstep, John and I, nervously smoking cigarettes. Miteo, who was sleeping in the cotton warehouse, heard us talking and ambled over, rubbing his eyes. He decided to stay up with us. Every fifteen minutes he walked down to the healer's hut to get news. "They're still trying," he said on each return. "The baby won't come out." Our dread and anxiety grew.

Eventually, John went inside to try to sleep, leaving Miteo and me sitting alone in the night air. It was a gentle evening, cloudless, with enough moonlight to draw shadows from the somnolent huts all around us. The mango tree across the yard loomed in delicate silhouette against a sky dense with a legion of glittering stars. The beauty seemed almost cruel, almost mockingly intense, given the grotesque human struggle taking place just down the hill.

Using my lantern, I went inside to get a *Newsweek* magazine and gave it to Miteo to pass the time. I watched him study the photographs. After a while he went down to check on Kabanga again. The healer was taking a long time, and I was growing increasingly certain Miteo would come running back at any moment breathlessly telling us to hurry with the truck. But it didn't happen. Not this time. He returned with the same message: no change.

I handed Miteo the magazine and he began flipping through it again. The lantern light played off his sleepy face, giving soft illumination to his smooth, thin cheeks. For a moment all of Africa's past and future, its very soul, seemed concentrated on that face—brave and hopeful, weak and tired. Sitting on my doorstep at that strange night hour with a young woman dying a few hundred yards away, I watched Miteo's face and a mad confluence of feelings and images began to pass through me.

I became suddenly conscious of how quiet it was in the village. It was as if someone had just flipped off a noise switch. By day, the space outside these huts was thick with the sound of young children wandering everywhere. I thought about how they converged on my yard each time I stepped out to play and how they mobbed fish-farmers' meetings soon after they began. Scores of children. Hundreds of children. Too many of them. But now the village was strangely bereft of their shouting and laughing and crying. The children were asleep, lying on reed mats, silently growing older to have a multitude of children of their own, all of them driven on by a social force seemingly impossible to stop.

Miteo's voice interrupted my thoughts. I stood. He had just returned from another trip down the hill. The healer was making little progress, he said. Disappointed, we took our seats on the doorstep.

I looked up at the stunning night sky again. The stars were clear and sharp, like ice crystals spread across the universe's window. Their presence distracted me for a moment. How many were there, I wondered. How many stars was I looking at from this obscure post in Africa? One hundred million? Five hundred million? One billion? Yes, perhaps one billion stars. I found myself wishing little Mulumba were awake so I could pick his star and so leaven this tense wait with his laughter.

But then an unsettling thought came to me: There weren't enough stars. There weren't enough points of light in the sky for

Mulumba to have his very own. With almost five billion people in the world, he would have to share. Looking up, that fact seemed impossible to me. It seemed impossible that there were more people in the world than stars in the sky. Impossible, too, was the thought that in a little more than one hundred years ten billion people will inhabit the planet, ten Mulumbas for every star, all on a smallish sphere already sagging from the weight of a population half that size. A majority of those people, too, will come from Third World settings like Kalambayi, fathered by men like those I worked with. They are the world's future.

I turned to Miteo. He was still looking at the *Newsweek* magazine. I watched him flip past articles on war in Cambodia, pollution in the Soviet Union, drugs in the United States, deforestation in Brazil. After a while, I looked away and gazed back up at the night sky. The sky had changed. It had lost its earlier beauty and enchantment. With all those stars, so many stars, it looked frightening now.

I was near fits wondering what was taking the healer so long. Another hour had gone by. Too much time. Kabanga was surely close to death by now. Miteo went down to check again. He was gone a long time and when I saw him running back I expected the worst. But the news was different. "They freed the baby!" he said. "They freed the baby! The healer got it out, and he says Kabanga is going to live."

My feeling of relief was strong but mixed. Kabanga was okay. Her bleeding had stopped and we wouldn't have to drive her to Bibanga. But the baby was dead, a tragedy. The parents would bury it the next day and resume lives heavy with shame, having failed to earn for themselves the revered status of life-givers.

Exhausted, I went inside to sleep, first saying goodnight to Miteo. I shook his small hand and thanked him for staying up with me. Then, from my room, I heard the creak of the warehouse door as he went back to the cotton to lie down and drift away.

12

<small>OCTOBER CAME AROUND AND WITH IT MORE FREQUENT SHOWERS.</small> But not enough rain had fallen to raise the Mvunai River, which was still at its dry-season depth of about three feet. The river was crossable on foot at this level, and all the canoes had been tied up downriver beyond the still-standing, go-nowhere Mvunai bridge. I dismounted my motorcycle and cursed. It was five o'clock and Mbumba Katonda, the local canoe operator, had promised to take me across. But he was nowhere in evidence. I would have to carry my motorcycle to the other side.

The humid afternoon air had been thickening for hours under an angry sun. It was pure syrup by the time I reached the river, heading home from a day of work in Kalundu Musoko. Perspiring, I walked down the trail that led to the river's edge. Along the way I came upon an old blind man with a grizzled beard sitting cross-legged about fifty feet from the water.

"Don't go down there," the old man said, hearing me and gesturing toward a clump of reeds along the bank. "My wife and daughter are bathing."

The man's irises were white, completely clouded over with cataracts. The milky sheen gave him that strange look common to cataracts victims of being both pitiably sightless and able to look right through you the way a ghost or an extraterrestrial might. Having warned me of the bathers, the blind man motioned for me to sit next to him and wait, which I did. We began talking. I quickly discovered that despite his condition he was exceptionally cheerful and full of wry humor.

"I hope you brought some food," he said turning to me, his eyes missing mine by several inches. "These women take so long to bathe we may starve waiting."

I laughed. I did have some food and reached into my knapsack.

"Want some peanuts?"

He took a handful and turned back toward the riverbank. "Are you women going to finish bathing today or next week?" he yelled. "I'm not the only one waiting now. There's another person here, too."

A flash of realization passed through my mind: The man didn't know who I was. He didn't know I was white, a foreigner. If he had, he would have said a *mutoka* or a *patron* was waiting. But he had simply said *muntu mukuabo*, "another person." My ability to speak Tshiluba was good enough that he evidently attributed my accent to another tribe. He took me for a Zairian. After more than a year and a half in Africa, I was having my first conversation with a villager completely free of cultural preconditions. The situation intrigued and amused me, and I wasn't about to blow it by letting on.

The old man and I talked for about fifteen minutes. He told me he was returning from the mission hospital at Bibanga, where an American doctor had informed him nothing could be done for his eyes; he had waited too long before seeking treatment. Had he gone five years earlier, the doctor had said, his sight could have been saved.

"Why didn't you go sooner?" I asked.

"*Katuvua ne falanga to,*" he said. "We didn't have any money."

I told him I worked for the government teaching fish culture. He was from a region east of Kalambayi and had never heard of the project. Again, the whole time we talked, nothing he said suggested he knew I was white and from another continent. We were just two travelers pausing at a riverbank in Africa, speaking Tshiluba. To pull this off, to become this immersed in culture and language, had been one of my goals in coming to Africa. As I talked to the old man, clucking at his descriptions of hardship, guffawing at his jokes, offering my own, there spread through me a feeling of having walked a long way and reached the circled endpoint on a map. For every child my white skin had pumped with horror, for every fried grasshopper I had eaten sure it would kill me, for every line of Tshiluba I had mangled to the chuckles of those around me, here now was my glory. I accepted the bad times and the defeats when they came. And I accepted this for what it was: a victory.

"Have some more peanuts," I said, putting another handful in the man's palm. Discarded shells were accumulating at our feet.

Just then the two women appeared on the trail, walking toward us. With disquiet, I saw that the old man's wife was blind, too. Not from cataracts, apparently, but something else. She was being led by their daughter, who was in her twenties. I greeted the women and walked past them to the river's edge, searching up and down both shores for people. I needed at least three other people to help me carry my motorcycle across, but there was no one around. The situation was upsetting. Chances were good I would wind up waiting a long time.

I turned and watched the old couple walking away, slowly, sightlessly, each holding one of their daughter's elbows. As I watched, the question leapt into my mind: Should I ask them? Should I ask these blind people to help me carry my motorcycle across this river? The answer came back just as fast: Of course not. The idea was ridiculous. They'd never manage it. Still, with all its Third World ironies, the notion lingered in my mind for a moment. I imagined the scene: stranded development worker leading blind helpers across bridgeless river, mud-smeared motorcycle on their shoulders as everyone splashes along praying no one falls.

I said farewell to the departing trio and sat down on the bank. Twenty minutes later, four men transporting corn on rickety bicycles rolled down to the river. Three of them agreed to help me. With a collective heave we lifted the motorcycle and headed into the tea-colored water. Two men held up the rear while the third man and I gripped either handlebar. The one in front with me immediately complained about the weight, increasing the nervousness I always felt during such crossings. "It's not far," I said. "It won't take long."

The cold water rose to our ankles, then reached our knees. Further out, it roiled loudly past our waists, tugging us in a diagonal line. The footing was tricky and we moved slowly, negotiating dips and crests in the river-bottom sand. Near the middle I hit a hole and the bottom of the engine dipped into the water without harm before I could recover. A few more seconds passed and the shore grew closer and finally we arrived. With tired arms we let the motorcycle down heavily, all of us soaked to our stomachs. Water dripped from the tires and the engine.

After thanking the men and handing out cigarettes, I decided to take a bath in an eddy a short distance downriver. I took off my clothes, laid them in a patch of reeds, and waded in with a bar of soap. I washed and rinsed myself by submerging several times in the water, shaking my hair as I came up. When I had finished, I walked back along the bank toward my motorcycle, feeling the late-day sun drying my skin. I paused before leaving and looked across the river at the spot where I had sat with the blind man. Then I looked at the river itself, its water swirling and hurrying by. It felt good to be across. I started the motorcycle and headed home.

13

It was six o'clock and getting dark fast when I reached my house in Lulenga. I cooked a plate of fried rice, ate it, and then tried to read awhile in bed. But the day of sun and river crossings and rutted roads soon drew curtains across my eyes. I was asleep after five pages.

The next morning I awoke and looked out my front window at something remarkable. There was snow on the ground—lots of it, several feet of it. Children were playing in it. I stepped outside and decided there was far too much for me to go to work; driving through it would be impossible. It continued to accumulate as the morning wore on and by eleven o'clock there were five- and six-foot drifts. It wasn't real snow. It was cotton. A snowfield of picked cotton lay in my yard. A real dumping.

Today was the day of the annual cotton sale and people throughout the village were bringing their fluffy white harvests to my yard. They covered the grass with it, preparing to put it inside the peeling, moldering, tin-roofed warehouse. The cotton arrived in homemade baskets of all sizes, carried by people of all ages. The women came first. They transported huge, four-foot-tall baskets on their heads, their neck muscles rippling under the weight. The men followed. They worked in pairs, carrying wood poles on their shoulders with baskets of cotton hanging down in between. Next came the children and the elders, who carried lesser quantities in smaller baskets. Three-year-old Mulumba from next door diligently did his part. He trailed his sister, picking up the bolls of cotton she sloshed and spilled from a load too big for her head.

By noon the whole village was standing outside the warehouse and cotton was everywhere. I poured a third cup of coffee and surveyed the scene from my door. Women with babies strapped to their backs untied them and let them wiggle and crawl inside baskets of cotton. Barefoot men adjusted their straw hats and nervously speculated among themselves as to how many kilos they had. Together it looked like a lot, but it was actually a meager harvest and no one was happy about it. The villagers had been forced to plant the cotton last Christmas, and now, just as they did every year, they were about to sell it at a low, fixed price to Cotonnière, the Belgian cotton company.

A company official arrived with a black metal box full of money, and a hush fell over the crowd. The buying was about to begin. I had been in Mbuji Mayi during last year's sale, and I decided to take the day off to watch this one. I wanted to see for myself if all the horror stories I had heard about the buying process were true. I had seen enough of how the cotton company worked in other ways to suspect they were. I had seen enough, in fact, to have personally led a secret war over the past year to sabotage the company's operations.

Cotton represented one of the final obstacles to the continued spread of fish culture in Kalambayi. By October of my second year when officials came to buy the cotton harvest, the fish project was doing fairly well, having survived a number of challenges. The minor civil war had come and gone, the widespread suspicion of me had ended with the first few fish harvests, and now enough men had ponds that fresh tilapia were entering village markets three or four days a week.

Still, there was the problem of cotton. Bumping along on its own inertia and sanctioned by a corrupt post-independence government, the old colonial system of forced cultivation endured, causing real hardship for everyone in the villages. It kept a lot of would-be fish farmers away from the project; men were too busy tending their half-hectare cotton fields to build and manage ponds.

And tending those cotton fields was something Kalambayans hated with an intensity impossible to exaggerate.

"Look at it," Kayemba had said one day as we were walking back from his ponds. He pointed with disgust to a field of shriveled, damaged cotton plants. The stems were black and spindly, and only half bore bolls. "Insects got it one month after I planted," he said. "It was the little red ones with the short legs. They're the worst kind. Now, there's nothing I can do. Only with God's help will I get one hundred kilos."

Cotton is a difficult crop to grow under any conditions, requiring a great amount of weeding and attention. Worse, it's extremely vulnerable to pests, making the heavy use of insecticide imperative. But the Kalambayans didn't have insecticide. They didn't have fertilizer either. To save money in the face of falling world cotton prices, Cotonnière had done more than just cut back on road and bridge repair. In the past three years it had stopped supplying villagers with the chemicals they needed. This despite the fact that the company received World Bank loans each year meant to improve conditions for peasant workers. The result of the company's cutbacks was that Kayemba and everyone else in Kalambayi planted and weeded and nurtured their plants as ordered, only to lose half their harvests to insects and bad soil. Cotonnière got less cotton this way, but it paid virtually nothing for what it got.

The gall and cruelty of the system were mind-numbing. I remember early on asking several fish farmers what would happen if they simply refused to plant. Their jaws dropped like stones. "Why Michel," they said, "we can't do that. We'll get arrested. The soldiers will come and take us away."

The soldiers came from the government office at Kabala, where state functionary Bashiya Mulumba ran things. There was a harmony of interests between Bashiya and the Belgian cotton officials in Ngandajika. Cotonnière wanted its cotton, but didn't want to invest. It got its cotton by relying on Bashiya, who took advantage of the cultivation to squeeze money from villagers. Several times a year he generated cash for his superiors in Mbuji Mayi by roaming through Kalambayi with a couple of armed soldiers, inspecting cotton fields. Anyone caught without a field was arrested or fined on the spot. Even people who did plant were routinely fined, told by Bashiya that their fields were too small or that the planting had been done too early or too late.

Villagers were virtually powerless against this system. The notion of organizing any kind of workers' strike was out of the question; the boot heel of dictatorship was always inches above, ready to flatten all attempts. On the few occasions I tried to explain to farmers how labor unions work in other countries and how one might work in Kalambayi, they emphatically shook their heads no. Their fear of Bashiya and the cotton company was much too great for anything that assertive. My Peace Corps supervisor in Mbuji Mayi, meanwhile, reminded me that any overt attempt to organize farmers would win me a prompt expulsion notice from the Zairian government.

There was one alternative to a full-blown strike, however, and the fish farmers and I eventually pursued it. We waged a quiet campaign of guerilla tactics against the cotton company, throwing wrenches into the system every chance we got.

It began when a couple of farmers in Bajila Membila told me they had reduced the time they spent on their cotton fields by spacing the plants wide apart and sowing peanuts and sweet potatoes in between. Government soldiers passing through the valley a few weeks before hadn't noticed the technique and the men had passed inspection. This was truly interesting news. As an extension agent I felt duty bound to pass it on to every fish farmer in every village in Kalambayi. The farmers, in turn, passed it on to their friends and relatives. Not everyone adopted the method, but when planting season arrived in December an encouraging number of creative cotton fields began to decorate the landscape.

Another interesting idea came from Baba Mpiana. He was a burly-chested workaholic who lived in Katombe with his six wives and six fish ponds—both records in Kalambayi as far as I knew. With so many ponds, Baba was always looking for the easiest and most effective way to feed his fish. One day he was walking by the cotton warehouse in Katombe when something caught his eye.

"There's a large pile of cotton seed sitting in there," he told me during my next visit. "It's left over from last year's planting. There must be fifteen sacks worth of it. I was wondering if you thought it would make good compost material for my ponds."

I gave it some thought and told him I thought it would. "But are you sure it's okay to take it from the warehouse? What if Cotonnière finds out?"

"It's leftover seed," he said. "Nobody's going to miss it. Besides, I'll take it when nobody's looking."

"Okay. Give it a try. Just don't get caught."

Under cover of darkness, Baba used the UNICEF wheelbarrow to transport several loads of seed from the warehouse to his compost bins. I visited the ponds two weeks later and saw that the soft, nutrient-rich seeds had decomposed quickly in the water, leaving an unusually thick plankton bloom that made his fish grow by leaps and bounds. I turned and looked at Baba. He was all smiles, thinking the same thing I was: We had struck gold, pure gold. We walked around the ponds slapping our knees and giggling like two schoolboys who had just gotten away with a tremendous prank.

Again I spread the news through Kalambayi and project farmers everywhere started raiding cotton warehouses for leftover seed. They entered at night, tiptoeing, leaving with sacks and wheelbarrows full. The ponds responded by turning dark green, and fish growth took off on a sharp, upward curve. It was a small triumph over Cotonnière, one whose irony gave us all a lot of satisfaction. The company was no longer providing fertilizer for cotton, but it was now providing us with a hell of a lot of fertilizer for ponds. I felt doubly satisfied knowing that I was living rent-free in one of the company's warehouses while fomenting anti-cotton activity every chance I got.

The fish farmers and I agreed that the next step in our campaign would come the following December. That's when Cotonnière truck drivers would make their annual delivery of new cotton seed. The men planned to ask for four or five times more seed than they needed to plant, dumping the surplus in their ponds. We all got a lot of laughs just thinking about it.

"Yes," Banza Bankani said, "I'm going to walk up to that truck driver and tell him I love cotton so much I won't be happy until I've planted a whole valley, top to bottom. And then my wife's going to plant a whole valley, too. She loves cotton just as much as I do. So please, *monsieur* truck driver, give me all the seed you can. Twenty sacks? Yes, I think that should do it."

Banza was a talented, twenty-six-year-old guitarist who spent most of his free time sitting on a log bench behind his house singing ballads to the grass and sky. With his sweet voice and entertainer's charisma, I was sure he'd take Cotonnière for all the seed it was worth.

Unfortunately, though, our little successes against the cotton company didn't last forever. I had had a strange feeling all along that it was too easy, that we were getting away with too much. As it turned out, I was right. Three months after the farmers started pilfering from the warehouses, Baba Mpiana got arrested.

He had already been released by the time I got the message and reached his house in Katombe. He told me to have a seat. "They found out about the seed," he said.

I sat down and almost stopped breathing as he recounted the story. Someone connected to the government office in Kabala apparently had passed by his ponds, seen the seeds, and informed Bashiya. Baba then was arrested and detained for an hour while Bashiya and his assistants warned him that using company seed for anything other than planting was a serious offense. Several times during the detention my name came up. Bashiya asked Baba if I was aware he had misused the seed. To protect me, he lied. He also said he knew of no other fish farmers using seed in their ponds—another lie. In the end, he was fined two chickens, told to obey the law, and released.

The story sent fear blowing through me like a cold wind. I felt bad about Baba's arrest, but worse about what might happen next.

"Do you think they're going to send out soldiers to check all the other ponds?" I asked him. We were slumped in chairs outside his house.

"That's what I kept waiting for them to tell me," he said. "But they never did. I think they believed me—that I was the only one. But you better tell the other farmers what happened just in case."

I planned to start that very day, I said.

"The thing I don't understand," he continued, "is that it was extra seed. They don't even need it. I didn't think anyone would notice."

I told him I was pretty sure it wasn't the cotton seed they were concerned about. "You broke a rule," I said. "They're afraid of that. If they let you get away with it, then other people might start breaking rules too: all kinds of rules. Then Bashiya and Cotonnière would lose control of things."

Baba didn't seem to grasp the dynamic I was getting at because as soon as I finished he repeated his original point over and over again. "But they don't even need the seed," he said. "What does it matter to them?" I decided not to push my explanation. Baba didn't have a revolutionary mind. He just wanted bigger fish.

Rising to leave, I thanked him for not revealing my part to Bashiya and we agreed to split the cost of the chickens.

Baba's arrest alarmed me and made me appreciate the seriousness of the game we were playing. Like a fool, I hadn't given much thought to what would happen if we were found out. Now that I knew, I realized I had been acting irresponsibly. I was advising the farmers to take advantage of the cotton company, advising them to do things they probably wouldn't do otherwise, but they were the ones taking all the risks. I think most of them saw me as an authority who could let them bend the rules and then protect them if they got caught. But I had no such authority, and I should have made that clear from the start. Now, at my suggestion, there were several dozen fish farmers throughout Kalambayi with cotton seed sitting in their ponds, and suddenly they were all subject to arrest. I was starting to feel a lot deeper in this thing than I wanted to be.

The next two days were tense. I traveled through the villages quietly spreading the news of Baba's arrest and advising farmers to remove their seed. Then we all held our breath and waited for Bashiya. We waited for him to dispatch soldiers to the ponds, fulfilling a nightmare vision of interrogations and large-scale arrests, all of it threatening to wash the project down the drain. But Baba was right. Bashiya had believed him. A week passed, then two, and no government patrols came.

Afterward, to my surprise, almost all the fish farmers pledged to continue using seed in their ponds. Unlike Baba's ponds, which lay along a heavily traveled path in Katombe, most of the other ponds in Kalambayi were in isolated spots away from the eyes of possible government informants. Just to be safe, though, the men decided to start spreading grass over the top of their compost bins, covering the seeds. I stressed to everyone that I was powerless to protect them should they get caught. But I admired their determination and privately decided that if there were any more arrests I would claim responsibility for everything, taking my chances with Bashiya.

Thankfully, however, there were no more discoveries. We survived the incident with Baba, and the secret campaign of stealing seed and planting thin cotton fields continued. It wasn't a full-fledged workers' strike. It didn't come close to crippling Cotonnière. But it was the best we could do.

───

So things stood when the cotton company came around in October to make its annual purchase. On the morning of the sale, Banza, who lived down the hill from me, carried his cotton to my house and came inside. "Watch what happens now," he said. "This is the worst part."

By noon the crowd of villagers standing in my yard with their harvests had been waiting several hours. They kept their eyes on the double doors at the center of the storage building. The doors were wide and heavy like barn doors, and when they opened the sale would begin. The entrance to my living quarters, where I stood watching everything, was fifteen feet to the left of the double doors.

There was a stir in the crowd and someone pointed down the road to indicate three Zairian employees of Cotonnière were finally arriving at the warehouse. Two of the men rode bicycles and the third, Muamba Mulunda, the company *Chef de Secteur*, rode a pale-red Yamaha 100 that burned outrageous amounts of oil and left a locomotive-like stream of smoke wherever it went. The men traveled through the villages conducting one sale each day, and they were always late. Craggy-faced, with a big stomach and baggy new clothes, Muamba was the man in charge. He carried the black metal box with the money. The two other men were his assistants. They weighed the cotton and recorded it in a company log book, looking over the tops of downward-adjusted sunglasses as they wrote.

Before the sale began, *Chef* Muamba entered my house and introduced himself. He behaved in a way that made it clear he wanted to be treated like someone important, insisting on speaking only in French and asking whether, by chance, *monsieur* had any beer. No, I told him, *monsieur* didn't. He was disappointed. We exchanged pleasantries, and he returned outside to begin the sale.

In the yard, the two assistants were telling the villagers to combine all partially filled baskets of cotton into single, tightly packed baskets. This would reduce the number of weighings the assistants would have to make. A dozen or so thin children promptly climbed on top of selected baskets. As if atop white, fibrous grapes, they began using their feet to mash the cotton down to make room for more on top. They did this in a rhythmic, dance-like fashion, with children along the ground clapping out a beat.

I left my doorway and began moving past the cotton-mashing youth. I found Banza and Mbaya Mutshi, another fish farmer, standing toward the back of the crowd and I stood with them. The company representatives had just opened the warehouse doors, revealing an interior empty of everything but old wasps' nests and graffiti. Just inside the doors, at a spot visible from the yard, the men placed a wooden table. Above the doorway they hung a round, spring-loaded scale with a red needle. The sale was about to begin.

Presently, a man with a pointed beard and the ragged look of a scarecrow jumped up to the elevated warehouse doorway and looked out on the crowd, signaling for silence. Everyone stopped talking. Children stopped mashing cotton. A baby cried.

"*Mioyi yenu iyi*," the man said, greeting the crowd. "I've been sent here to announce that before any man can weigh his cotton, he must first agree to pay me 20 zaires that will go to Mbaya Tshiongo."

Mbaya Tshiongo was the village chief. The man speaking was his brother. A low murmur passed through the crowd.

"The cotton officials here are guests of our village," the speaker continued. "Last night Chief Mbaya killed a goat for them. Now everyone must give me 20 zaires to pay for the goat."

The murmur grew louder. A chorus of complaints began.

"No one asked us if we wanted to buy these men a goat," yelled Komba Tshibingu from the back of the crowd. "And none of us ate any of it, so why should we pay for it?"

Smiling wryly, diplomatically, the speaker said: "Yes, but these men are our guests. It doesn't matter if you were asked or not. The chief killed a goat for them."

The crowd began hissing and whistling.

"I refuse to pay," a man yelled hotly from near the road. "I grew this cotton, and I'm the one who's supposed to get paid today. Those cotton people get traveling money when they're on the road. Why should we pay them again and feed them again?"

Other villagers grunted in agreement.

During the standoff, Banza, Mutshi, and the other fish farmers present didn't speak up. They stood in groups along the edges of the crowd. Given Baba's arrest, they had decided to keep a low profile throughout the sale.

In the doorway, just behind the chief's envoy, the Cotonnière officials had finished setting things up for the sale. They were now seated at their table, a triumvirate, looking profoundly bored with the drama before them. They had already eaten their goat and no doubt had advised the chief to impose this tax to pay for it. Smoking and whispering to each other, they casually sat back and watched peasant farmers grapple with corruption's bottom line.

The shouts and charges continued until the crowd of village men finally gave in. Grumbling, one by one, they brought their baskets forth and hung them on the hook extending from the bottom of the scale. Each farmer's eyes watched carefully as the red needle gave quantitative expression to months of sweat.

"One-hundred-two kilos for Kalala Ilunga," the scale assistant yelled to the bookkeeper assistant.

"One-hundred-two kilos for Kalala Ilunga," the bookkeeper assistant repeated, scribbling the number in the company ledger.

After the weighing, the farmers dumped their cotton in the warehouse and walked away, most of them shaking their heads and muttering that the scale had been rigged. The village's total production came to 13.2 tons—an eight hundred kilo drop from the year before. I silently wondered how much of that was due to the planting technique the fish farmers and I had spread around. At least some, I thought.

Muamba pulled out his black metal box and set it on the table. He was ready to start the paying. But first he stood and reminded the crowd that new cotton seed would be arriving in December and that everyone except the very old and very sick had to plant. As he spoke, Banza and I exchanged glances. A grin crept onto his face and I could almost hear the words, "Yes, yes, a whole valley, top to bottom."

Next Muamba informed everyone that the company would be paying twelve cents per kilo for the cotton handed over that day. No bargaining was permitted. The farmers could take it or leave it. A government soldier wearing a beret and ill-fitting fatigue uniform stood next to the table, leaning on a semiautomatic rifle and drawing on a cigarette. He had just arrived on loan from the government office at Kabala and his presence reinforced the message: Take it or leave it.

Each farmer waited for his name to be called, then approached the table. The money was counted out on the wood surface, totaling $5 or $10 or, if the farmer had worked extraordinarily hard and pests had spared him their worst destruction, $20.

While Muamba was paying the farmers, three men riding cargo-laden bicycles arrived and began setting up a small market along the dirt road behind the crowd. The men were merchants who followed the Cotonnière officials from village to village like seagulls behind a fishing trawler. On reed mats they spread pots and pans, bars of soap, bolts of cloth, bicycle tires, fish hooks, cigarettes, and other products. Most of the items had been bought at the Cotonnière supply store in Ngandajika and were sold in the villages at significantly marked-up prices.

But flush with money, many villagers didn't care about prices. They took their bills from Muamba, cast a nod at the smoking soldier, and headed across the road to examine cloth and try on straw hats. I took leave of Banza and Mutshi and walked over to inspect the wares myself. I quickly noticed that sudden wealth was leading many people toward frivolous purchases. One merchant was doing brisk business with his "Temple of Heaven Essential Balm," a skin ointment sold in small, highly decorative tin containers, the backs of which read: MADE IN SHANGHAI, CHINA.

A few hundred feet from the merchants, under a stout mango tree in the center of the village, another wooden table had been set up. Behind the table sat another official-looking figure accompanied by another sloppily dressed soldier with a semiautomatic rifle. The official was Bashiya. He had come from Kabala to collect taxes. Another seagull behind the good ship Cotonnière.

"We have to do it this way," Bashiya told me when I walked over and discreetly posed a few questions. "Any other time of year the people will lie and try to tell us they don't have any money. But now they have no excuse. I can see them putting the money in their pockets from here."

Bashiya, who was in his late thirties, seemed to wear power well. His thick frame filled a neatly pressed suit and his calculating eyes, set behind wire-frame glasses, sailed out with sure superiority to greet the overpolite farmers who stepped up to his table. He recorded the payments of the annual tax in a large black notebook. The amount ranged between $1 and $2, depending on a man's age and the size of his family. Women were exempt from paying—except prostitutes, who paid the $2 maximum.

"Prostitutes?" I said.

"Yes," Bashiya replied. "They're merchants, aren't they? In one night, a prostitute can make twenty-five or fifty [cents].

Then, the very next night, she might make the same amount. Some of that money should go to the state, don't you think? *C'est just, n'est ce pas?*"

"But how do you know who the prostitutes are?" I asked. "Is there an official government list or something?"

"No. We just walk into each village and ask. Finding out who they are is easy. Getting them to pay is what's hard."

I asked the next question out of a love for theater.

"What does the state do with the money it collects?"

Bashiya shot me a disapproving frown, as if to ask why I wanted to spoil our little chat with such a hostile question. He went on to turn in an impressive performance nonetheless, ticking off state expenditures. "We support schools, we fund health clinics, we build bridges, we repair roads—everything we can do to meet the needs of the people." But as he spoke, I found myself only half-listening. My mind was wandering back to the bridgeless Mvunai River where just the day before I had almost asked blind people to help me carry my motorcycle across waist-high waters.

The tax table grew crowded with men come to pay. I left Bashiya and headed back toward the warehouse, where a few dozen farmers still waited for their money. I sat on my doorstep and watched a while longer before deciding I had seen all I wanted to see. I went inside and closed the door, but the sordid circus of fraud and thievery reached my ears through the windows. Suddenly I was relieved to remember I had promised Mutshi I would feed his fish that afternoon. I put on my boots, walked past the farmers in my yard, and headed for a string of ponds outside Lulenga, glad to be leaving the market ordeal behind.

Within minutes I was out of the village and alone, moving through the drowsy sunlight toward the valley floor. I passed no one along the trail. Indeed, looking around, I saw that the entire valley was empty of people—no one farming on the hillsides, no one drawing water from the river. Everyone was up at the warehouse. It was so quiet I felt a passing urge to shout something into the air to let the valley know I was there and to vent all the feelings of revulsion and anger building inside me since morning.

When I reached the ponds, I took off my boots and walked barefoot up and down the dikes, inspecting the fish. The grass was warm and soft under my feet. As I walked, I noticed that all of the farmers had taken the precaution that day of covering their compost bins with extra-thick layers of grass. I took a stick and lifted the grass above one bin. Underneath were thousands and thousands of cotton seeds busy decomposing and generating fish food. The sight made me feel a little better.

By the time I walked back to my house, the cotton sale was winding down. From behind his table, Muamba yelled, "Kakumbi Muadianvita," and a shy-eyed farmer stepped forward. With long, thin fingers he scooped up $11 from the table and turned to leave.

Late-afternoon shadows were stretching through the village when the last of the farmers had been paid and walked away from my yard. Across the road, a handful of men and women bargained over goods at the roadside market, but soon they were gone too. Only at the government tax table did activity continue at an energetic pace. Bashiya's military attaché roamed through the village personally inviting to the table all men who had discourteously walked away from the cotton sale without paying their respects.

In the warehouse yard, bolls of fallen cotton lay on the ground, sprinkled evenly through the grass. Discarded baskets and parts of broken baskets littered the yard too. There lay in the debris a sense that a party had ended and everyone had gone home. It was a sense of release, but release without satisfaction. Another hard-gotten crop had been sold. A few hundred dollars had been dropped, as if from a passing plane, into their poor village. But it was a quantity so ridiculously small it tempted many villagers to blow it, to spend it recklessly and bitterly in one shot. Home they went with their $5 or $10 or $15. Home to drink bottles of *tshitshampa*. Home to rub "Temple of Heaven Essential Balm" on always-sore muscles. And home to wait for December, when the Cotonnière trucks would labor down the village roads dropping off sacks of cotton seed meant for sowing on Christmas Day. Then the hoeing, the planting, the weeding, the picking, and, next year, another party.

In the fading last light of day, I watched Miteo and Ditu, the boys from next door, comb the grass outside the warehouse for bolls of fallen cotton. Their plan was to collect a full kilo and sell it to the Cotonnière officials the next day for twelve cents. As the boys worked, I could hear Bashiya across the way threatening to imprison an inebriated village man who claimed that he had already spent all his cotton money and couldn't pay his tax. Bashiya waved his hand, and his soldier assistant backed the man against the mango tree, slapping him across the face and then poking a finger hard in his chest—once, twice, three times—until the man pledged to borrow the money and return shortly.

Watching this final obscenity, I almost got the feeling Bashiya was putting it on for my benefit. The soldier's blunt fingertip was indirectly meant for my own chest, each stab a replay of the day's message: Build your little fish ponds with your little villagers, get away with your little fringe maneuvers if you can, but don't for a second think you're changing anything on a grand scale. Things are going to be this way long after your brief visit is nothing but a memory relived in slideshows to your friends.

That evening Banza and Mutshi stopped by my house and we drank a bottle of *tshitshampa*. They insisted on buying. They had money. Banza had made $10.50, Mutshi, $14.

"Did you see?" Banza said, speaking to me. "Did you see how it works?"

I nodded and said I did.

"I heard a rumor," he continued, "that they are supposed to pay us fourteen [cents] per kilo, but when they get here they pay only twelve."

I had heard the same rumor. So had Mutshi, but he didn't believe it. He stuck to the more established view.

"That's not the way they do it. What they do is fix the scale so it reads ten kilos when there are really twelve. It's a lot easier for them that way."

The two men argued the point while we drained the last of the *tshitshampa*. Then they said goodnight and went home.

The next morning, *Chef de Secteur* Muamba came to my house and asked, if, by chance, *monsieur* had any motor oil to spare for the intemperate Cotonnière motorcycle. My impulse to say no was countered by a desire to do everything necessary to get him out of the village. I gave him half a liter from my stock and watched as he rode off to the next village and the next cotton sale, a cloud of foul-smelling smoke trailing him. Later that day Miteo and Ditu told me they had presented Muamba with their small sack of collected cotton. But the *chef* had brusquely ordered them to dump it in the warehouse without giving them their twelve cents. "I can't pay you for this cotton," he had told the children. "You didn't grow it. You stole it."

14

WHILE THE FISH FARMERS AND I WERE SKIRMISHING WITH Bashiya and the cotton company, Mbaya, my worker, was waging a fight of a different kind. Having just turned twenty, prime marrying age in Kalambayi, he was doggedly searching for a wife.

Unfortunately, his first proposal ended in brutal rejection. It wasn't that he was abusive or humpbacked or anything. He just lived on the wrong side of the tracks. He lived along the upper stretch of the Lubilashi while his *l'ame soeur* lived sixteen miles away along the river's lower reach. Riding my motorcycle down the road connecting the two regions, letter of proposal in my pocket, I began to sense the match was doomed.

Geography and history were the villains working against the marriage. The territory of Kalambayi ran roughly east-west for forty miles along the Lubilashi. The chiefdom had been founded along the lower part of the river, and the villages there had grown large and densely populated over time. With this concentration of people had come modest amenities: the chiefdom's only secondary school, a multi-building Catholic mission, and the sprawling outdoor market on Wednesdays in Katombe.

But nothing of comparable modern sexiness leavened the landscape farther upriver. Once you passed Kabala, the land turned more rural; the villages became smaller and farther apart. The roads, moreover, were the worst in Kalambayi, bush-choked and frequently impassable.

In the universal habit of us-them classifications, the people of upper and lower Kalambayi held prejudices against one another. The downriver people looked on their more isolated upriver neighbors as something akin to poor country hicks. They called them *Bena Tshisuku*, or "bush people." The upriver people, in turn, tended to see the downriver villagers as self-important, bourgeois snobs who lived in villages too crowded for comfort.

This was all absurd, of course. Up and down the river everyone lived in the same basic, traditional way. Everyone was poor. Still, the silly prejudices endured, producing silly consequences. When the UNICEF wheelbarrows were donated to the fish project, for example, a fit of arguing and fractious blather broke out among the fish farmers until everyone agreed on one thing. The snobs would get a wheelbarrow and the hicks would get a wheelbarrow, and only in emergencies would the tools be used in tandem.

Aware of all this, I was naturally less than ebullient that morning when Mbaya handed me his letter of proposal. I was in my house preparing to head downriver to visit farmers. "Give this to Kalanga Fortuna," Mbaya said, his chest expanding.

Kalanga was a fish farmer and tailor in Katombe who had an attractive fourteen-year-old daughter. Mbaya had met her during a recent trip downriver, and now he wanted to marry her.

When I found Kalanga later that afternoon, he was seated under a palm tree outside his house, busy at work behind a treadle sewing machine. The machine was mounted on a cast-iron frame and looked like something out of a 1915 Sears Roebuck catalog. This passed for highly evolved technology in Kalambayi. As Kalanga sewed, his naked and filthy three-year-old son chased chickens around a family hut that tilted slightly to one side. Kalanga took Mbaya's letter, shooed flies from his face, and began reading. A moment later he let go a mirthless laugh. "A *bush man*?" he exclaimed. "I didn't go to a mission school and sew clothes all my life so my daughter could marry a *bush man*!"

Mbaya was standing in the doorway of my house when I returned to Lulenga just before sunset. "What did he say?" he asked.

"She's already taken," I said.

"What? That's not possible. She told me she was free."

"She's already taken, Mbaya. Forget about it."

Rightly suspecting rejection, Mbaya sulked for several weeks. He snapped out of it, though, and resolved to wipe away the stain on his honor by finding another mate. This time he chose a good upriver girl from Ntita Konyukua and her father accepted.

Having sidestepped the upriver-downriver obstacle, Mbaya now faced a more daunting problem: how to pay for his wife-to-be. As part of every marriage, the suitor had to make a dowry payment of $100, two goats, a rifle, and a four-meter-long piece of cloth. It was a truly fantastic sum in this society where a scrawny piece of dried fish divided ten ways was the nucleus of a family meal and where children ransacked my garbage pit every day for tin cans. Asking a young man to come up with so much wealth was just a few notches short of asking him to produce the lost treasures of Atlantis.

The means of acquiring the money were limited. Cotton farming was out of the question, of course. Only a fool would take that route now. And fish farming, although it provided a dependable source of protein and a steady income supplement, was not a get-rich-quick scheme. Besides, it carried a fifty thousand stroke start-up cost. Instead of these, most men met the dowry payment by simply saving and scraping for several years—raising a few extra chickens, farming extra-large plots of corn, and cajoling everyone in the extended family to help with contributions.

But Mbaya had another strategy. With less than seven months left on my Peace Corps contract, he sat me down for a serious talk.

"You know I like my job," he said, "and I want to keep working for you till the day you go back to your people. But do you think you could help me with something?"

There was a dramatic pause. I waited.

"Do you think you could pay me my next seven months' salary in advance so I can get my wife?"

I did the arithmetic. With a salary of 700 zaires per month, Mbaya was asking for 4,900 zaires. His plan was to use the money to buy twelve sacks of manioc and pay to have them transported by truck to Mbuji Mayi. A shortage of food in that diamond-mining town would allow him to sell the manioc at a considerable mark-up perhaps doubling his money. With the cash he gained, he would be able to make a large-enough down payment on the dowry to take his bride while he paid off the balance.

As it happened, I had some extra money at the time and I agreed to the advance. A few weeks earlier I had received from my mother two $20 bills sent from home the usual way: hidden in the hollowed-out interior of a hardback novel to avoid the flypaper fingers of Zairian postal workers. I also agreed to the plan because Mbaya had been a rock of loyalty and friendship since the day he came to work for me a year and a half earlier. His duties kept him at my house much of the time, and we had grown close. So close, in fact, that many of Mbaya's friends and relatives were perplexed when they learned he was looking for a wife. "Why do you want to get married again?" they asked humorously. "You're already married to Michel."

The fact that Mbaya and I spent much of our free time together wasn't the only source of such comments. Much of his work was considered women's work—cooking, washing clothes, drawing water. I didn't realize this made him an object of village jokes until one day I asked him why he always returned from the village water source in a state of great agitation. "They laugh at me," he said. "The women laugh at me because I'm always the only man there. They call me *mukaji wa Michel*. Michel's wife."

The jokes were upsetting to Mbaya, but they didn't change the fact that working for an expatriate and earning a salary were matters of prestige and honor in the village. Thus Mbaya never considered quitting. He remained a conscientious worker and a conscientious son to his parents, using part of his income to help feed the large tribe of children that gathered under his family roof each night.

The most impressive thing of all about Mbaya, though, was his honesty. He had a key to my house, and the opportunities to steal were unbounded. Yet in two years he never took so much as a thimbleful of salt. In fact, he gave *me* money. "This was in your pants pocket," he'd say, handing me a 10- or 50- or 100-zaire note he'd found while washing my clothes at the river. This always moved me. Would I be as honest in his place, I wondered. If I had three brothers and five sisters and parents broken with poverty's worries, would I pass up ten cents that belonged to the foreigner with the motorcycle and cassette player and 35mm camera with power winder and flash attachment? I wasn't sure.

There was one part of Mbaya's job that was never formally articulated in the work agreement. It just developed on its own. At the end of bad days at work, when I'd dismount my motorcycle and walk into the house covered with mud, muttering stories about birds eating fish and ponds leaking water and roads destroying my motorcycle—at the end of bad days like these, Mbaya would administer therapy. He'd listen and shake his head and wait until the whole sad chronicle had passed my lips. Then he'd tell me what a great person he thought I was and how no one blamed me when things got screwed up. "It's okay, Michel. *Kakuena bualu to.*"

He always ended with that phrase. *Kakuena bualu to.* It was a common Kalambayan response to setbacks in life. Literally, it meant, "There's no problem." But a closer translation would be: "Hey, take it easy. Everything's going to turn out all right. And if it doesn't, there's really nothing you can do about it so why not play it cool?" The advice was fatalistic, but following it was often the only way to preserve some measure of sanity.

On occasions when I was really down and Mbaya couldn't bring me around, he'd suggest we play one of our favorite games. It involved my dog—a stumpy, short-haired puppy I had selected from a village litter. The dog's name was Kalambayi and he had a ravenous puppy appetite.

In the evening, after Kalambayi had finished a typically huge bowl of *fufu* by himself, Mbaya would turn to me. "Let's do it," he'd say. We'd watch Kalambayi leave the kitchen and curl up next to the rocking chair for his ritual post-meal nap. As soon as his ears had slackened and his eyes had shut for good, we'd tiptoe outside, open the warehouse doors, climb to the top of the mound of cotton and there bury ourselves under the bolls. Then we'd call him. "Ka-lam-baaaaaa-yiii," we'd yell. Giggling, we'd listen as he ran furiously about the yard barking and whimpering and wondering where the heck we were. We'd call him again. "Ka-lam-baaaaaa-yiii!" Totally confused, he'd stick his head inside the warehouse, catch our scent, and come charging up the pile of cotton all paws and tail. Right before he'd reach us, we'd leap up from the cotton and, in a blizzard of flying bolls, we'd all go rolling down the mound barking and squealing and tackling each other until exhaustion set in and whatever depression had plagued me had passed.

The stiff and sterile patron-servant relationship found between most expatriates and their African workers simply never had a chance with Mbaya and me. Only four years separated our ages. I was too young to feel like his boss, and he was too honest with his feelings to maintain the reserve of an employee. "I think you look funny," he told me at least once a week, trying to get me to shave off my beard.

We were friends. I needed Mbaya. And when he told me he wanted a wife, I was glad to help.

"Now you're sure this plan to buy and sell manioc will work?"

Mbaya and I were standing by my sitting-room table, and my fingers were ready to count out 4,900 zaires. "Yes," he said for the third time. "It will work."

Thus assured, I began counting: "10, 20, 30 . . . 100, 200, 300 . . ."

But as the bills piled up higher and higher on the table, reality began to sink in for me. Forty-nine dollars! With a gun put to their heads and an order given to come up with $5 by the end of the day, half the men in Kalambayi would be dead at sunset. And here I was about to hand Mbaya $49. Quivers of apprehension passed through me.

". . . 1,000, 2,000, 3,000 . . ."

Higher and higher the pile grew. Had Mbaya ever even seen this much money before, I wondered. Could he manage it? I was beginning to hyperventilate just counting it. What was it doing to him? I glanced up, expecting to see a face clouded with anxiety. But he looked serene and collected. He smiled. You're overreacting, I told myself. He knows what he's doing. Be cool. *Kakuena bualu to.*

". . . 3,000, 4,000, . . . 4,900." I threw in another 100 to make it an even 5,000.

"There," I said. "Five thousand zaires." I stepped back from the pile as if it were gold dust and a sneeze would blow it away. Mbaya scooped up the money and left the house.

A week later, he clambered on back of an eleven-ton, rusting and road-scarred Mercedes truck. It was the first merchant truck to come to upper Kalambayi in three weeks, and it was bursting with corn and manioc and people. "See you in a week," Mbaya yelled down from atop his twelve sacks of manioc. "See you in a week," I said. The truck rolled plaintively out of the village, and as I watched Mbaya grow smaller in the distance, his face beaming with confidence, a surge of emotion passed through me. I was proud of this guy.

Within twenty-four hours of Mbaya's departure, my life went into a funk. I dragged myself home from an eleven-hour workday and promptly tried to blow myself up by using too much kerosene to light a cooking fire. When the flames died down, I called Miteo from next door and sent him to fetch water to boil rice. By the time he returned, the fire had gone out and I had to light it a second time, almost blowing myself up again. When I finally finished cooking, I discovered something that my dog, despite his fierce appetite, wasn't crazy about: charred rice. He ate it anyway, of course, avoiding the more horribly burned pieces, but he pouted the rest of the evening.

Things continued at this piteous level for the next few days. Then they got worse. I ran out of clean clothes toward the end of the week, and my dog and everyone else in the village began to sniff and frown conspicuously in my presence.

But somehow I survived, and the seventh and final day of Mbaya's trip found me sitting on my doorstep wishing I had Roman candles to welcome him home. I waited anxiously. But afternoon gave way to twilight, and twilight to night, and still I was waiting—in vain. He never came. Not on the seventh day. Not on the eighth day. And not on the ninth.

While I tried to imagine what was holding him up, my domestic crisis intensified. On the tenth day, losing weight and becoming a growing olfactory blight on the village, I decided to act. I found Ilunga Ngoyi, Mbaya's best friend, and asked him to work for me. I explained that there had been a slight, unexpected delay in Mbaya's return.

The delay turned out to be more than slight, however. The two-week mark came and went, and still no Mbaya. I grew concerned. Was he ill? Had there been an accident? Had he been robbed? Whatever the case, I fully expected a letter any day explaining the situation.

No letter came.

Meanwhile, Ilunga was complicating my life.

I jumped up from the sitting-room table one evening and spit a mouthful of fried tilapia out the front door.

"Ilunga!" I yelled into the kitchen. "What did you do to these fish?"

"What? What is it?" he said, running out. "My cooking doesn't please you?"

With a fork, I lifted the side of one of the remaining fish on my plate and, to my horror, saw a pristine network of entrails. I showed Ilunga. He slapped his forehead. "I completely forgot to clean them."

At the three-week mark, I noticed something peculiar happening in my kitchen. My supplies of powdered milk, sugar, salt, palm oil, and kerosene somehow had developed hyper-accelerated half-lives since Ilunga's arrival. They were disappearing on their own. Just as strange, in the last week and a half I had been dramatically cured of my life-long habit of leaving money in my laundry. Ilunga never found a thing when he washed.

Then there was the case of the brown drinking water. "Why is it brown?" I asked Ilunga, holding a cup under his nose. Pressed, he admitted that he had stopped going to the village source and was instead filching water from his grandmother's clay holding vase at home. The women at the water source had been laughing at him. "I'm not your wife," he told me ruefully, "and I don't want to go there and have them call me that."

Four weeks. Mbaya had been gone four weeks. He had vanished. His parents had heard nothing. I queried travelers from Mbuji Mayi, but no one had seen him. Disappointment and worry washed over me each day like ocean tides. What in the world had happened? I debated whether to go look for him, but no one in his family was sure where he was staying, and the thought of walking the crowded backstreets of Mbuji Mayi calling his name struck me as useless and absurd.

About this time, what had started as a murmur in the village rumor mills was now on just about everyone's lips in Kalambayi.

"Mbaya is gone," people were saying. "He's made a fool of Michel. He's taken his money and left for good."

"Impossible," I told myself. I ignored the talk.

Five weeks. Ilunga's thievery continued. I confronted him and warned him to stop. With every day, meanwhile, my pining for Mbaya grew. The person who had once saved me from fever was now killing me with his absence. I longed for his friendship, his work, his honesty. I clung to the hope of a letter. But the days continued to pass without a word, and I began to feel myself slipping in to the throes of a slow death. I struggled, descending, through the stages.

Denial: "There's got to be a good explanation. Mbaya would never stay away this long intentionally. He'll be back any day and he'll explain it all and I'll see he hasn't betrayed me. He has *not* betrayed me. I'm sure of it."

Anger: "Another day. How could he do this to me, dammit? Why didn't he tell me his plan might take this long? He knows I need him here. I'm paying two salaries—his and Ilunga's—and getting peptic ulcers in return."

Depression: "No one to wrestle with in the cotton warehouse. Can't play Dylan—makes me think of him."

And, finally, after seven weeks, acceptance: "The rumors are true. Mbaya is gone. He's used me. There can be no other explanation now. He's taken 5,000 zaires of my money and escaped to the anonymous slums of Mbuji Mayi where I can never hope to find him. This had been his plan all along, to maintain a front of honesty 'til near the end and then make the big kill."

Then, just when the hurt was unpacking its bags for a protracted visit, a letter. It was written in Tshiluba, barely legible, and full of spelling errors.

> *Michel,*
> *How are you? I have not died. I have not left you. But there have been problems. I do not know when I will be*

*home. I am staying with my cousin. This is the third letter I
have sent. Have you gotten the first two?*
   Mbaya Bukasa

I took the letter down to a string of ponds outside the village
and read it again, quietly trying to imagine what "problems"
could justify Mbaya's staying away from his job and his family
for seven weeks. Unable to think of anything convincing, I threw
the letter away and pronounced our relationship over.

Eight weeks. It was late Sunday afternoon. The gloomy
loneliness that had settled onto my house was most conspicuous
on Sundays, my day off, and I had taken to drinking *tshitshampa*
as a countermeasure. I was growing aware of my increased
drinking generally, but it would be a few more months before I
admitted the truth about the habit.

On this Sunday, my neighbor Lengos and I were sitting
outside over a bottle. He was explaining, I believe, how his
brother had recently spotted a mermaid in the Lubilashi, when,
in the distance, walking down the road into Lulenga, Kalambayi
running circles around his ankles—Mbaya. I rubbed my eyes
and slapped my face and pinched my skin, but he was still there,
walking closer. At the sight of his signature smile and dark,
leaping eyes, I knew I couldn't stick to my decision. I couldn't
play the role I had intended, that of the proud, rejected partner
who would be strong and refuse when the guilty half returned. I
was a weakling. I rushed up to Mbaya and hugged him.

After a long, overwrought greeting, with both of us
laughing and then almost crying, Mbaya told me his story. He
told how Kabemba Pascal, the truck owner, had gouged him,
charging a criminal rate to transport his manioc. He told how
the price of manioc in Mbuji Mayi had been lower than he had
expected. After expenses, he had only 3,000 zaires, a 2,000-zaire
loss. Then he told how he had foolishly lent that sum to his

diamond-digger cousin, who promised to pay it back after two days but who immediately disappeared. Mbaya had searched the streets of Mbuji Mayi for his cousin for weeks before giving up and returning home without a single zaire in his pocket.

I needed clarification on the last part.

"Nothing?" I said. "You don't have *any* money?"

"Nothing," he said, shamefaced. "I had to borrow money for the truck ride to Kabala. I walked the rest of the way."

Five thousand zaires—gold dust—lost forever.

We both knew what was coming next. I launched into a severe lecture outlining my case against him. He should have made sure a message got to me sooner (his first two letters were given to unreliable friends); he should have returned after four weeks no matter what; he should have better appreciated my situation, and so on. The speech went on for a while, but the sight of Mbaya ten pounds lighter from languishing moneyless in the city made my grievances seem a bit frivolous. I left out a lot of details and rehearsed passages.

When I finished, Mbaya was silent for a moment. Then he looked at me with timid eyes.

"*Kakuena bualu to,*" he said. It was clear from his tone that this was more a question than a statement.

I looked back and my response was automatic. "*Kakuena bualu to,*" I said.

It was true. There was "no problem." Mbaya was free to come back, and I wouldn't ask him to pay back the salary for the two months he was away. But on a deeper level, there *was* a problem. A serious problem. Mbaya's failed money-making project pointed up with shattering force the limitations at work in his life. Later that day, I began asking detailed questions about his trip and discovered that, aside from the loan, the real reason the project failed was that Mbaya hadn't properly calculated the costs, market prices, and profit margin involved. He hadn't done this because he couldn't. Six years earlier, a contaminated cup of drinking water had left him deathly ill and forced him to drop out of school at a fifth-grade level.

Now, at twenty, he had great trouble with multiplication and division. Unable to make accurate calculations himself, he had let the merchants he dealt with calculate for him, and they had taken advantage of him at every step: the truck owner, the marketers he sold to, the tax collector in the market. I reproached myself for not having recognized Mbaya's vulnerability beforehand. He had received enough education to want to try this project but not enough to make it succeed. I should have made the trip with him.

It was late and the village was sleeping when Mbaya and I ended the marathon of talking our reunion had become. He left the warehouse and walked wearily toward his family hut, a silver arc of moon guiding him past grass roofs. After he left and I was alone, the meaning of his trip continued to grow in my mind, pointing toward an inescapable conclusion. Mbaya was a cripple. I had always hoped his future would somehow amount to more than just farming with a hoe and raising fish like the others. But what hope of advancement beyond the village level did he have? What opportunities?

In addition to the limitations imposed by the country's grievously depressed economy and the bleak future facing the whole continent, Mbaya could barely read and write, and he had trouble with basic arithmetic. He was lame. Like so many other Kalambayans his life would be one of manual labor and commerce no more sophisticated or profitable than selling bananas one by one in the village market. Perhaps I had known this fact all along. Perhaps the trip to Mbuji Mayi was just elaborate confirmation of it.

Mbaya's story wasn't unique, of course. Failure was as abundant as air in Kalambayi. It was there in Chief Ilunga's first harvest, there in Kanyenda's numbing poverty, there in the sullen faces of cotton farmers gathered around my house on payday. But Mbaya's problems affected me differently. His were more like my own. We practically lived together, bound by a compatibility so great it was almost spooky. Indeed, according to most villagers, we were married. For these reasons I felt more deeply the sadness of his failure.

There was another factor at work here too. Mbaya was my looking glass. On my bedroom wall there hung a small rectangular mirror whose surface had grown covered by a thick layer of dust. I had brought the mirror from the States stuffed inside my duffel bag, but the monstrous struggle I saw outside my door each day lessened the urgency of making sure my hair was combed just right every morning. The mirror went largely unused. But regularly seeing one's reflection may be a psychological need I hadn't fully appreciated because, having scorned my mirror, I found myself using the closest thing around. I used Mbaya. When I looked at him I saw my own reflection. We were of close enough age and disposition that this was easy to do.

What I saw in Mbaya wasn't a spitting image of myself, but a version of myself. It was a version cast by accident in this inhospitable Third World environment just as I had been cast by accident in the gilded West. We were essentially the same person. Chance had just put us at different ends of the global river, with its upper and lower stretches just like the Lubilashi. Realizing this, realizing that Mbaya was me trying to make it in a different place, my greatest hopes had gone with him when he left with his twelve sacks of manioc. I wished for his success as if it were my own project. And when he walked back defeated, I saw myself walking back, and at that moment the whole tragedy of African poverty was laid bare to me as it never had been before.

Who was I? What did I want to do with my life? To answer these questions had been one of the reasons I had left home for work in Africa. Was I a writer? A teacher? A businessman?

A social worker? Living on this distant continent, divorced almost entirely of things familiar, I had hoped to give myself the freedom to unlock the right role. A bounty of opportunities lay at my feet. I just had to pick one.

And Mbaya? Who was he? After being with him for so many months, I knew these same roles, these same potentials, lay in him. None would ever be unlocked, however. When he came back penniless and dejected that Sunday afternoon, it was clear the key had been thrown away.

Yes, except for the future, the similarities between us were great—age, demeanor, likes, dislikes. So great were they, in fact, that I was almost afraid to wipe away the dust that had gathered on my bedroom mirror and take a look. I was afraid I might really see Mbaya looking back, and at that moment I would become him. My work boots would give way to ragged sandals, my body to bony black shoulders and calloused feet. And all the books in my house would suddenly appear as nothing but pages and pages of lines and squiggles, and numbers would confuse me so much I'd have no choice but to stay on this land and drag a hoe through the soil, hoping to someday save enough money for a wife.

And after a few months my friend Michel would leave and I'd hug him and wave goodbye. I'd have a vague feeling that part of me was leaving too. I'd want to go with him. I'd even ask him to take me along. But we'd both know I couldn't go because I was really already married, not to a woman, but to this village and this land. I was already taken.

15

At least Mbaya didn't lose everything in Mbuji Mayi. He was gone a long time, but when he returned to Kalambayi he was still alive, his heart was still beating. In a real sense, it was something of an accomplishment. Many Kalambayan men left for Mbuji Mayi and returned in coffins. Nothing but bad things seemed to happen in that city.

One evening I was sitting in my bedroom taking off my boots after a day of work when the news ripped through the village. Another coffin was coming.

"Kasongo Mujinga is dead," my neighbor Mulumba was telling his wife outside. "Someone heard it on the radio from Mbuji Mayi."

I listened through an open window as Mulumba continued. "There was nothing anyone could do. The dirt fell on top of him. It covered him up. He had stopped breathing by the time they found his body."

I knew immediately what Mulumba was talking about. Kasongo, twenty-five, had left Lulenga three months earlier to prospect for diamonds in Mbuji Mayi. Like hundreds of other local men, he had gone hoping to make it rich digging along the banks of the Mbuji Mayi River. And like so many others, he wouldn't be coming back the way he left. The wall of his mining pit had collapsed, burying him under a ton of dirt.

The irony was grim and unnerving. Before leaving for the city, Kasongo had talked to me several times about doing fish work. He had planned to return home to build a few ponds if his prospecting trip didn't bear riches.

But there would be no ponds now. Kasongo was dead and his family was in mourning. His mother and sisters began their public weeping that night, walking through the village with their heads thrown back in anguish, screaming that God had buried their son alive, and now the body was coming home so they could bury it a second time, dead.

Again, as grotesque as Kasongo's death was, it wasn't an uncommon way to die in Kalambayi. During my two years, more than three-quarters of the villages lost at least one man to the devouring diamond pits of Mbuji Mayi. This shocking death rate didn't diminish the flow of prospectors to the city, however. Almost every village man journeyed out of the bush and into Mbuji Mayi at least once in his life. Some went for a few months. Some, like Kanyenda Mushia, went for ten years. They went searching for that one-in-a-million find that would put $5,000 or $25,000 or $50,000 in their pockets the way cotton and manioc and fish could never do.

So great was the lure of diamonds, in fact, that during my second year much of the challenge of my job shifted from finding new fish farmers to hanging on to the ones I already had. About 20 percent of the men I worked with took off for Mbuji Mayi during my tenure, leaving their ponds in the temporary custody of wives and children. Mutombo Mukendi left for the city less than a month after Kasongo's death. Mutombo was a gentle-spirited fish farmer with a body so large everyone called him "the tree." The afternoon he told me he was departing, I shook his mammoth hand, wishing him luck, and begged him to be careful. Saying goodbye this way to men headed to the mines was always a strange and terrifying experience for me. What do you say, after all, to someone you're not sure you'll ever see alive again?

"They're wasting their time," Mupeta Mudinda used to tell me each time a new man left for Mbuji Mayi. "They think they'll get rich, but there's no money in diamonds. If you manage to stay alive, you come back after three or four months with a thousand zaires in your pocket. What kind of work is that?"

Mupeta was the schoolteacher in Lulenga. He was twenty-six years old, intelligent, and was a qualified critic of the mining process. In his late teens he had dropped out of school to try his hand at prospecting. But after two hard and luckless years, he had given up on the mining work and returned to finish his high school studies, joining the trace element of people in Kalambayi with diplomas. When I moved to Lulenga, I found him struggling on an inconsiderable teacher's salary. I persuaded him to build a fish pond.

For most of the time I knew Mupeta, his diamond-digging days assumed the air of a bad war experience. He never talked about the mines other than to mention what dangerous, grueling work it had been and how he never wanted to go back to it. But in the end he did go back. I lost Mupeta as a fish farmer because, as much as he hated the prospector's life, he hated the poverty, limitations, and frequent irrationality of village life even more. He hated the fact that he had to plant fields like everyone else and that there were few people in the village with whom he could discuss even half the things he read in the collection of worn-out books he kept inside his house.

For several months, Mupeta carried on a debate with himself, trying to decide whether to leave the village and all of its frustrations. This went on without my knowledge. Then something happened to tip the scales for good, sending him running to Mbuji Mayi. There was a scandal: Mupeta collided with the village soccer team.

It started with an ultimatum. The soccer team gave Mupeta seven days. If, after seven days, he hadn't ripped up one-quarter of his cornfield, the players would do it for him. At issue was the fact that Mupeta had planted his corn right behind the goalposts at one end of the soccer field. The team was embarrassed by this. Visiting squads would think they practically played in the middle of a farm, they said. But the corn had grown several feet by the time the team complained, and Mupeta refused to remove a single stalk. Thus, the countdown began. The whole village held its breath, secretly relishing the excitement of a conflict pitting a schoolteacher against the young toughs of the soccer team.

When, after three days, it became clear that the players were serious, Mupeta went to Chief Mbaya seeking adjudication. But the chief's reasoning powers were clouded by the fact that his son was the team's star forward. He ruled against Mupeta, declaring that the corn had to go. Buoyed by the decision, the players began inviting everyone in the village to watch the destruction party on Sunday afternoon.

"They're barbarians," Mupeta told me after the meeting, speaking in French with an expansive vocabulary born of anger. Five days had passed since the ultimatum was made. Time was running out. "Do you realize what a serious offense it is to destroy someone's crops? It's primitive. The fact that the corn doesn't even interfere with their playing makes it twice as primitive."

We were sitting at Mupeta's pond, feeding his fish, both of us having decided this was the best place to retreat and discuss the crisis. I had special feelings for this pond because I had dug half of it myself. Mupeta's teaching job had left him little time for pond construction, so for two and a half months, working mostly on weekends, we had shoveled together, lifting and throwing two thousand cubic feet of dirt.

But those determined digging days seemed fixed in an innocent, faraway world as Mupeta and I now girded for the humiliating public showdown facing him in two days.

"They've got to be bluffing," he said of the team. "They won't do it. I know they won't."

He was wrong. Sunday afternoon arrived and so did the soccer team. Mupeta appeared at my door at 4:00 p.m. "It's done," he said. "They pulled up the corn. I watched them do it."

I offered him a chair. "I'm sorry," I said.

"Don't be," he responded abruptly. "It doesn't matter anymore. It just doesn't matter."

"What do you mean? Why not?"

"Because I'm leaving, that's why. I've been humiliated. It's impossible for me to stay here now."

"Where are you going?"

"To Mbuji Mayi—as soon as I can."

His hardened air of resolve took me by surprise. "But you said you'd never go back."

"Well how can I possibly stay here? I'm the only person in this whole village with an education, but you'd think I couldn't read or write the way I have to scramble and deal with this village mentality. I'll go insane if I stay here any longer."

In most respects, he was right. The chiefdom was a dead end for him, the last place he had expected to be after twelve years of school and rising expectations. Never would it provide the clothes and stereos and other trappings of modern life featured in the *Newsweek* magazines I gave him and which he hung covetously, page by page, on his bedroom walls. Only one thing could provide those things. "Diamonds," he said. "I'm going to mine again."

I tried to talk him out of it, raising the same issues of safety and low pay he had raised with me on other occasions. But there was no changing his mind. He stayed only long enough to harvest his pond. Then he packed everything up and left for good with his wife. Shaking his hand goodbye, I felt those usual farewell feelings invade me. I was sickened and frightened by the thought that his could be the next mining death broadcast on the Mbuji Mayi radio station.

So now Mupeta was gone and Mutombo was gone and Kasongo was dead. And there were about a half dozen other fish farmers presently prospecting for diamonds in Mbuji Mayi. "Come visit me when you're in the city," Mupeta had said before leaving. Four months later I decided to honor his invitation. After all these months in Kalambayi, I knew relatively little of substance about the mining process that so affected my work and the lives of the men I worked with. I wanted to visit Mupeta and explore as much as possible the city's diamond trade. As it happened, I already had the perfect guide for this: Mbaya. During his eight-week nightmare wandering through Mbuji Mayi, he had practically memorized every street and alley. I figured this made him as qualified as anyone to lead me through the vast ghettos where the diggers lived and down into the mining pits where so many of them died.

———

Steeling ourselves for the slow and tiring seventy-mile motorcycle ride, Mbaya and I set off for Mbuji Mayi on a morning in late December. We would be gone three or four days, long enough for me to pick up my quarterly paycheck, buy some supplies, and take a trip to the mines.

It was an hour before we were out of Kalambayi and bouncing down the northern side of the Katanda hills. We followed a dusty road past a succession of villages and through long stretches of open countryside. Women floated over the crests of hills, carrying firewood. Funeral drums, their beat wild and sad, rushed toward us from ceremonies in several villages. Up ahead the Lubilashi appeared, bowing northward into the distance.

During the three-hour trip we saw no more than a dozen trucks, each itching and rolling along the abysmal road with a knot of people and merchandise rattling in back. Soldiers at three military roadblocks along the way waved us through when they saw the government emblem on my motorcycle.

Three miles outside Mbuji Mayi the dirt road gave way to something fantastically rare in Zaire: asphalt. We entered a paved road. I let go a whoop and relished the smooth surge in speed. The road continued along a ridge for a short distance before descending sharply to the Mbuji Mayi River and the city of eight hundred thousand people along its banks. A quilt of shabby, tin-roofed houses spread itself across the valley floor and up the sides of surrounding hills. To the north, the spire of a large Catholic church rose high above the roofs, cutting into a sky made somewhat hazy from the smoke of the city's hundreds of thousands of daily cooking fires.

Central to the view of the city was the helter-skelter spread of crude mining pits that stretched out from both banks of the river. The pits gave the area the look of having suffered heavy aerial bombardment. Miners with shovels and pickaxes worked all along the river except to the west, where a barbed-wire fence—interspersed with watchtowers, searchlights, and soldiers with rifles—kept peasant diggers out of the diamond-rich area controlled by the government diamond company. Taking in this sight from the ridge, speeding closer and closer to the filthy slums along the valley floor, I was reminded like a slap in the face what a coarse, lawless, overcrowded prospector's town Mbuji Mayi was.

A few minutes later, Mbaya and I crossed the city's main bridge and I dropped him off near the neighborhood of Kasavubu, where he had family. We agreed to meet in two days. I then rode for ten minutes through a maze of dirt streets, arriving finally at the regional Peace Corps office.

Located in one of the few relatively affluent areas of the city, the Peace Corps office was a white stucco building with a bureau inside for the regional director and bedrooms for visiting volunteers. Like most houses of any value in Mbuji Mayi, this one had a twelve-foot-tall security wall around it with pieces of broken glass protruding menacingly from cement on top. The wall was a precaution against the city's high crime rate, which was spurred on by hungry diamond diggers who often stole anything they could to get food for themselves and their families. Thievery was at its worst in March and April when the flooded Mbuji Mayi River inundated mining pits, interrupting the city's income and causing widespread hunger and misery.

When I arrived at the office after dropping off Mbaya, I knocked on the back gate and Tshiteya, the resident cook, let me in. Inside I picked up my mail and found Karen Sundberg sitting in the courtyard. An attractive, fair-skinned fish volunteer posted twenty-five miles south of Kalambayi, Karen, like me, had just arrived to pick up her pay. We promptly made plans to visit Mbuji Mayi's largest outdoor market the next morning, both of us needing to pick up supplies. I also hoped to find Mupeta there. According to a letter he had sent me a few weeks before, he had put off diamond digging for a while by taking a job selling shoes in the market with his brother.

The thirty-minute walk to the market the next day took Karen and me through the city's main commercial district, which had the look of a frontier town in the American West. The dusty streets were lined with one- and two-story shops, each shop possessing a wide veranda and a plaster-faced front. As we walked, a steady flow of overloaded trucks and taxis trundled by, expelling nose-searing fumes from misfiring engines. Most of the city's people moved on foot, however, carrying goods on their heads or pushing crude, metal carts. Deep gullies, forged by rain and noxious open sewers, ran along most streets.

When we reached the market, Karen and I paused. It was huge—a crowded, twenty-five-acre spread of stalls and outdoor tables buzzing to the accelerated tempo of commerce. Seventy-five percent of the men in Mbuji Mayi were diamond diggers, and this was where they and their families came to spend whatever cash they squeezed from the mines. Surveying the vast throng of people bargaining and hustling and haggling over wares, Karen and I braced ourselves and went in.

To the uninitiated, an African market can be a startling thing. You don't visit such a place. It's poured all over you. You walk in, move about, absorb a billion bits of sensory data, and then walk away with your body limp and your faculties tingling. An African market is a sunburst of colors: brightly patterned *pagnes*, orange and pink and gold bars of soap, deep-crimson palm oil, multi-colored species, yellow bananas, amber papayas, red tomatoes. It's a landscape of odors: fresh bread, spoiled fish, tangy oranges, pungent peppers, woodsmoke, human sweat, human urine. It's a carnival of noises: talking, shouting, singing, chopping, pounding, bleating, barking, crowing, and always, always laughing. People laugh in African markets. Despite their clamor and confusion, the markets maintain a cheerful air.

Pushing and squeezing through the crowd, Karen and I collected at various tables the vegetables we had come to buy. We moved next to a labyrinth of narrow alleys lined with stalls in the fashion of a bazaar. The alleys were thick with the steely, Latinesque sound of Zairian pop music blaring from cassette players in various stalls. The music was scratchy, from pirated tapes, but the upbeat mix of horns and silky-fluid vocals seemed to energize the market-goers, moving everyone along as if by gentle electric current.

In the section of the market reserved for the sale of shoes, we looked for Mupeta. After some effort, we found his brother, who told us it was Mupeta's day off. He gave me directions to Mupeta's house, suggesting I visit him there the next afternoon. I said I would, and Karen and I continued through the market.

Rounding a corner, we nearly bumped into two men begging for money. They sat crouched against an alley wall, their hands held up imploringly. One man was an albino with pink, mottled skin and the other a toothless old man with crutches and a face cratered long ago by acne. To the latter I handed 20 zaires. His lolling head straightened for a moment. "May God give you many days on Earth," he said.

These words were still lingering in my mind when, a few minutes later, I came across something that jolted me and made me stop in the crowded alley. Karen, who didn't notice I had stopped, kept walking. She came back after a moment and found me still staring at the sight. "What?" she asked.

I pointed. Standing before us were Bruce Lee and Jesus Christ. Bruce Lee was shirtless, his muscles like steel bands and his body set in a challenging position, ready to rip out the heart of some wretched foe. Jesus Christ, arms outstretched and beckoning, wore a robe and a thorn of crowns. They were posters, one a promotional poster for a movie, the other a wall calendar from The World Council of Churches. They were hanging side by side from packing crates stacked in a V formation and facing out toward the alley like some consecrated shrine. The display was shocking and weird, but not out of stride with the character of this city, I thought. Karen and I stared at the posters for a moment before the stall owner asked if we wanted to buy one. We told him we didn't and began walking back to the Peace Corps office.

⸻

"There are two ways to dig for diamonds with a shovel," Mupeta was telling me. "The one you choose depends on how hungry you are."

We were sitting outside his mud-brick house in Kasavubu, the crowded, noisy, relentlessly dreary Mbuji Mayi neighborhood where a large number of Kalambayans lived. I had found the place despite the atrocious directions his brother had given me. Now we were discussing diamonds. I was going down to the riverside mining area with Mbaya the next day, and Mupeta was opening up on the subject, preparing me for what I would see.

"One way to dig," he said, "is to dig a large hole and to layer it so that you have large steps that lead down gradually to the depth where the diamonds are [about fifteen feet]. This is the safe way to dig. There's little risk of the dirt caving in on you because the walls of the mine are layered. They're short and stable. But this method takes a long time. It takes a team of five men about two weeks to dig a hole like this. You need to have enough money and food to support yourself and your family during this period.

"If you don't have enough money, and you start to get hungry, then you have to dig the second way, which is more dangerous. You have to dig down quickly to the diamond level and find diamonds quickly in order to feed yourself. So you dig a steep hole, with no steps, or perhaps one. You go straight down. It's faster that way. But that's when you get into trouble. A tall wall of dirt is almost always unstable. It may come falling down on you while you're digging. Before you know what has happened, you're buried under a mound of dirt. Then they read your name on the radio."

He was referring to the government radio station in Mbuji Mayi, the one that had broadcast Kasongo's death back to Lulenga. Three times a day—at 12:30, 4:00, and 6:00 p.m.—it announced the names of people who had died in and around the city the day before. It cost seventy-five cents to have a name read, the goal being for relatives in the city to notify relatives in the villages to come help take the dead home for burial. According to Mupeta, at least one or two diamond diggers were on the list every day, having suffocated in collapsed mines.

"Do you think it's safe for me to go down there?" I asked him, referring to the riverside digging area. I had heard that conditions at the pits bordered on anarchy. Different gangs competed for control of different sections. The gangs had their own Mafia-style protection system and they intimidated independent diggers. I also knew that government soldiers patrolled the pits, alternately controlling and being controlled by powerful digger gangs.

"You're going with Mbaya, right?"

I nodded.

"Well, you're going to see a lot of men standing around buying and selling diamonds. They're nervous because most of them don't have government licenses to handle diamonds. They bribe the soldiers. So don't ask any questions or get involved in anything. People are going to think you're a big diamond *patron* or something from Europe because you're white. They're going to be suspicious. If you see a fight or an argument, walk in the other direction."

I asked Mupeta if he had ever seen or been involved in fights at the pits. He threw back his head and enjoyed my naiveté with a laugh so loud I almost took offense. Violence was a permanent fixture of the digging area, he said. He told me a few battle stories, including how he once absorbed the butt of a soldier's rifle during a government shutdown of the mines and how, on another occasion, he had watched a man named Kalonji Muenda, one of Mbuji Mayi's most notorious gang lords, get into a fight that resulted in his opponent biting a large U out of his ear and spitting it on the ground. "Now Kalonji's ear is like a symbol of how tough he is," Mupeta said. "He carries the wound with him. You see him digging at the river or walking along the road or at a bar drinking beer, and he has this big, perfect U missing from his ear."

While we were talking, Mupeta's wife brought out a meal of *fufu* and dried fish. The conversation changed over dinner. Mupeta inquired about his old fish pond back in Lulenga. He had sold it to me for $20 before moving away, and now Miteo and I were feeding the fish. Everything was progressing nicely toward a February harvest, I told him. The village was well too, I added, except for the soccer team. The players had mysteriously lost every match but one since rending his crop. Mupeta laughed at this. "It sounds like they need to replant some corn behind their goalposts."

After the meal, we walked to an outdoor bar where we sat on empty beer crates and drank a quart-sized bottle of stout Zairian beer. Surveying the ramble-down shacks that lined the neighborhood's narrow dirt streets, I found it hard to tell whether the standard of living here was higher or lower than in the villages. For many, it was clearly lower. There was no shortage of children with distended stomachs bulging under tattered shirts. There was no shortage, either, of large rats that ran about unafraid through most houses at night, Mupeta said. And for all its intoxicating promise of modernity, Mbuji Mayi was a city where the vast majority of residents lived in slums like this, with neither electricity nor indoor plumbing.

I rose to leave just before sunset, mounting my motorcycle and accepting Mupeta's wishes for a safe trip to the mines. Then I followed a dirt road back to the city center, battling holes, gullies, and exposed rocks the whole way.

───

Mbaya was in a foul mood when he arrived at the Peace Corps office the next morning to escort me to the diamond pits.

"I found Nsomue," he said morosely.

Nsomue was his cousin, the one who had finished off Mbaya's money-making scheme by "borrowing" 3,000 zaires.

"And?" I asked.

He made a hissing sound through clenched teeth. "He's spent all the money," he said. "But he promised to pay me as soon as possible. He says he's working to get the money back."

We both knew what that meant. *Wayi kuabo.* End of story. He would never see the money again.

We began the hour-long walk to the river. It was 6:30, and a few people were out in the city's commercial district. After passing the main market we entered the monotonous ramble of neighborhoods that would continue all the way to the river.

Most of the men in the neighborhoods had already left for the diamond pits, leaving behind women and young children who sat outside houses listlessly passing the early morning hours. A young woman with a child suckling at her breast stared at us dully beside the rusting carcass of a Toyota pickup truck. A teenage boy with polio-withered legs crawled outside a dirty Red Cross dispensary. A naked baby girl sat in the clearing outside one house, enthusiastically putting dirt in her mouth as she watched us pass.

About a mile from the river, the street we were following began to descend with increasing severity. As it did, it grew wider and more eroded until, close to the river, it was nothing but a series of gnarled gullies and ravines cascading down a hillside crowded with ramshackle houses. Like mountain goats, we picked our way. I was concentrating so hard on not falling into one of the gullies that it was a few minutes before I looked up and noticed the diamond pits. We had arrived. An ugly warren of mines and excavated dirt stretched out haphazardly just below us, continuing for several hundred yards across a flat area to the river. More pits lay on the opposite bank, visible through a faint morning mist hanging above the river.

Like figures in a dreamscape, thousands of men stood scattered across the dirt, busy disfiguring the earth. Many were shirtless; most were barefoot. And as if spewing from giant gopher holes, dirt flew skyward every few hundred feet, launched by the shovels of unseen diggers inside mines.

The scene was stupefying, calling to mind all the fantastic crudity of open-pit gold mines in Brazil. This was the digging domain of the freelance prospectors. The government mining company, equipped with cranes and dump trucks, left this area to the peasant diggers while claiming for itself better areas farther upriver. The fence in the distance separating the two areas was guarded with machine guns mounted on tripods.

When Mbaya and I reached the bottom of the hill, we were greeted by the sound of pickaxes striking rocks and shovels entering dirt. Mbaya's brother worked with a team of diggers along this stretch of the river and we hoped to visit him.

While Mbaya asked a resting digger for directions, I walked to the edge of the first pit I came to and looked down. It was about thirty by thirty feet at the top and was dug according to the first (and safer) method Mupeta had described, with three giant steps leading down twelve feet to the bottom. Three men worked below, two tossing dirt out of the mine with shovels while a third used a crowbar to dislodge a large rock. The dirt was dark red, like spilled blood, and the dust from it settled on the diggers' bodies, turning their hair a lurid orange. It was 7:30 a.m. and already the men were sweating heavily as if they'd been working nonstop through the night. They wore weary, haunted looks.

I walked to a second pit. A digger near the top was startled by my white skin. He recovered and smiled, his teeth flashing white against a brown face streaked with dirt and perspiration. His limp, yellow T-shirt read: PA. SPECIAL OLYMPICS.

"*Oh, monsieur blanc*," he said, launching into poor French. "Are you come for buying the diamonds?"

I shook my head no. The digger lifted his shovel up to me. "Then why not you come down for digging the diamonds with us for a time?"

I jokingly thanked him and refused the offer.

Mbaya tapped my shoulder. He had gotten directions to his brother's digging team, and we set off through the confusion of mines and men. As we walked, I was quickly struck by how young many of the diggers were. Some couldn't have been more than ten years old, and at least a third were younger than twenty. Clearly, there were no government regulations covering age or anything else here. The two soldiers I saw standing near the river seemed to have no greater purpose at the moment than to smoke cigarettes and absent-mindedly finger the pistols on their hips.

Mbaya and I came to the deepest mine we had seen yet. "They're almost to the diamond level," he said, pointing to the diggers.

The men were far below, working quickly. This was the stage at which trouble often broke out.

The diamonds lay in a horizontal vein about fifteen feet below the surface. When a group of diggers reached this level, hostile gangs of five to ten men often arrived to try to oust the rightful mine owners and harvest for themselves the fruits of two weeks of work. Faced with an attack, diggers could flee, fight, or, if they were connected to a larger federation of diggers, call together enough men to persuade the gang to back off. The soldiers who roamed the area usually intervened on one side or another depending on which side offered the largest payoff.

Such confrontations didn't occur at all mines, but they happened enough that a feeling of tension and vigilance hung in the air. The diggers were constantly looking around, apparently ready to scramble from their holes at any moment to confront an advance. I, too, remained on alert. I secretly inspected the ears of every man I saw, prepared to turn around at the sight of a horseshoe-shaped void.

Mbaya was getting annoyed because we couldn't find his brother's digging team. I followed him past a long series of mines, all the while trying to determine the best moment to do something slightly risky. I looked around and decided now was a good time. We had passed two soldiers since arriving, but here, farther upriver, none was in sight. I took off the knapsack I was carrying and pulled out my camera.

The act made Mbaya frown. He had told me several times that he didn't think taking pictures here was a good idea. Without government permission, photographs were forbidden in most of the country. The state was particularly sensitive about mining areas like this, considered "vital" to the country's national security. But I wanted some photos, so I started snapping.

I had taken a half-dozen shots at two mines when, adjusting for a vertical shot of a digger climbing out of a pit, I heard Mbaya.

"Look," he said.

I turned. He was pointing. I followed his finger. Fifty yards away to the right was a soldier I had somehow overlooked. He was standing at the edge of a mine, outfitted in a standard military combination of beret, mirrored sunglasses, and fatigue pants tucked inside combat boots. He didn't say anything. He didn't gesture. He just stared at me as if giving me time to realize what a stupid thing I was doing and how he was prepared to demonstrate just how stupid it was.

I gave myself a couple of swift inward kicks and decided the best thing to do was to approach the soldier voluntarily. I walked over, camera in hand, beating back thoughts of dank tropical prisons and trying to remember how much cash I had in my pocket.

"*Bonjour*," I said.

"*Bonjour*," the soldier said curtly. "*Qui etes vous?*"

Feeling the hot scorch of his mirrored sunglasses against my face, I introduced myself. I told him I worked for the department of agriculture. But my hopes of impressing him were flattened by his stern, unchanging expression.

"Is it okay if I take some photos here?" I asked.

"Why are you asking me now?" the soldier said scornfully. "You've already been taking photos."

"No, no," I said. "That's not what I was doing. I was just adjusting for light and distance."

I was sure he knew I was lying, and I sensed that things were about to get unpleasant.

"Why are you here?" he asked. "And why have you brought a camera?"

They were good questions. If I wasn't the first "European" witness to wander through these mines, I was probably part of a group so small that the suspicion in the soldier's voice was justified. Was the *mutoka* a spy?

"Curious," I said. "I was just curious."

"*Pas des photos,*" he said bluntly, with anger. "*Absolument pas des photos.*"

"*Oui, oui,*" I said, putting away my camera. "*Ça va. Je comprends.*"

I waited for him to ask for my film or, worse, to order me to follow him to some military office where I would be questioned at length. But he said nothing more, and I bade him good day.

"I told you so," Mbaya murmured, working hard to match the brisk pace that now carried me, sighing, farther upriver.

"He must have been hiding," I answered. "I never saw him."

We put several hundred yards between us and the soldier before stopping. A crowd had gathered around a certain mine. We went over to have a look. At the bottom, three men held square sieves made of fine wire mesh. The men had reached the final stage of the mining process. They were looking for diamonds. With great care, they removed shovel-loads of dirt from the mine floor and sifted the dirt through the sieves.

Although some mines turned up nothing, a typical find, according to Mupeta, was three to five small diamonds of varying quality. Such a find might bring in about $75. For a team of five diggers working for two weeks, that came out to a dollar a day. The diggers sold the diamonds to government-licensed buying agents or to various hustlers, smugglers, and loan sharks who stood around the mines wearing poker faces, ready to deal.

The diamonds weren't worth more because they were of low quality, valued not for jewelry but for various industrial uses. Among other things, their super-hardness made them useful as blades for cutting other diamonds or as drill bits in underground exploration.

Altogether, the diamonds along the Mbuji Mayi River—one of the largest deposits of its kind in the world—brought in hundreds of millions of dollars to the national treasury in Kinshasa. Yet virtually none of that money found its way back to the provinces in the form of development projects. It accumulated instead around the president, Mobutu Sese Seko, and a small class of corrupt elites around him. Mobutu's personal fortune, built on diamonds and other natural resources in the country, has reportedly grown to $5 billion, making him one of the wealthiest men in the world. Five *billion*.

Moving through the mines that made the president so rich, Mbaya and I were having problems. We had been unable to find his brother's digging team and we were now walking more or less aimlessly through the digging area. Since arriving, we had passed several dangerous pits—the kind dug according to the second method Mupeta had described—and now we looked down at another one. I cringed. The team of diggers had dug almost straight down, with only one narrow step, so that the mine resembled a giant trench. Vertical planes of dirt, frightfully vulnerable to the laws of gravity, led down, down, fifteen feet down, to two men hurriedly sifting dirt at the bottom. The men were hungry.

A cave-in at such a mine wasn't a mere possibility; it was a constant threat. The members of the team not digging or sifting dirt stood near the mine, keeping an eye on the walls. If a crack appeared, streaking across the dirt face, the watchers would scream and the men at the bottom wouldn't even look up. They would know what was happening. They would scramble up ropes or makeshift ladders, trying to reach the top. And if they didn't make it, if they disappeared under an avalanche of red dirt, the mad rescue would begin. Word would rocket through the mines and for a moment, the fractious, strife-ridden mining ethos would be put on hold. All the nearby diggers, irrespective of gang or allegiance, would come running from every direction, soldiers too, trying desperately to save those trapped below.

"You have between ten and fifteen minutes," Mupeta had told me. "After that you recover a body, not a person."

Any man who had spent more than a month digging in Mbuji Mayi was sure to know someone—a friend, a relative, an acquaintance—who had been swallowed by a mine. Back in Kalambayi one afternoon, Kalanga Fortuna, the fish farmer and tailor in Katombe, had told me about a digging accident involving his best friend years before. Without warning, a mine wall had given way and his friend had vanished.

"I was up top when it happened," Kalanga said. "The dirt dropped so fast that no one was sure exactly where he was when it happened. We had to guess. Other diggers came, and we chose a spot and started digging. We kept digging and digging and I was screaming: 'Where is he? Where is he? Too much time is passing.' We didn't find him on the first try, so we started digging at a different spot. As we worked I kept thinking: 'Time. Time. Time. Time.' It kept going and going and then I knew it was over. We weren't reaching him fast enough. When we found him, we pulled him up and shook his body. He didn't move. We kept shaking him and yelling at him to wake up, but he was dead."

Not all the mining victims die of suffocation, though. In the hysteria of the rescue, shovels kill too.

Kabaseli Kazadi, a mechanic who worked for the government fish project in Ngandajika, had two teenage sons who were caught in a mine. I saw Kabaseli a few days after the accident, and he explained what happened. "My oldest boy told me he saw the crack in the wall first and screamed and started climbing out. But the mine wall fell down on him and pinned him against another wall. The force broke his arm in two places. His whole body was buried except for his head. His head was sticking out of the dirt, and he was screaming for help. Other men came and dug around his head and pulled him out.

"But my other son was far below. About fifteen or twenty diggers were trying to find him. They dug in one spot and found nothing. They dug in another spot and found nothing. Then a shovel struck something. It was his head. Blood started coming up from the dirt and spreading everywhere in a pool. The diggers pulled him out. He was alive, but his head was badly cut from the shovel. He's in the hospital now, and we don't know if he'll live."

He did live, I learned later, and eventually both he and his brother resumed prospecting.

Mbaya and I were still standing near the edge of the dangerously wrought mine, peering down at the men working fifteen feet below. The disbelief that had been mounting inside me all morning was coming to a head. I turned away and glanced up and down the riverbank at orange-haired men and swinging pickaxes and dirt spewing skyward from mines. Even knowing the village hardships that pushed them here, it was hard to see what made these men accept the risks and wretchedness of this Hobbesian place. It was hard to understand why so many of them played Russian roulette, spinning the chambers round and round until one fell into place with a click that said, "Dig straight down and we'll see."

Only a few answers seemed to make any sense at all. First, as far as I could tell, the fact that digging might kill the miners was a threat similar to what cancer is to a cigarette smoker, only raised to a higher power absurdity because the risk was immediate. If, his stomach aching, a prospector had to dig vertically, he did so under the assumption that the worst wouldn't happen to him, even though he watched it happen to those around him every week.

Second, there was hope. It sustained the men, sparkling in their minds like the small diamonds they unearthed and held up to the sun's rays. The hope was of making a really big find.

From time to time, under a particular ton of dirt, a team of diggers found a particularly large deposit of diamonds. Then into their pockets tumbled several thousand dollars, sometimes more. It didn't happen often, but the fact that it happened at all apparently was enough to fuel the dream, enough to cause men to leave family and friends and fish ponds back in the villages, where poverty was permanent, guaranteed.

Every man knew that hitting the big money was like participating in a lottery: If you didn't play you didn't win. To have any chance at all, you had to pick up a shovel and dig. So every day along the banks of the Mbuji Mayi River, thousands and thousands of men played. They maimed the earth and they maimed each other. A few got rich, a lot more died, and the rest stayed poor. Meanwhile, the president prospered and the industrial world got its diamonds for use in oil exploration and for crafting fine jewelry.

Tired and directionless, Mbaya and I walked away from the steep-sided pit we had been viewing, both of us agreeing it was time to leave the mines. I was afraid of what we might see if we stayed any longer, afraid of the lifeless, twenty-five-year-old bodies that might be exhumed before the morning was out.

We took a different course back to the city, heading west along the river for several hundred yards until we reached a paved road. We were walking along the road's shoulder, gravel crunching under our feet, when I turned around and saw a red jeep coming in the distance. On impulse I stuck out my thumb.

"What are you doing?" Mbaya asked.

"Hitchhiking," I said.

"What's that?"

"If you have luck, it's a way to make cars stop."

We had luck. The jeep rattled to a halt. It belonged to a Catholic mission in the city. From the passenger window a robed Zairian priest silently waved us in. As we made our way toward the city center, passing a dirty roadside blur of bicycles, shirtless diggers, and merchants carrying goods, I felt myself growing more and more anxious to leave this vile and violent Third World city. I had seen up close the kind of world Kalambayan men entered when they came to Mbuji Mayi, and it had left me in a dark mood. Only the knowledge that I would be back in Kalambayi later that afternoon provided relief.

While the priest and his driver talked in the front seat, I kept looking out the window. I tried to recall the last time I had hitchhiked and almost laughed when I remembered it was during my fisheries training in Norman, Oklahoma. I had wandered down a country road looking for a place where I could teach myself how to raise fish. The driver who picked me up then had been a Christian, too, one who was certain I was going to save Africa from all its suffering. That seemed like such a long, long time ago now.

16

I MANAGED TO AVOID TWO THINGS DURING MY FIRST TWENTY-one months in Kalambayi. I avoided attending one of the mud-hut Christian churches found in every village, and I avoided the worst crisis that can befall a fish-culture extension agent. But with three months left on my two-year work contract everything changed: The fish crisis happened, driving me, praying, to a Sunday church bench.

Katenda Kambowa was the fish farmer standing at the center of this drama. A short, solemn man with deepset eyes, Katenda was one of the last people I helped to build a pond and his was by far the most problematic. Soon after he began digging, a dam-burst of misfortune flooded through his life, leaving us both wrecked.

It started with a toothache. Two weeks into the pond construction, Katenda's tooth erupted in a fury of pain. Desperate for help, he sought me out in Katombe where I was spending the night in Ilunga Clement's backyard guest hut. The flame of the candle I held quivered when I opened the door, casting weird shadows against Katenda's body. His mouth was so swollen, his face so distorted, that at first I half-believed I was seeing one of the macabre night spirits that Mbaya was always warning me about.

"It's my tooth," Katenda managed.

Deep inside his mouth, inside a right rear molar, he had an infected cavity. It had begun as a funny pinch of hurt six days ago, he said, and now he spent all his time hunched over in a chair, unable to eat, not wanting to talk and wishing he didn't have to breathe.

Perhaps no aspect of Africa's poverty is more obviously cruel than the fact that poor people have teeth that go uncared for. Eventually, those teeth rot and burst with pain. When that happened in Kalambayi, people came to me.

"Please give me some gasoline," Katenda said, handing me a small tin cup.

We walked over to my motorcycle parked outside. I disconnected the fuel line where it entered the carburetor and gave Katenda a half-inch shot. He put the gas to his lips, poured it in and swished it around. The sight made me wince. It always did.

According to villagers, a little gas this way helped kill the infection and reduced the pain. The first time a man came to my house asking for gas for this purpose I refused. The idea repulsed me and its effectiveness seemed dubious. But people kept coming and coming—some walking tens of miles, crying, begging, mouths swollen—until finally I agreed. From then on, three or four times a week, I doled out gas to the sick of mouth. On some days, in some villages, I drew such crowds that an observer might have thought I was a missionary dispensing Bibles or a famine relief worker dispensing supplies. But that wasn't the case. I just had gasoline and the villagers around me had teeth that wouldn't let them sleep at night.

Katenda spit out the gas, thanked me, and began the two-mile walk back to his village, Bena Mbaya. The treatment worked. The next day he was able to eat. After four days the swelling went down. After five days he was back to digging his pond.

As it turned out, though, the toothache was just a warmup. It had slowed Katenda down. It hadn't stopped him. The really debilitating blow would come later—when he finished building his pond.

For eight weeks, always with a tattered straw hat cocked on his head, Katenda dug his pond, tangling with some of the driest, hardest, angriest red dirt Africa had to offer. The site had seemed perfectly normal when we chose it. It lay next to a stream in a wide, flat valley outside the village. But when the digging began, the dirt at Katenda's site proved to be inexplicably hard, like nothing I had seen before in Kalambayi.

Where it was possible, Katenda shoveled the dirt directly. Where it wasn't, he attacked it first with a giant wooden club, breaking it up jackhammer fashion into pottery-like shards and then shoveling it. In the afternoon after school, his thirteen-year-old son Juney (as in Juney Kennedy, the American president, Katenda told me) helped him dig. But eventually the work overwhelmed the two of them.

When this happened, Katenda took all his money, $2, and bought eight bottles of *tshitshampa*. He set the bottles on one of the half-finished pond dikes and threw a digging party, inviting all the men in his village to dig in exchange for face-numbing shots of whiskey. A dozen men ventured forth and for eight hours, beginning at ten in the morning, dirt flew over the pond in dusty, erratic trajectories until, in a happy spasm of drunken enthusiasm, the men wound up digging the pond a full six inches deeper than necessary.

"Stop! Stop!" Katenda had to yell down at the besotted diggers, flailing his arms from atop one of the dikes. "Stop digging! It's done. Put your shovels down and go home and sleep."

Looking up, the diggers dropped their shovels, smiled dully and began the slow walk home.

It was over. The pond was finally finished. Now, like all new ponds, it stood awkwardly empty, yearning for water the way a naked man yearns for clothes. Katenda opened a bamboo inlet pipe and sent a silvery stream splashing in.

Then something very, very bad happened.

——

Digging a fish pond always required a considerable leap of faith on the part of village farmers. There was no guarantee the ponds would work, after all. They were built not with concrete or plastic, but with mere dirt. All the digging—tip to the ground, push it in, pull it up, throw the dirt, fifty thousand times—was based on a faith that this crumbly, gritty, humble soil would hold tons of water. But would it? Would it hold water every time? Wasn't it possible that somewhere, sooner or later, the soil would be faulty? Perhaps porous? Somehow unworkable?

The chance that this would happen generated in me a fear that never went away. I called it the "what if?" fear. What if, I asked myself, a villager accepted the gospel of fish culture, invested countless sweat-hours of work in a model pond, and then the thing really didn't work? What if, when added, water just vanished into the pond-bottom soil? What would I do? I wasn't sure. It was like contemplating violent death. Even after helping build several dozen ponds without a glitch in Kalambayi, I couldn't dislodge the "what if" fear from my brain. Every time ground was broken for a new pond, the fear thumped inside me, faintly perhaps, but always enough to let me know it was there. With Katenda it thumped too.

For several days, Katenda added water to his pond. It gurgled in. It gushed in. It spilled onto the pond-bottom slope—and nothing happened. A four-inch-deep pool formed at the lower end of the pond and stubbornly refused to grow deeper. After a week, with water entering twenty-four hours a day, I grew very concerned. Most ponds were full after three or four days.

"It's the soil," I told Katenda, theorizing with outward confidence during my weekly visit. "It's just really dry here. Add another inlet pipe. With double the water, the pond will start filling up."

When I came back the next week, having done a week's worth of fretting and worrying, there were not two but four bamboo pipes entering the pond, each delivering a generous three-inch-wide column of water. But to my dismay, the pool at the bottom was still barely ankle deep. The water was simply disappearing. Katenda told me that when he closed the pipes the pond was completely empty in twenty minutes.

"It's not working," he said. "My pond isn't filling up with water."

An icy block of panic clamped itself down somewhere near the pit of my stomach. I couldn't believe what I was seeing. Failure was impermissible. The stakes were too high. Staring at the pond, I could only think of how much Katenda's eight kids eventually would suffer—at meal time—if all of papa's weeks of work turned out to be wasted time.

"It's not working, Michel," Katenda repeated. "The water refuses to stay."

"Okay, okay—let's think about this," I said nervously, wondering if Katenda could hear the "what if?" alarm bells clanging between my ears with their message: *This is not a drill. This is not a drill.*

"Are there any termite colonies below the pond bottom or below any of the dikes?" I asked.

"No. I've already checked."

"Did you leave any tree stumps or roots in the dikes when you were digging?"

"No."

"Did you pack the dirt tightly?"

"Yes, yes, I did."

"Well then what's the problem, Katenda?" I snapped, frustrated, scared. "Why isn't your pond filling up with water?"

"I don't know," he said. "I thought you would know."

I *was* supposed to know, but I didn't. At least, I wasn't sure. I suspected the water was passing through small cracks in the super-hard clay. The only thing to do, I decided, was to stay the course. I told Katenda to keep adding water, hoping that the pond-bottom dirt would loosen and seal the passages that were allowing water to escape.

"We'll just have to wait," I said. "There's nothing else to do." He agreed.

"It's in God's hands now," he said, "not ours. We need to pray to Him for help."

Katenda was a deeply religious man, and back at the house, as I was preparing to leave, he repeated his point. "I'm going to pray as hard as I can for God to make my pond work," he said. "And Michel I want you to do the same. You're involved in this too. I want you to pray for my pond when you go to church on Sunday."

I stiffened for a moment, unsure of what to say. Should I tell him the truth, that I wasn't a believer? I was fairly confident he already knew this. Virtually everyone else in Kalambayi seemed to. From the day I arrived in the chiefdom, my habit of not going to church had caught people's eyes, causing them to shake their heads. Like my lack of children, it placed me in an orbit of hopeless oddity. This was a society where everyone held some kind of spiritual belief, whether in Christianity or sorcery or mermaid worship, or, more likely, some combination of the three.

But when I looked at Katenda's face—so earnest and heartbreaking, a face as big and sad as the history of Africa—I decided I couldn't tell him the truth. I would honor his request. What could it hurt? I was running out of solutions anyway. "All right," I said. "I'll pray for your pond at church."

"You promise?" he asked.

"I promise."

—❦—

Four days later, Saturday, I was up to my forehead in thick savanna grass, perspiring heavily and asking my neighbor Lengos what church I should visit to fulfill my pledge to Katenda. With my Peace Corps contract winding down, Lengos had finally decided he wanted a pond, and we were in a valley outside Lulenga searching for a site.

Or at least I was searching. Lengos was spending half his time anxiously looking up and down the valley as if we were being followed. Every few minutes he would stand on his tiptoes, thrust his head above the grass like a periscope, and peer in every direction. I was familiar with this behavior. Lengos was one of my best friends, and he had a serious problem: He was young, unmarried, and strikingly handsome, with a pair of sparkling, angry-sad eyes that drove young women all over Kalambayi into fits of desire. He found it necessary to disappear into the bush from time to time to escape the three or four jealous and competing women who usually courted *him* simultaneously. Now, to the detriment of the pond search, he was convinced a recently spurned beauty was stalking him, ready to break his kneecaps.

His paranoia was making me angry. "Will you please stop looking around and concentrate on the pond?" I said.

Lengos stared down at me, still on his tiptoes. "You mean you didn't hear that?"

"Hear what?"

"That sound. Like someone sneaking up on us."

"I didn't hear anything. All I know is I'm the one doing all the work here."

"Hmmm. Well, all right. But I'm *sure* I heard something."

He took one last look around and began hacking the grass with me again.

"Now what was it you were telling me," he asked, taking us back to our original conversation.

"I was telling you about Katenda's pond. It won't fill with water, and I'm not sure what to do about it. It's worrying me to death. It's failing."

"Yes, that's terrible," he said. Then he laughed unexpectedly. "Wait a minute. How do I know my pond won't turn out the same way as his? No one's put a curse on your work or anything have they?"

"*Mon Dieu,*" I said. "How can you make a joke about this? This is serious. I can't sleep at night because of it, and I told

Katenda I'd go to church and pray. Now you've got to tell me the best place to go."

"Okay," he said. "I'll help you. But what do you want? Do you just want to go and watch a church ceremony or do you want to participate in one?"

If I just wanted to watch, he said, I could go to the one-room Catholic church near the soccer field or to the Presbyterian church down the hill. These were both rather conservative, orthodox places established by missionaries years before. If I wanted to get more involved, however, I could go to any number of local Christian sects that have taken the faith—in whole or in part—and infused it with doses of African ritual and mysticism. I could, for example, paint my face white as a sign of inward purity and dance and pray all night under the stars with the Bena Lupemba Church. Or I could worship in the Pentecostal Protestant Church where members, caught in the spirit, speak in tongues and practice faith healing.

But Lengos didn't recommend any of these. He had a better idea.

"You need to go see the priests of the Bena Malemba Church," he said.

"Who are they?"

"They're the priests who walk on fire."

This must have been a rather secretive, shadowy church because, unlike the others, I had never heard of it before. "They really walk on fire?" I asked. "Barefoot?"

"Yes. That's what makes them so powerful. And I think they can help with this pond. But they don't meet regularly and they don't meet in a building. The priests roam through Kalambayi and start building bonfires in the bush spontaneously, outside different villages. Then word goes out to the worshippers."

I was fetched by the idea of seeing the fire-walkers. I told Lengos to come get me if there was a ceremony the next day. Otherwise, I planned to visit the Catholics.

When, after another hour of searching, we couldn't find a good pond site, Lengos and I called it quits. The late-afternoon sun was falling fast, leaving the valley awash with a radiant rush of amber light. I was anxious to get up to the house because I wanted to drink. My blood was whistling its afternoon call for *tshitshampa*. It was a call that had grown louder and more urgent each day as my remaining time in Kalambayi shrank and I had ever more frequent senses that I had not accomplished all I wanted to.

As for Lengos, he had his own reasons for wanting to call off the pond search: His heart wasn't in it. It hadn't been from the start. He was too vulnerable to the distractions of youth, too bothered by all those women who chased him, to be a serious fish farmer just now. In the end, we never resumed the search.

Tired and thirsty, we followed the path back to the village that afternoon with Lengos insisting on walking in front. He did this as a precaution against attack, keeping those stunning eyes of his opened wide for aggrieved nymphs skulking in the grass, ready to leap forth in ambush.

The next morning I received word from Lengos that there would be no fire-walking ceremony that day, so I went to the Catholic church in Lulenga to pray for Katenda's pond.

The mud-and-thatch structure was full of people and music when I arrived. I took a seat on a log bench toward the back. To my left, a group of five musicians was playing a traditional village song using tom-toms and percussion shakers and a xylophone made of wooden keys. The song, overlaid with Christian lyrics, had a fast, thumping, infectious beat. It swirled around me, leaped inside me, passed between my toes. In front of me were about two dozen men and women worshippers sitting on benches. Covering the dirt floor was a multitude of children. Virtually everyone was clapping and singing and swaying to the music. Already I was beginning to sense this was going to be a church service like none I had ever attended before.

At the head of the church, with adults seated before him and children at his feet, with drums beating and xylophone zinging, Mutombo Mulengela, the church catechist, stood dressed in a gray, short-sleeved suit behind a wood pulpit. He swayed back and forth, eyes closed, rocking to the beat like everyone else. Twice he raised his arms and cried out in the swell of music, "Yes God. Come to us. We are your children. Come to us now God."

As if to answer his plea, a four-foot-wide ragged hole in the church's grass roof was busy letting in a thick column of sunlight. In slightly slanting rays, the light passed in front of the pulpit and illuminated the width of two benches. The hole had been caused by a recent wind storm. Looking up, I could see clouds and blue sky.

After about five minutes, the musicians abruptly stopped playing and everyone stopped clapping and singing. An older woman then rose from a bench and knelt before the pulpit. With her hands cupped to her mouth and her head cocked heavenward, she released in the local fashion of extreme joy a yelping banshee-like scream that seemed to never end. The ear-piercing sound startled me terribly, but clearly pleased all the other congregants very much. They nodded their heads and clapped their hands in approval, leaving me to wonder just what Lengos had meant when he called this church *orthodox*.

When the woman finished screaming, she calmly stood, made the sign of the cross on her chest, and took her seat. The signal had been given. Sunday mass had officially begun.

Mutombo welcomed the congregation with a brief prayer. Then he guided everyone through a catechism he read from a book at the pulpit. As things progressed, the shaft of sunlight poking through the damaged roof periodically disappeared and returned as passing clouds obscured the sun.

The homily was about a group of Old Testament believers put to death in ancient Egypt. Telling the story, Mutombo used most of the common Tshiluba names for God, including: The Creator of Earth and Sky, The Fish Net, The Man with Many Eyes Like a Basket Used To Hold Chickens, The Light That Hurts the Naked Eye, The Man Who Can Cross on Top of Water Like a Spider, and, the catechist's apparent favorite, The Hatchet That Does Not Fear Chopping the Thorns of Palm Tree Nuts.

"Obey my laws and you will have eternal life in heaven, said The Hatchet That Does Not Fear Chopping the Thorns of Palm Tree Nuts," Mutombo explained to the congregation.

After the homily, Mutombo requested a moment of silence, instructing everyone to pray for personal needs. This was my cue. As best I could, I prayed for Katenda's pond to hold water. When I finished, I silently surveyed the people still praying on benches around me, their heads bowed and their eyes closed. What were they praying for? I wondered. The survival of a child stricken with dysentery? A yield of one more sack of corn from the next harvest? The safe return of a son digging diamonds in Mbuji Mayi? So many needs. So much to pray for. No wonder Christianity—or rather the hybrid, village-ized Christianity found here—has taken such hold. "Obey my laws and you will have eternal life in heaven," Mutombo had just told the flock. That sounded pretty good to people whose present life offered $170 a year for hard work and shots of motorcycle gasoline for toothaches.

The mass ended and the musicians launched into a final, fiery piece of music that escorted the congregation outside into the noonday sun. Having fulfilled my obligation to Katenda, I left the church and went off to do what I did most Sundays. I drank *tshitshampa* all afternoon with Lengos and a few other friends until I could barely find my way home.

The prayer didn't work.

I arrived at Katenda's pond Monday morning aching for good news. I found instead the same depressing sight. The water was only four inches deep, the pond still a huge, worthless, gaping embarrassment. Katenda stood on the upper dike waiting for me, his appearance the pure image of a crestfallen man.

"I sit here for hours," he said, "and just stare at the water. Every once in a while I start to think it's nudged up a little and I get excited and I grab my measuring stick. But then I put the stick in and see that there's been no change and I sit back down and keep watching. It never changes."

I faced the truth. The pond was a failure. Left to itself, it clearly would never fill with water. After a lot of thinking, Katenda and I decided there was only one thing left to do, and it would be painful. He would have to line the pond bottom with a layer of riverbank clay taken from the stream fifty feet away. Transporting and applying the clay would be almost as much work as digging the pond itself, but it was the only way to try to salvage the pond.

"I'm sorry," I told Katenda later, choking on a black sludge of guilt as we sat in chairs outside his house. "This has never happened before. The soil seemed okay to me. It was an unlucky site."

"It's all right," he said. "It's not your fault. It happened and I have to accept it."

"But I feel responsible," I said. "It's like I deceived you. I told you the site would work."

"Look, you didn't do this," he said. "It was God who did it. God doesn't want me to have a pond."

As sympathetic as I was of Katenda's situation, I was growing quite weary of his reliance on the heavenly boss to explain everything.

"You know Katenda, I really don't think God has much to do with all this. It's the soil. It was hard, unlucky soil. And besides, it's not over yet. The clay might work."

"You're wrong," he countered. "God has everything to do with this. And if the clay does work it will only be because He has changed His mind and decided I can have a pond."

A sharp feeling of frustration and déjà vu moved through me. With minor variations, I had had this exchange a hundred times before with a hundred different village farmers. Like Kanyenda and his DDT spirits, all the men stuck tenaciously to the view that accidents and free will played no role in steering human life. God controlled events. Or if not Him, then some black-magic spirit. And if not that, then something else—the soul of a deceased ancestor perhaps. I considered it a failure that in two years I had been unable to alter the views of even one farmer in this respect.

Back in Lulenga that evening, Lengos was equally stubborn. I told him about the pond's continued failure and he said he wasn't surprised. I had prayed for assistance at the wrong church, he said. The Catholics didn't have sufficient command of God's ear to get Him to fix a leaky pond. If I truly wanted results I would have to visit the Bena Malemba fire-walkers. They had real power. "They make crippled people walk and crazy people sane," he said. "I've seen it myself. And they can do something about this pond."

My skepticism of spiritual remedies, fairly great to begin with, had grown stronger since the Sunday mass. Still, I was becoming increasingly fascinated with this cult.

"Okay," I said. "When can we see the fire-walkers?"

"I'll let you know when they come around again."

But Lengos let me down. The Bena Malemba came two weeks later, holding a worship session in a valley outside Lulenga, and he failed to alert me.

"It was *fantastique*," Lengos said afterward. "There must have been five or six priests who walked across the fire. And they cured a lame woman."

I was too upset with him for forgetting me to care much about his description. He tried to mollify me by saying he had spoken briefly with one of the priests about the leaky pond and had been assured the matter would be given the cult's attention.

Two more weeks went by and there were no more opportunities to see the fire-walkers. But back in Bena Mbaya, the health of Katenda's pond began to change. The repair technique worked. After lining the pond bottom with clay, Katenda started adding water until, with steady sureness, it rose to the top of the dikes and stayed. Never have I been so happy, so utterly relieved of dread, as the moment I crested that valley ridge and looked down at the deep pool of water gleaming and glittering in Katenda's pond. A few days later we stocked the pond with 250 fingerlings. When the last of the fish entered, Katenda and I collapsed on the dikes sighing the thunderous sighs of two men who had just outrun several salvos of bullets.

On the way home that afternoon, I cornered every person I knew, spreading the news—"It works! It works! Katenda's pond has fish!"

"Of course it does," Lengos said when I reached Lulenga and told him. He promptly informed me that it was the Bena Malemba priests who had rescued the pond. "Give credit to those who deserve it," he said.

"I'll give credit to the clay Katenda used, if that's okay with you," I said. "Besides, how can I credit a group of priests I've never seen before." My desire to view the Bena Malemba had not diminished, but my faith in Lengos to take me to them had. "I'm still not convinced they exist."

"They exist," he said. "I'll take you to see them soon."

A week and a half later, he kept his word, arriving at my door late at night. "They're going to be in [the village of] Kalula tomorrow morning," he said. "I'll be by to get you."

I went to bed excited, but unsure of what to expect the next morning from these men reputedly able to cure everything from polio to ponds that won't hold water. Lengos swore the

Bena Malemba were Christians, but the fire-walking ceremony sounded African in its soul, as African as the flaming sunsets over the Lubilashi each evening and the wood-carved *mukishi* fetish perched outside Kanyenda's home.

It was cloudy and windy and unusually cool at 5:30 a.m. when Lengos came rapping at my door. Using my flashlight in the darkness, I started my motorcycle and Lengos hopped on back for the two-mile ride to Kalula. As we drove, the wind grew stronger, seeming to portend the approach of a thunderstorm. In head-on bursts it blew against my face and chest. Palm trees swayed and banana leaves flapped wildly in the night-stabbing shine of my motorcycle headlight.

It was still dark when we reached Kalula. Lengos told me to park next to a trail that led into the valley. The village had a deserted look. No one was stirring. The only noise other than the continuing swoosh of wind came from a lonely-sounding cowbell clanging under someone's eave. I began to wonder if we had the right place. "Yes, yes," Lengos said. "We're almost there."

We entered the bush and walked a few minutes, passing no one. Then, to the left, about three hundred feet away in a clearing, a crowd appeared in the night air. There must have been two hundred people. From the distance their bodies looked sinister—dark and oddly misshapen, huddled in a large circle around the glow of a bonfire. The wind-whipped grass hissed all around them, and as we got closer I could see that the women in the crowd were wearing *pagnes* draped over their heads for extra warmth.

Wanting to get as close as we could, Lengos and I made our way through the spectators until we reached the circle's inner space and stood facing the bonfire. The fire had been burning all night and was now a long, red heap of coals. From fifteen feet away, I could feel its warmth spreading over my chest and arms. I looked around at the men, women, and children crowding along the edges of the inner circle. Their faces, faintly illuminated by the fire, contained looks of fascination and reverence as they watched the priests.

There were four priests. They stood inside the circle wearing red silken skullcaps and matching robes that hung to their bare feet. Down the chest of one, the oldest, flowed a long black beard. All four men stood in a line to the right of the fire chanting prayers before a group of sick and crippled people who had come to be healed. There was a young boy on crutches, a cross-eyed, mentally retarded man, and three women who Lengos said were barren. To secure for themselves the fire's curative powers, the priests rubbed cooled ashes on their cheeks, leaving them lightened.

Then, one by one, they did it. The priests walked across the fire. My hands tightened into fists as the first one went across. His arms were outstretched and his lips moved to the rhythms of unintelligible incantations as his bare feet touched glowing coals. His face never flinched. The others followed.

The wind, meanwhile, had not relented. It blew harder and harder as the priests performed their ritual, and I was sure it was going to storm very soon. I remember looking around and thinking how strange and spooky everything seemed— the ghostly orange faces of people in the circle, the continuing swoosh of wind, the hypnotic chants of the priests as they crossed the fire, the crippled child waiting to be cured.

So compelling was the scene that for a moment it was easy to imagine this was the only thing happening on Earth, that we were on a vast, angry plain with nothing but darkness and empty space stretching away forever all around us. It was as if after two years I had arrived, finally and indisputably, at the secret place where village ills truly were cured. On this valley slope, amid these powerful priests, the laws of sickness and suffering so uncompromising by light of day, so confounding to locals and foreigners alike, were laid low by the ageless strength of African magic. The magic really existed. Here was proof. Or so it seemed for a while. So it seemed until the ceremony's strange, disillusioning end.

After the priests had crossed the fire once, they circled around and passed a second time. Then a third time. Then a fourth. On each crossing, the last of the four men, the one with the beard, did something disturbing. Instead of taking four measured steps across like the others, he lingered for a moment in the middle of the fire, standing motionless on the coals. He seemed to be testing his endurance. The pauses became slightly longer each time and it was very uncomfortable to watch.

Following their fourth trip across the fire, the priests walked back to the group of afflicted people. The men seemed to be in a trance now. They jumped up and down in place, springing into the air and chanting their prayers more loudly. The bearded priest jumped higher than the others and chanted the loudest.

It was starting to get light out. I looked up and saw storm clouds rolling across the slate-gray sky from the north. A few minutes later it began to rain: not hard, but in scattered drops. Lengos and I put on the raincoats I had brought. Some people in the crowd began leaving, hurriedly scooping up children. But most stayed.

The priests moved back to the fire and walked across it four more times. Then all but the bearded one returned to the sick people and continued to pray, their backs turned to the fire. The bearded one stayed to make more trips across. Again he paused in the middle of the fire each time and the pauses grew longer and longer, unbearably so.

On his fourth pass he stopped so long I feared he was burning his feet. On his fifth pass he stopped completely.

Seconds went by—one, two, three . . .

He didn't move.

. . . four, five, six . . .

He didn't move.

Watching, I began to hear my heart pounding in my ears. The man's feet had to be burning by now. A faint, nervous rumble rose from the crowd. The other priests, praying off to the side, didn't see what was happening.

More seconds passed—seven, eight, nine, ten, eleven . . .

The mumbling and commotion in the crowd grew louder. Finally a woman yelled out: "Get off. Get off the fire." But the priest didn't move. He didn't lift his feet. He was manifestly out of control, bent on burning himself up. There were more shouts, and finally the other priests looked over. They rushed to the fire, grabbed the man's arms, and pulled him off. He fell to the ground and immediately started rubbing the tops of his feet and yelping in pain as if he had just woken from a dream and realized what he had done. He tried to stand but couldn't.

It was raining harder now. People were leaving in a panic. Inside the circle, a woman lifted the crippled boy and hastened away. Lengos was pulling at my sleeve. "Let's go," he said. "Let's go back to the village."

I didn't respond. I kept watching the injured priest, barely believing what I had seen.

"Come on," Lengos repeated. "He's all right. It's raining. Let's go."

But the priest wasn't all right. His feet and ankles were badly burned. He tried to stand again only to collapse back to the ground with a grimace. Two of the other priests took his arms, wrapped them behind their necks, and helped him up. Then the trio moved past the fire to the path, their red robes now dirty and getting wet, their ash-covered cheeks streaked with rain. The ceremony was over. The priests headed back to the village behind the crowd.

17

Inside a white, U.S.–government envelope, the letter arrived. I opened it. It was from Brian Steinwand, my Peace Corps boss in Kinshasa. After a few opening platitudes, he quickly got to his point. "Why don't you stay in Kalambayi a third year," he wrote. "Postpone your return to the States and keep working. We need you where you are."

I finished the letter and laid it on my desk, not wanting to read it a second time. Brian had written before and this was his final, last-minute plea. A recent diplomatic squabble with Washington had prompted the Zairian government to stop issuing visas to new American volunteers. As a result, it was uncertain whether another extension agent would ever arrive to take my place in Kalambayi as previously planned. Hence, Brian wanted me to stay. He wanted me to sign up for a third year. He didn't want the post to lie vacant.

The letter left me torn. There were many reasons to accommodate Brian's request. I agreed with him that it would be a shame to leave the post empty. Kalambayi was now one of the top fish-farming regions in the country, and there was still great room for expansion to the east, on the other side of the Mvunai River. My hard-won knowledge of local conditions, moreover, would surely make a third year even more productive than the first two.

Yes, a strong case. Stacked up like the tons of cotton under my warehouse roof, all the facts argued I stay. They argued I keep working with these peasant farmers. All the facts but one, that is: *tshitshampa*. Slowly, for the past two years, I had begun downing more and more of the local spirits until now I was afraid. I was afraid of what living in Kalambayi was doing to me. I was drinking too much.

I picked up Brian's letter, folded it in half and turned it over in my hands. Trying to produce a decision, my mind wandered back to the beginning, back to the day I took my first burning swallow.

———

It was in Lulenga, barely twenty-four hours after I arrived in the chiefdom and unpacked my duffel bag. My neighbor Mbaya Mutshi came to my door, led me to his house for a visit, and then disappeared. He came back a few minutes later with a bottle of clear liquid in his hand. "*Tshitshampa*," he said, pointing to the bottle. "*Tshitshampa*," I said, taking an empty glass.

I remember the hollow pop of the corncob plug coming out. Then the clink of bottle against glass. Then the tumbling splash and the searing smell of twice-distilled alcohol rising to my nose. Then I remember drinking it. It scorched my throat and made my eyes water. I coughed violently while Mutshi slapped my back, laughing like he had just seen the funniest thing in the world. Between gasps for air, I swore I'd never drink *tshitshampa* again.

But I broke the pledge about a week later. This time I was at a funeral. This time the experience was less horrible. I had another shot a few days after that. Then another a day later. Then, pretty soon, I forgot about the original pledge altogether. *Tshitshampa* was the drink of choice of village men, consumed whenever someone inside a circle of chairs had twenty-five cents in his pocket. I had no choice, really, but to learn to drink it too. It was part of adjusting to village life, part of lowering the barriers between myself and the men I hoped to work with. Or at least that's the way it seemed in the beginning.

Again, the adjustment to *tshitshampa* wasn't an easy one to make. For good reason, the alcohol was also called *mala a kapia*, "the drink of fire." Anything beyond small quantities inflamed the mind, making the drinker abusive and insensible. I staggered home and retched pathetically in my grass outhouse the first few times my attention lapsed and I drank too much. But with time I learned to handle it. I grew to imbibe regularly, confidently, without much effect. The fact that I was one of the few expatriates in the entire country who didn't hate the stuff, who, instead, actually began to like it, didn't bother me. I snickered inwardly when visiting volunteers steeled themselves and knocked back a shot at village gatherings just to be polite. "Another?" I'd ask, lifting the bottle. "No, no. That's all for me, thanks."

As more time passed, however, the evidence started piling up, especially toward the end. There was the near suicidal swim in the Lubilashi after splitting a bottle of *tshitshampa* with Wateketa, the river ferryman. There was the night I spent with Ilunga Clement slowly draining his pond and drinking shots and finally cutting the dike so sloppily that the water rushed out and we lost a quarter of the harvest. There was the morning, hung over, I transported stocking fish in stale water and all one hundred died before I reached Kayemba's new pond.

And there were Sundays, my days off. I didn't have to ride my motorcycle on Sundays and could drink free of caution. These weren't good days for me. With no work to do, nothing on which to train my mind, I grew restless and depressed. Time seemed to slow down, then stop altogether, allowing the data around me to lurch forward with greater definition. The village houses seemed smaller and cruder on Sundays, the distended stomachs larger, the funeral drums louder, the cough of the child next door harsher. By one o'clock, a book tossed aside, I'd feel that tug, that need to do something. I'd find Mbaya or Kayemba or Lengos and we'd find a bottle of *tshitshampa*. Then we'd find another. Then, by nightfall, I'd find myself out of control, doing stupid things.

One Sunday stands particularly tall in my memory. It came three weeks before I left Kalambayi and represented the ugly, evolved product of all the others. When it was over, it sent rising through my mind the red flags of a final warning.

The day began typically, with a tedious, sun-drenched morning giving way to afternoon and a desire to drink. I met Lengos at his house at 1:00 p.m. and we went to the funeral of Mutatu Katenga, a Lulenga elder who had died of malaria the day before. For the occasion the surviving family had built a palm-branch pavilion under which libations flowed and a group of men danced in a tight circle, their gyrating hips controlled by a group of musicians seated off to the side.

After expressing our condolences to the family, Lengos and I intercepted a bottle of *tshitshampa* passing through the crowd and began pouring each other shots. Soon the alcohol was running through our blood, driven along by the furious beat of the tom-toms and xylophones. As the afternoon wore on, a familiar, fiery haze settled over my faculties and stayed with me through the string of bizarre events that followed.

After a couple of hours, Lengos and I left the funeral. We proceeded to roam through the village with pitched animation, looking for another bottle of *tshitshampa* to buy and take to my house. We wound up at the village whorehouse, a large mud-brick structure on the east end of the village behind which was one of the best stills in Lulenga. The house matron took our order and we settled woozily into chairs outside to wait. A group of prostitutes wearing bright *pagnes* and garish red lipstick milled lazily under the eave. They were certain we had come for something else, of course, and one of them, Kabisenga wa Mulumba, ran inside and came out wearing decadent, tight-fitting corduroys. Pants! She had her eye on me and tried several times to sit on my lap. But I was having enough trouble staying in my chair by myself. I pushed her away, finally handing her 25 zaires. "No, for the bottle," I said. "*The bottle.*"

When the *tshitshampa* came, I grabbed Lengos by the arm and we left quickly, with the prostitutes only half-jokingly looking for a spear with which to punish us for arousing their hopes. At my house we uncorked the bottle and listened to Zairian pop music tapes. The shots we poured grew larger, the sunlight outside fainter, the walls inside softer. Then, after what could have been two minutes or two hours, I looked up and was startled to find the house suddenly full of people. Half the crowd from Mutatu's funeral had arrived, bringing with them more *tshitshampa*.

Banza Bankani turned off the cassette player and began making his own music, playing fast dance songs on his guitar and singing full-throated lyrics that nearly lifted the roof. A soup of grinding hips and bobbing elbows washed through every room. I acquiesced to the crowd's presence and began dancing myself. I remember thinking how wonderful everyone looked, how right the moment felt. At one point, I tried to record Banza's singing with my cassette player. But the moment I hit the record button everyone in the house began singing along loudly, creating a sound less like music than a pack of crazed souls speaking in tongues.

I'm not sure if it was before or after Lengos tried to teach my dog how to dance that the fight broke out. In the yard, where the party had by then spilled, Kalombo Ilunga and Kayemba Lubanda stood inches apart, hurling abuse at each other while other men held them back. They were arguing over who had put the hole in the door. I looked. There was a hole in the door. To protect the house from further abuse, Mbaya began shooing everyone out and slamming shut the house's side-hinged windows. Before I could get out of the way, one window caught my arm, leaving a long, red scrape above the elbow. But by that point I was impervious to pain. The world had begun to corkscrew around me, and people and things had taken on vague, fluid shapes.

It was early morning when I woke up in my yard, lying on my back. My head was raging and the starscape above hurt my eyes. Lengos, still conscious, was lying next to me. He was shaking me and speaking softly in my ear in the limited English I had been helping him with: "Say to me what it is about that you are not standing."

I didn't answer. I couldn't. With every ounce of coordination left in my body, I picked myself up and silently toddled inside.

Had his vocabulary been larger, Lengos might have said more that early morning as he tried shaking life into me. He might have asked the same question I had been asking myself lately: Are you an alcoholic?

It had come that far. The habit that had begun as a few two-finger shots of *tshitshampa* in the afternoon with fish farmers was, by my final six months, out of control. In the beginning I drank to be sociable. I drank for entertainment—to relieve the monotony of village life. But now I was drinking seven days a week, and charging more frequently into heavy, disruptive binges. At least once every three or four days a bout fouled my memory wires and made it hard to go to work the next day. Not by any charitable stretch of the imagination could this be called normal consumption.

The reasons people give to explain their drinking often have the ring of contrived excuses. Perhaps mine have the same ring. I don't know. I have no way to account for the excessive consumption except to say this: Everything seemed worse in Kalambayi toward the end. The dark moods and frustrations that come from living day after day with utterly poor people intensified for me with time. I discovered that clouting myself with shots of *tshitshampa* helped reduce the feelings some.

You can't, without injury, attend two hundred funerals in two years and watch stooped, elderly people approach your house begging for gasoline to pour on aching teeth. You can't without inner lacerations, take a two-month-old diarrhetic baby in your arms and listen while the parents tell you his name is your name. Living amid such things is like drinking the local water.

Sooner or later you pay. If your ability to feel goes further than that of a dog or a cat, you eventually find yourself reaching for something—religion, sorcery, a plane ticket home, *tshitshampa*—anything that allows you to explain it all or blot it out completely. I reached for *tshitshampa*. It was my final defense. In the haze of a late-afternoon intoxication, my mind was less quick to dwell on the full meaning of the stagnant, hopeless lives around me.

Everything, as I said, just seemed worse toward the end. I looked around after two years and was terrified by the fact that a majority of the people I cared most about in the world had ten cents in their pockets on a good day and could expect to live, on average, no more than forty-five years. And what had I done for them really? What had I changed? The fish farmers had built more than one hundred ponds, and that was a lot. Fresh tilapia were entering village markets at a rate of two metric tons per year. I was proud of that fact. I was proud that, where before they had stood still, several dozen farmers were now walking a course out of absolute poverty. But it was a slow, hard, grinding course. Even with their ponds the men were poorer than anything I could call acceptable.

And as if local conditions weren't a sufficient source of frustration, developments outside Kalambayi contributed to the strain. Like Mbaya, 90 percent of the villagers I knew couldn't identify continents or oceans on a map. It didn't do much good, then, to tell them what I was reading in each month-old *Newsweek* sent to me courtesy of the Peace Corps. I didn't tell them that the world was falling apart. While the project farmers and I were busy building fish ponds in the heart of Africa, record-hot weather and drought across much of the planet were putting the words "global warming" and "greenhouse effect" on the lips of environmentalists worldwide. The news was all the more fantastic and tragic received here amid the elephant grass and swaying palms of this struggling backwater. It made my small contribution seem even smaller, even less relevant. I hadn't gone overseas expecting to save the planet, but neither had I expected it to be so much worse off when I came back. The whole world had a drinking problem. It was drunk on over-consumption.

As for my own case, a pattern of alcoholism in my family made my drinking particularly frightening. The pattern suggested I was ripe and ready to fall. First, there was my estranged grandfather. I saw him four times in my life, the last when I was ten years old and he was thin and sickly and so desperate for drink he went to my grandmother's house just as we were sitting down to Christmas Eve dinner. Later, at the package store, I sat in the car with my father and watched the cashier hand over a brown paper bag to a trembling old man whose age was fifty-four only on his birth certificate. Ten blocks away, he got out of the car. Staring down at the sidewalk, bottle in hand, he said Merry Christmas. Then he said goodbye.

More recently, there was my "father," Kanyenda Mushia. When I first met him and witnessed his destructive binges, my reaction swelled with the concern and self-safe sympathy of the unafflicted. But waking up in my yard that early morning with a blinding headache and the stars blurry above me, I realized my relationship to Kanyenda had grown beyond the cultural symbolism of an adopted son. With disturbing vividness, I saw an unwanted inheritance bayoneting my future.

It was time to get out. It was time to leave Kalambayi, with all its *tshitshampa* and reasons to drink it. I couldn't stay a third year.

The decision was made. Back at my sitting-room table, I pulled out a clean sheet of paper and wrote a letter to Brian, my Peace Corps boss. I wrote quickly, wanting to get the task over with. When I finished, I sealed the letter, penned an address, and sent it off to Kinshasa.

18

My departure was two weeks away and I needed two goats. I was glad Mupeta, the Lulenga schoolteacher, had sold me his fish pond before moving to Mbuji Mayi the previous August. Miteo and I had fed the fish for the past six months, and now it was early February, time to harvest. The excitement of at last draining my own pond and gathering fish I had farmed myself was quite great. My plan was to sell the entire catch, buy two goats with the money, and throw a fête for the Kalambayi fish farmers.

It was late Sunday afternoon when, shovels slanting against our shoulders, Mbaya and I walked down to the string of ponds outside Lulenga to begin the harvest. We dug out a portion of my pond's lower dike and reclined nearby as the water ran out in subdued gurgles. Above the horizon, the sun hung orange-pink, soft and perfect, coloring the valley with that lustrous final light that made "even ugly people look beautiful." Soon the orb sank behind a low ridge, passing with such speed that, watching, you could almost feel the Earth turning and hear the creak of its unfathomable weight. Africa was sliding beyond the sun's gaze.

The sunset carried in its beauty a particularly strong sense of ending that evening. I was going home. Everyone and everything seemed to know it. Spent cornstalks, yellow and brittle from the December harvest, whispered ruefully in fields by the ponds. Women washing along the stream shook water from their clothes, waving them up and down as if already saying goodbye. On the pond dike, an unspoken awkwardness sat between Mbaya and me like a third party. Two more weeks.

At sunrise the next morning, we returned to the pond to drain the last of the water. "It looks like a lot," Mbaya said when a field of dorsal fins thrust up from the muddy pool. The sight was a relief to me. I was running short on cash, and a good harvest would pay for the goats and leave me with enough money to squeak through the last two weeks.

Mbaya and I plunged into the empty pond. I reached for a big fish and it took off through the mud, flapping on its side. It stopped and I reached for it a second time. But again it took off, this time slinging mud in my face and making a fool of me. Mbaya laughed. "All this time and you still can't catch fish," he said. When, several minutes later, the same thing happened to him, I wasn't the only one returning the laugh. Chuckles and howls streamed down from the dikes. I looked up. A crowd had gathered, composed of more than a dozen of my friends and neighbors and other fish farmers. More people were approaching on the trail.

I suddenly felt the specter of Chief Ilunga's first harvest descend on the pond. I had completely forgotten about the post-harvest giveaway ritual. It hadn't occurred to me that everyone would come to my harvest, too, expecting me to share. I grew worried and unsure of what to do. This was *my* pond and *my* fish and I needed the money.

Plucking the last of the baby fish from the pond-bottom muck, Mbaya and I ordered people out of our way and hoisted the holding basin onto the dike. For a small pond it wasn't a bad harvest: twenty kilos—enough to buy two medium-sized goats. But the pleasure this total brought me lasted only as long as it took the crowd of onlookers to close in. Before I knew it, they were standing around me, about twenty people now, congratulating me, fidgeting, waiting for me to act, tapping my skin with expectant stares. And not just people. The grass, the sky, the clouds, the sun, the empty pond—they were watching, too. What was Michel going to do with his harvest? Stalling, I cleaned my glasses with my shirttail. I shifted my weight from foot to foot. I glanced down at the basin of fish at my feet and jumped. A thousand cold fish eyes looked up, stabbing me—"Well?"

The words came out before I had time to stop them. "Go get some banana leaves Mbaya." He returned and I scooped out a handful of fish and handed it to Miteo for all his help in feeding the fish. Then came Kalenga Ngamala, Mupeta's teenage sister whose back was badly deformed from tuberculosis of the spine. Then came two of Mbaya's uncles. Then, one by one, the others. When it was over, about eleven kilos of fish remained, barely enough to buy one goat.

After the handshakes and fulsome thank-yous, the crowd dispersed and I walked over to the canal to clean up. Scrubbing splotches of dried mud from my face and arms, I realized with surprise how little the loss of the fish bothered me. To cover the cost of the goats I would have to use the last of my living allowance money. For other expenses, I would have to borrow from volunteer Brandt Witte when he came to evacuate my things in the Peace Corps Land Rover. But I would get by. I wasn't upset. It could hardly be called sacrifice to share a few kilos of fish with people who, for the past two years, had shared everything they had with me—their food, their homes, their lives, their stories. Two years ago, fresh from the self-absorbed, self-first West, I would have sent these people away. Now the change was something I would carry home with me.

At the canal, I splashed water on my face and arms, rinsing the last of the soil from my skin. Feeling renewed and strengthened, I rose and walked back to the pond.

It was 7:30 and Mbaya was about to head to the market. I wanted to sit by the ponds for a while, I told him, and would be up later. The sun had risen two fists into the sky, but the valley air was still cool as I walked down the line of ponds, taking in their familiar charm. Water bugs skated serenely across the gold ice of reflected light. Fish surfaced, causing ripples. Long strings of frog eggs lined the pond edges like valuable necklaces, teasing the blades of grass that dropped down from the bank, unable to grasp.

I sat down next to one pond and started thinking. I thought about going home and about the future. Although life had not always been easy in Kalambayi, it had been relatively simple; my purpose had been clear. I got up every morning and traveled to different villages and taught men how to raise fish. Looking ahead, I already missed that simplicity. The future now appeared as a strange looming on the horizon, full of complexity and uncertainty. What would I do outside this ring of rivers? What would be my purpose? I still wasn't sure.

All I knew with certainty was that what I needed—what the whole world needed, in fact—were fish ponds. Not strictly for food, but for places to sit and think. The sense of perspective and calm I had gleaned during quiet times by the ponds was something I had come to count on in Kalambayi. Whatever anxieties I experienced during my stay would have been much worse without them.

The therapy now seemed worth sharing. Why not, I wondered, put ponds—thousands and thousands of them—all over the world? The planet would surely be a better place and the future less frightening to contemplate if world leaders could be made to sit next to fish ponds and take off their shoes and throw a few stones for a while. Greed and hate and overactive ambition do not survive long next to a shimmering pool of fish. There could be a pond in the Rose Garden, a pond in Red Square, irrigated ponds in the Middle East. And Kalambayans like Chief Ilunga and Kanyenda Mushia could be roving ambassadors of the new order, showing others how it's done, colonizing the world.

Yes, the idea sounded nice. But perhaps, I concluded, my thinking was a bit too fanciful, too ambitious. Perhaps I should just settle for a pond for myself. Wherever I go I'll search the back roads and backwoods near where I live until I find a pond. It'll be like Oklahoma all over again. And if I can't find one, I'll dig one. Then, from time to time, I'll retreat to the placid water to think about life and about Kalambayi and about what's important. Perhaps then I won't go too far astray; I won't lose my center, no matter what the future brings.

———

Fearing the afterlife consequences of breaking two years' worth of promises, I rode my motorcycle to the Lulenga soccer field, dismounted, and tossed the keys to Mbaya. "Go ahead," I said, "get on."

Since the day I met him, Mbaya had been bugging me to teach him how to ride. He worked on my resistance with the diligence of a lumberjack attacking a mammoth tree, stroke after stroke, day after day. But fearful of injury—both to him (by way of accident) and to me (by way of jealous friends demanding to ride, too)—I refused to fall. "Not today, Mbaya."

"But you'll teach me before you leave?"

"Yes, okay, before I leave."

Now, my departure less than two weeks away, the tree had fallen. Mbaya held the keys in his hand and stared at the motorcycle. Then he did something that surprised me. He backed off.

"Here," he said, handing the keys to Kayemba, who was standing in the field with us, "you go first."

Kayemba was the only other person in Kalambayi to whom I had been making the same promise. He had arrived that morning from Ntita Konyukua. He was a first-rate fish farmer whose sense of humor and honesty had lured me into a friendship too deep to say no when he asked to ride. A year and a half earlier, however, I wouldn't have thought him capable of operating a motorcycle. He couldn't even stock a pond properly. When he finished digging his first pond he had insisted on understocking it because, he claimed, rainstorms would deliver additional fish from the sky.

"The sky?" I asked.

"Yes," he told me. "That's how fish get into rivers and lakes. They come down as tiny babies inside raindrops."

Thankfully, he wasn't averse to revision, and I was eventually able to disabuse him of the crazy notion. But now my task was more challenging: teaching him the inter-workings of clutch, brake, and gear sequence.

Kayemba took off his straw hat, put on my helmet, and mounted the motorcycle. After four tries he released the clutch without stalling the engine and proceeded slowly across the soccer field. I ran beside him shouting instructions above the whine of the motor, which was spiraling higher. "Shift, Kayemba. Shift into the second gear." Thinking I meant for him to give more gas, he throttled the accelerator and the laborious whine grew unbearable. "No, *shift!*" I yelled. Panicked now, he slammed on the brakes with all his might. The abrupt, shuddering stop sent him sliding off the seat and onto the soccer-field dirt without harm. I grabbed the handlebars just in time to keep the motorcycle from falling on top of him.

The crowd of children swelling along the edges of the soccer field burst into applause at this, apparently thinking I had instructed Kayemba to fall off as part of the training and he had done a competent job of it. My dog approved, too, running circles around the motorcycle, barking loudly.

Somewhat traumatized, Kayemba decided to take a break, and Mbaya stepped forward. While I held the motorcycle, he positioned his dirty, sandaled feet above the gear and brake levers. Then, with Zen concentration, he released the clutch and began rolling. After some initial awkwardness, he got the hang of things, and all I had to do was run up and down the field waving him clear of the bamboo goalposts. After a while, even this was unnecessary, and I joined the crowd of children in cheering him on through lap after lap of confident, glorious riding.

Watching, I was reminded of my own first time riding a motorcycle and the exhilaration I felt when fear gave way to that heady wave of motion that has no equal. The enormous grin on Mbaya's face said he was having the same experience. But the experience seemed to be more than physical for him. Part of the reason he had wanted to ride my motorcycle so badly, I suspected, was that it represented everything that separated my world from his in Kalambayi. More than the photos I could show him or the stories I could tell, more than the wealth of things that filled my house, my motorcycle was Mbaya's way of glimpsing my world. On it, he vicariously experienced the freedom—the *feeling*—of the privileged Western life I led.

From an insulated college campus I had come to Africa and lived in comparative comfort amid all its exotica. I had collected memorable experiences like beads on a string, and now I was moving on to other work, other places, other experiences, with relatively little worry about money and how I would stay alive. Those things would take care of themselves. I would keep moving through the world with the same speed and energy with which I had moved through villages in Kalambayi on my motorcycle, kicking up dust and getting where I wanted to go. Yes, it summarized wonderfully my Western world, my motorcycle. It was expensive and complex and fast, and to the rider it offered mobility and choice unavailable to people shackled to the soil, unavailable to Mbaya until now, until this brief moment.

I watched him turn another corner and head down the length of the field, picking up speed. His smile grew wider; the sensation was intensifying. For the first time in his life, he was really moving, really going somewhere, traveling, in a sense, beyond the boundaries of this forgotten patch of Africa. He made another turn and charged down the field. Again the smile. "Yes, Mbaya," I thought, "that's what it's like. That's the feeling. It *is* good isn't it? It really is." His flight was short, just a few times around a sun-baked soccer field, but it would have to do. It would have to last him through a million strokes of a short-handled hoe spread over years and years of a hard lifetime.

After Mbaya, Kayemba got back on the motorcycle. Although he never managed to get above second gear, his riding improved and there were no more falls. After a dozen or so slow trips around the field he was satisfied. Hungry, we decided to go to my house for a celebratory bowl of *fufu*. Kayemba rode the motorcycle, and Mbaya and I followed on foot in the strong midday sunlight. I sighed with relief that the lesson was over. Mbaya grinned all the way home.

***

The final two weeks passed rapidly in a whirl of departure preparations and final visits to farmers. I reminded the men that no extension agent would be replacing me soon because of the diplomatic dispute between our respective countries. For the men who already had ponds, this wasn't a problem. "You don't need me any more," I told them, priming them for my absence. "I've got nothing left to teach you." It was true. They knew as much about fish culture as I did now. They were independent, able to eat fish forever.

At first, though, many of the farmers didn't believe I was leaving. I had become a regular fixture in their lives, and they saw the relationship continuing forever. That they no longer needed me for technical advice wasn't the point. We had forged friendships and shared binding experiences. Why would I want to leave? Had they done something wrong?

Some of the men even viewed my exit as something of a betrayal. Katombe Jean was one of them. He was a hulking, somewhat thick-witted farmer whose early resistance to proper fish culture methods had fostered rocky relations between us in the past. Since I was about to abandon the project, he said when I came for my last visit, would I please help him stake that second pond he had been meaning to dig? The tone of accusation in his voice pricked me like a needle. I said I would.

Under a hostile afternoon sun, we began hacking through the tall grass near Katombe's first pond in Ntita Konyukua, looking for a site. We worked for more than an hour, sweating and grousing, unable to find a good place. Katombe grew increasingly irritated each time I explained why a site was unworkable. He gestured with his machete and suggested I was wrong. I had just rejected another site and turned away when he exploded. "*Nyama!*" he yelled at me from behind. "*Nyama!*"

I froze. He was calling me an "animal," a grave insult in Tshiluba. I turned around and saw that the worst was happening. Katombe was facing me with his machete raised high above his head, ready to slice me in half like a ripe papaya. "*Nyama!*" he yelled again to my face. I closed my eyes and threw up my arms to fend off the blow.

The blow never came. "An animal ran by your feet," Katombe explained excitedly. "A *muidi!*" I opened my eyes and saw that, indeed, the face staring at me wasn't that of a murderer. A real animal had passed between us, darting across the trail we had cut through the grass. Although this explained Katombe's agitated state, it did little to ease my fear of injury. What was a *muidi*, I wondered. Was it a big animal? Did it have sharp teeth? And, most important, where was it now?

There was no time to pursue these thoughts. Katombe put his finger to his lips, signaling for silence. We were hunting now. Machete still raised, he cocked his ear and listened. The animal was apparently close, hiding somewhere in the thick sea of grass next to the trail. Motioning for me to stay put, Katombe moved twenty feet to the right. Then, together, we shifted our position five feet to the left. Now we were set. Katombe explained with his hands that we should charge forward through the grass at angles that would intersect where he believed the animal was hiding. I nodded that I understood. With his fingers he began counting: One, two, three . . . "Go!" he shouted.

I hurled myself into the five-foot-tall grass and tried to run, but it was impossible. I lunged and stumbled instead. To my right, I heard Katombe screaming as he moved through the grass: "Aaaahhhh!" Assuming this was a form of self-protection, I started screaming, too: "Aaaahhhh!" By the time I reached the animal, still stumbling, it was over. With impossible speed and accuracy, Katombe had located the *muidi* in the grass and somehow pinned its neck to the ground with his machete. It was a black-furred creature with the look and size of a large badger. The animal squirmed and clawed and snapped its jaws until, pressing the machete blade harder and sliding it, Katombe broke its neck.

The exhilaration of the kill postponed the pond search and laid waste to old disagreements between Katombe and me. With our hearts still racing, we carried the animal back to Katombe's house and butchered it while his wife stoked a cooking fire under the eave. There was a loud sizzling sound when she dropped the meat into a pan of palm oil. Katombe and I, meanwhile, sat back in chairs nearby, enjoying with imperial satisfaction the good smell of our good fortune.

Sitting in the palm-tree shade, I reflected on the hunt and wondered if some combination of Kanyenda's *mukishi* fetish and the good luck ceremony of the pig hunt wasn't still having its effect on me. Perhaps these rituals would continue to protect me even after I left. I doubted it, though. With each passing day I had begun to feel the rhythm and texture of village life receding from my own. Kalambayi was already becoming a memory in my veins. Riding home from Katombe's house later that day, my fingers still slightly greasy from the meal and a souvenir *muidi* pelt tied to my motorcycle, I grew nostalgic.

The nostalgia was for all the good times in Kalambayi. For in truth, there were far more of them during my two years than the number included in this account. Missing are the indolent early mornings picking papaya leaves on the way to farmers' ponds; the late nights weeping with laughter at stories told around open fires; the steamy afternoons swimming in the Mvunai River and tossing glistening, naked children into the current from the high bank.

Missing, too, are many of the happy details of everyday life: the high-strutting roosters at dawn, the cool papayas at noon, the smell of scallions in the market, the gaudy crown of the village chief, the jags of lightning on the midnight sky, the roasted corn at harvest time, the high peep of lemon-yellow chicks, the baby goats trying to eat my shoelaces, the quirky chameleons with two eyes wandering, the million morning dewdrops dangling and glinting on the tips of grass blades, each almost falling, but never quite, to the ground.

These are the experiences and images I would prefer to remember above all others in Kalambayi. But they are fragments in my mind, cleaved into tiny pieces by the larger reality of want and failure. They lay scattered under memories of a moribund economy, of a cruel dictatorship, and of people dying of easily cured diseases. What, in the end, was the real story of Kalambayi? What did Mbaya Bukasa's life mean? What did Kanyenda Mushia's life mean? Back in the States, behind a humming word processor in a room overlooking streets with sidewalks and houses with porch swings, I would try to answer these questions and a string of unhappy chapters would necessarily step forth. There weren't enough *muidis* in all of Kalambayi to stop them.

19

THE LAST FEW DAYS WERE MARKED BY MOSTLY BAD EXPERIENCES, making the final taste of Kalambayi foul in my mouth. First, there was the ordeal of traveling through upriver villages haggling over the price of goats with merchants until I found two I could afford. Then there were the fêtes. We had planned two, one for the downriver farmers on Tuesday and one for the upriver farmers on Saturday, my last day.

The first fête began well enough. We gathered outside Ilunga Clement's guest hut in Katombe and slaughtered a goat and drank *tshitshampa* while his wife cooked. But after the evening meal, instead of the solemn reminiscing and goodbye speeches the party was meant to produce, bickering broke out. The men from Bena Mbaya got into a silly argument with the men from Katombe over alleged ill treatment of the UNICEF wheelbarrow. Both sides eventually stomped off huffing and blowing, and the party dissolved.

I went to bed in the guest hut in a bad mood and woke up the next morning feeling even worse: My knapsack was missing. I looked everywhere, finding nothing. It contained my camera and some clothes. The door to the guest house had been left open during the party, and a number of men, all of them fish farmers, had come in to get bottles of *tshitshampa* stored inside. The knapsack was taken then, I was sure. It had to have been someone I knew well.

Clement was furious. He wanted to hold a special witchcraft ceremony that would cause the thief to go insane, revealing his identity. But I refused. I knew I would never see the knapsack again, and hanging around would only fuel my bitterness. I bade Clement sincere farewell and headed back upriver feeling like I had been kicked in the groin.

On Friday morning I jumped out of bed and started packing. Brandt was coming that afternoon with the Peace Corps Land Rover. From under my bed I pulled out the old Air Force duffel bag my father had given me more than two years before. The bag was covered with dust: forgotten again. I took it outside and thrashed it with a broomstick until the blue-white color returned and my family name was again legible across the side. It was ready for another trip.

As I gathered my things, a steady rain began to fall on the tin roof. It sent a grating, metallic noise through the house that matched the buzz of my inner anxiety. Heaped on the anger I still felt over the theft of my things was a growing nervousness over leaving.

I tried to concentrate on packing. Into the duffel bag I stuffed clothes and books and journals and a few souvenirs. I assembled a pile of tools, motorcycle parts, and kitchen items that would go back to the Peace Corps. Most everything else I set aside to give to various friends. To Mbaya I would give all my Bob Dylan tapes and my cassette player. To Kayemba, my bicycle. To Chief Ilunga, my dog.

From my bedroom wall I took down a collage of photos that had served as my window to family and friends back home. There were photos of picnic gatherings and sailboat outings, a photo of a friend's new jeep, a photo of my father exultant after a ten-kilometer road race, sweatband around his head. Staring at the pictures now, I felt like de Tocqueville about to see America for the first time. The consumer culture, the elaborate needs, the sweaty scramble for profits—it all struck me as boring and threatening at the same time. The feeling had begun to bloom a few months earlier when I picked up a late-night signal from America on my shortwave radio. I listened stone-ignorant as a commentator lamented the growing problem of Americans with remote control devices taping TV shows with their VCRs and then "zapping" commercials as they came on. These outlaw "zappers," the commentator said, were threatening the very foundation of the television universe. They had to be stopped.

While I was packing, Clement arrived on foot from Katombe. My knapsack and camera had mysteriously appeared at his doorstep in the middle of the night, he said. A rumor had spread that I had cast a powerful *mutoka* spell that would kill the thief if he didn't return the goods. So be it, I thought. Clement winked and shrugged when I asked him who had started the rumor. We both laughed. I told him I would pick the stuff up on my way to Mbuji Mayi Sunday morning.

Brandt pulled up late Friday evening, mumbling half-incoherently about how savage roads had almost torn his Land Rover to bits along the way. The next morning, he and I loaded the vehicle while Mbaya slaughtered a goat under the mimosa tree. At 3 p.m. the living quarters of the cotton warehouse were empty, the goat was cooked, and off we went to Ntita Konyukua for the final party.

We held the fête in a dirt field outside the village's two-room schoolhouse. By five o'clock all the upriver farmers had arrived except Chief Ilunga, who came late after tracking an antelope he had wounded in the bush. Several musicians came, too. I had persuaded a group from Lulenga, headed by Ndala Musuma, the chief's son, to play in return for a goat-meat meal and all the alcohol they could drink. Musicians were the lifeblood of any respectable social gathering in the villages, and I made sure this last fête was well equipped.

By nightfall everyone had eaten. We arranged our chairs into a large U with the musicians at one end, and settled down to a session of high-intensity revelry. Mbaya and I moved about with bottles of *tshitshampa*, pouring generous shots into every empty glass. An hour later, just when the booze was beginning to raise people's voices and a tempest of dancing had broken out,

Ndala, the head musician, pulled me aside and said the players were interested in getting their pay.

"What pay?" I said.

"The 500 zaires," he said. "It's customary to pay us 500 zaires when we play at gatherings."

"I don't have it," I said. "I spent everything on the goats. You agreed to play for food and *tshitshampa*, and that's all I can give you."

He shrugged his shoulders ambiguously and returned to the group. The party continued.

Thirty minutes later, Kanyenda quieted the crowd and gave a drunken, sentimental farewell speech that included a rambling digression on how much he loved his fish and a reminder to everyone that, despite my departure, my name would live on through his newly born son. Encouraged by the audience to get on with it, he concluded by saying he spoke for all the farmers in thanking me for the work I had done.

I spoke next, holding up my pinkish, uncalloused hands and telling the farmers it obviously wasn't I who had dug all the ponds in Kalambayi. The men laughed. I congratulated them on their work and encouraged them to continue. When I finished, Banza Bankani broke out his guitar and sang a farewell ballad he had written for the occasion.

I was in good spirits. The fête was going the way it was supposed to go.

Then things started to unravel.

Ndala pulled me aside again. More trouble with the musicians. "The other players say you have to pay for the music. We always get paid. It's the custom. Otherwise we'll leave."

I reached into my pants pockets and pulled out the linings, letting them drop down like dogs' ears. "Will you just play as a favor to me?"

"I'll see what the others say."

Soon Kayemba approached me and asked if he could take my motorcycle for a few laps around the schoolyard—with the headlight on, of course. He wanted to show off his new riding skills. This was the third time he had asked. He was getting on my nerves.

"No," I said. "Someone might get hurt. There are too many people around for you to ride now."

Sulking, he went back to the party.

Meanwhile, the *tshitshampa* was running out. The farmers had provided all the booze up to that point, but now everyone was broke. I borrowed 100 zaires from Brandt, enough for four bottles, and gave it to Bukasa, whose wife had brewed a batch of ten bottles that afternoon. Bukasa returned and handed me a white, five-liter plastic jug. "Four bottles," he said. I poured *tshitshampa* into two empty bottles and put the rest in the Land Rover cab. The partying and dancing continued.

Katombe Jean and Kazadi Manda had something they wanted to discuss with me. We walked behind the schoolhouse.

"We've been wondering about something," Kazadi said. "How many women have you slept with since you've been in Kalambayi?"

It wasn't the first time I had been asked. With some embarrassment, I told the men the truth. "None," I said. The temptation had been there all along, of course, rampaging at times, but nothing stayed a secret in these villages, and on this subject I hadn't wanted to be an object of gossip. However, this *was* my last night. What did they have in mind?

"We'll ask around," Kazadi said. "You really should sample one of our women before you leave. We'll arrange something."

It was around ten o'clock and the party was thriving. Kayemba was leading a group of farmers in a traditional dance in which the men wore *pagnes* around their waists and moved in a circle, reversing directions every half minute or so. Chief Ilunga was standing on his chair, drunk and clapping.

The two bottles of *tshitshampa* I had filled earlier came back empty. I went to the Land Rover cab and began refilling them with what was left in the plastic jug. But after one bottle the jug was voided. I began to sweat with anger. Either by accident or intent to steal, Bukasa had given me only three bottles of *tshitshampa*. I called him over. He blamed it on his wife, but I knew he was lying. I shoved the jug in his hand. "I paid for four bottles," I said. "Bring me another one and don't be slow."

Kazadi and Katombe came back with bad news. There were three prostitutes in the village, they said, one was out of town, one was ill with fever, and the third had confessed that sleeping with a white man just wasn't her cup of tea. *Mutokas* were a little too spooky, thank you. The rejection stung.

Kayemba walked over, perspiring from dancing. I answered his question before he had a chance to ask it. "No," I said. "You can't ride my motorcycle."

"I don't want to ride the motorcycle."

"What then?"

"The musicians are leaving."

I looked. Ndala and the others were walking across the field toward the trail, tom-toms and xylophones slung over their shoulders. I bolted after them, picking my way through bodies in the crowd. When I reached Ndala, I grabbed his arm and spun him around.

"Where are you going?"

He pulled his arm free. "You haven't paid us."

"That wasn't the agreement," I said. "You said you would play for food."

"We always get paid. . . ."

"Stay," I said. "You'll kill the party if you leave. Stay and play." I was yelling now.

The men ignored me. They turned and resumed walking away. The crack of a final hammer stroke reverberated in my head.

I ran up to Ndala and tried to grab his arm again, but he turned around and stepped back before I reached him. "Don't touch me," he said.

The other musicians were putting down their instruments, all of them facing me. Several fish farmers had run up and were standing behind me.

"Don't leave," I said to Ndala.

"Pay us."

"I can't."

"You have to."

The hammer stroke rang louder in my head. The fête was finished without the musicians. I stared at Ndala, his eyes intransigent and hot, and I felt a sudden, flashing urge to hurt him, to send my fist crashing into his face. In fact, I wanted to charge swinging into the whole group of musicians and make them pay for everything I was feeling—the ugliness of the last few days and hours, the pain of friendships dying, the lacerating suspicion I held inside me that Katombe was right, that I was abandoning the fish farmers.

I launched into a barrage of insults. I called the musicians "animals" and "bums" and "lazy porcupines." With each sentence I edged closer and the urge to hurl myself into the group grew. It was as if, together, their bodies represented an oncoming train or the edge of a tall precipice and all I had to do was get close enough to make something happen.

And all of this over $5. I could have borrowed the money from Brandt, but I didn't. Ndala had broken a promise and was trying to take advantage of me. Still, nothing warranted this behavior. My reaction was ridiculously overdone. In truth, I think I *wanted* something to happen. I wanted a fight—bruises, blood—to go along with everything else. I wanted things to end with the simplicity of surface pain that would last a few days and then go away forever, not lingering like the interior kind. Or perhaps I wanted a fight because it would give me reason to hate Kalambayi. Hate would have made things simple, too. It would have made it easier to leave.

Ndala and I were barely two feet apart now, arguing face to face. I was close enough to do it, close enough to shove him back and detonate something really vulgar. Kayemba and Kanyenda took hold of my arms. "Let them go," they said. "It's nothing. Let them go."

I refused to listen. I argued on, ready to hit and kick and fall to the dirt like some pathetic village dog finally gone mad.

"Let them go, Michel."

I felt the hot pressure of their hands tightening around my arms.

"Okay," I yelled at the musicians at last. "Go, then. *Go*. We don't need you. *Ndayi*."

They began picking up their instruments and walking away.

"That's it, goddammit," I said, switching to English without realizing it at first. "Leave. Get the hell out of here. We don't need you. *Leave* goddammit!"

Kayemba and Kanyenda let go of my arms, and I turned around and began walking back toward the schoolhouse. It was only then that I noticed the near total silence that had fallen over the party. There was no music, no laughing, no talking. All the farmers had been watching the ugly exchange. The uneasy way they avoided my eyes now accelerated the shame and embarrassment uncoiling inside me.

The fête was over, its fire gone without the music. Most of the farmers went home. Inside the schoolhouse, Brandt unrolled a mat and went to sleep. The rest of us—Kayemba, Mbaya, Chief Ilunga, Kazadi, Kanyenda, myself, and a few others—pulled together some chairs and stayed up the rest of the night talking. I had calmed down after the falling-out with the musicians, reining in my absurd rage. I willed myself to enjoy these last few hours and not to let a few aberrant acts of thievery and pettiness contaminate the decency I knew to be the signature of these people.

It was past midnight now. In the schoolhouse field where we sat, it grew increasingly still and quiet. The farmers and I were the only ones awake in the entire village. The moon, now almost directly overhead, gave a silver-tinged clarity to the palm trees and thatched roofs all around. Just past 3:00 a.m., Kayemba went to his house to make some tea. He came back, floating across the moonlit field, with a kettle and some cups. We tried to wake Kanyenda, but too much *tshitshampa* had finally left him expired in his chair.

Kazadi raised his cup for a toast. "Go safely, Michel, and with God. And when you reach your land, tell your parents about us. Tell them we lived with their son for many days. Tell them we await his return as if he were one of our own children."

An hour before sunrise, a blanket of clouds sailed across the sky from the north. The moon and stars disappeared, and it grew cool. With the first light of dawn, we could see that a thin fog had settled onto the village.

Sleepily, we stood and stretched. "Do you think it will rain today?" I asked Kanyenda. He had just woken up and was still half-drunk. His eyes were glazed. With the uneven steps of a sleepwalker, he strode fifty feet to the center of the field. He stopped and looked up into the misty sky, putting his arms out as if about to catch a giant raindrop. Then he walked back. "Yes," he said. "I think it will rain."

Roosters were crowing. It was time to leave. I went into the schoolhouse to wake Brandt. While I was inside, I heard the crack of my motorcycle engine starting up and I remembered I had left the keys in the ignition. By the time I ran out, Kayemba was already motoring across the field toward the dirt road that ran through the village. I yelled for him to stop, but it was futile. He turned right on the road and disappeared through a pearly veil of fog. I ran to the road and cursed having taught him how to ride. I listened as the whining engine, still in second gear, grew faint with distance. Just when the sound was about to fade out completely, it grew louder again, returning.

The motorcycle came into view and I signaled for Kayemba to stop, but he passed me by, now going the other direction. "Just a little more," he yelled.

The anger wanting to mount inside me was checked by the realization that this was just Kayemba's way of postponing my departure. He knew that when he got off the motorcycle, I would get on it and leave.

After a few minutes, he returned and turned off the engine. He handed me the keys. The moment had come.

The other farmers gathered in close to say goodbye. We stood awkwardly facing each other in the wet, smoky air. The men looked strange to me. Different. Changed by the significance of the moment. I felt as if I were seeing them for the first time instead of the last.

Kanyenda shook my hand and gave me a *kashiba* whistle to hunt with in America. Chief Ilunga gave me a calabash pipe. Mutombo Mukendi smiled broadly, but insincerely, as if my leaving were some kind of bad joke and I had carried it too far. During the farewells, my mind was both dull and alert, needled by intense emotion and clouded by lack of sleep. I was participating in the scene, but also somehow detached from it, watching it. I watched myself accept the whistle and the pipe. I watched myself shake the last hand. I watched myself begin to cry, tears tumbling down my cheeks.

I got on the motorcycle and began the long ride out of Kalambayi. Brandt followed in the Land Rover. Mbaya rode along on the motorcycle, sitting behind me. Now that his employer was leaving, he was going to Mbuji Mayi to dig diamonds in the mines by the river. None of my desperate protests had changed his mind.

We passed through villages: Bena Mutombo, Kalula, Bena Muyumba, Kaponda. We passed brown huts slumbering under halos of fog hanging in the trees, white and mossy. We crossed Mujimbayi Creek and entered Bena Tshibango, where villages were just rising and a woman with a bulbous goiter on her neck waved from under a load of firewood. We rode along a ridge above the Lubilashi. The river wasn't visible, obscured by bleak clouds.

Near Tshibumba Creek, it began to rain. Mbaya got into the Land Rover, and I put on my raincoat and kept riding, raindrops popping against my chest and arms. Beads of water gathered on the speedometer glass as I rode. I glanced down at the beads. They were clear and empty. There were no fish inside them as Kayemba had once believed, no baby tilapia falling from the sky. There was just water. Just empty rainwater.